Igniting Courage Fueling Your Heart To Serve The Lord

Joshua Rhoades

Published by Joshua Paul Rhoades, 2024.

IGNITING COURAGE FUELING YOUR HEART TO SERVE THE LORD

First edition. December 13, 2024.

ISBN: 979-8230200413

Written by Joshua Rhoades.

Also by Joshua Rhoades

Courage Under Fire: David's Stand On The Battlefield
Jonah's Journey: Voices Of Redemption And Lessons In Obedience
The Furnace Of Faith: 12 Principles From The Heat Of Faith
Whispers of Hope: Inspiring Stories of Men's Prayers In Scripture
Frontier Legends: The Oregon Dream
Elijah: A Beacon Of Boldness
HOOK, LINE & SAVIOUR - Faith Reflections from Fishing
Driven By Faith: Motor Racing Inspired Christian Life
30 Day Devotional - Bold and Strong- Coffee Devotions for a Courageous Christian Walk
Authentic Christianity: The Heart of Old Time Religion
Consider The Ant - God's Tiny Preachers
Flee Fornication: The Plea For Purity
Renewed Hope- How to Find Encouragement in God
Sounding The Call - The Voice of Conviction
The Altar - Where Heaven Meets Earth
The Bible's Battlefields- Timeless Lessons from Ancient Wars
The Sacred Art of Silence - How Silence Speaks in Scripture
Under Fire- The Sanctity of the Traditional Biblical Home
Who Is on the Lord's Side? A Call to Righteousness
What Is Truth? - From Skepticism to Submission
First and Goal- Faith and Football Fundamentals
From Dugout to Devotion- Spiritual Lessons from Baseball
Par for the Course- Faith and Fairways
The Believer's Pace- Tools for Running Life's Marathon
The Immutable Fortress- Security in God's Unchanging Nature
Biblical Bravery
Deer Stands and Devotions: A Hunter's Walk with God

Jesus Knows- Our Hearts, Our Responsibility
Restoration - Setting The Bone
Spiritual 911- God's Word for Life's Emergency's
The Freedom of Forgiveness
The Jezebel Effect - Ancient Manipulations Modern Lessons
The Shout That Stopped The Saviour
The Time Machine Chronicles: Old Testament Characters
Anchored In Truth Exploring The Depths of Psalm 119
Biblical Counsel on Anger
Proverbs' Portraits The Men God Mentions
Stumbling in the Dark - The Dangers of Alcohol
Guarding the Wicket Protecting Your Faith and Game
The Champion's Faith - Wrestling and Achieving Spiritual Victory
Scriptural Commands for Modern Times Living God's Word Today Volume 1
Scriptural Commands for Modern Times Living God's Word Today Volume 2
Scriptural Commands for Modern Times Living God's Word TodayVolume3
The Greatest Gift
A Christmas Journey of Faith
Daughter Of The King: Embracing Your Identity In Christ
Determination and Dedication Building Strong Faith As A Young Man
Walking Through Walls God's Power to Part the Storms of Life
David's Song Of Deliverance Praising God Through Every Storm
From Weakness to Warrior: Gideon's Transformation
Why Did Jesus Weep?
Living For God The Call To Be A Living Sacrifice
My Mind Is In A Fog What Do I Do?
Turning The Page Written By Grace
The Calling and Greatness of John the Baptist
For Such a Time Esther's Courageous Stand
From Brokenness To Beauty Written By The Pen of Grace
The Ultimate Guide to Massive Action- From Plans to Reality
A Heart Of Conviction

Serving In The Shadows
Repentance Revealed The Road Back To God
The Chief Sinner Meets The Chief Saviour Reflections On I Timothy 1:15
Answer The Call - 31 Days of Biblical Action
The Birthmark of the Believer
Reflections on Calvary's Cross
The Kingdom Builder Paul's Bold Proclamation of Christ
The Animal Of Pride
The Reach That Restores Christ Love For The Broken
Paul- The Many Roles of a Servant of Christ
Unshakeable Faith- 31 Days of Peace in God's Word
O Come, Let Us Adore Him- A Christmas Devotional
The Shepherd's Voice
The Trail From Vision To Mission
Enabled- Living God's Purpose With Power
Held Back But Not Defeated
The Enoch Walk
The Power and Precision of God's Word
The Children Who Found Christmas
Hearts of Valor - Faithful in the Call
Why It Matters Finding Hope in Moments of Frustration
The Wild West Lives On McCall Family Adventures
Igniting Courage Fueling Your Heart To Serve The Lord

Dedication

This book is dedicated to you with the hope that it will challenge and inspire you to live boldly for Christ. Life is filled with moments that test your faith, your strength, and your purpose, and sometimes the weight of fear or uncertainty can feel overwhelming. But you, dear reader, have been called to something greater. You have been chosen to shine the light of God's love in a world that desperately needs hope and truth. This journey will not always be easy, and the path of courage often demands sacrifice, trust, and a willingness to step into the unknown. Yet, it is through those moments of surrender that you will discover God's strength carrying you, His love surrounding you, and His promises giving you the boldness to keep going. This book is not for the faint of heart—it is for those who are ready to push past fear, embrace faith, and fuel their hearts with the fire of God's purpose. You might feel inadequate, unprepared, or even afraid, but know this: God's strength is made perfect in your weakness, and He has equipped you with everything you need to fulfill the calling He has placed on your life. As you turn these pages, allow yourself to be vulnerable, to face the questions and challenges that stir your soul, and to trust that God's hand is guiding you every step of the way. Let this dedication remind you that courage is not the absence of fear but the determination to move forward, knowing that God is with you. You are not alone in this journey—He walks beside you, empowering you to live a life of faith, purpose, and joy. So, to you, who have chosen to embark on this journey of igniting courage, may this book become a source of encouragement, a spark of inspiration, and a reminder that you were created for so much more. Let it be your guide as you learn to trust God deeper, serve Him with passion, and live boldly for His glory. May your heart be set on fire for the Lord, and may your life reflect the incredible courage He has placed within you. You are capable, you are chosen, and with God, you can do far more than you ever imagined. This is your time to rise, to fuel your heart, and to ignite your courage for the Lord.

"Be strong and of a good courage, fear not, nor be afraid of them: for the LORD thy God, he it is that doth go with thee; he will not fail thee, nor forsake thee." Deuteronomy 31:6

Introduction

Day 1 - The First Spark: Embracing God's Call to Courage
Day 2 - Overcoming Fear: Trusting the One Who Leads You
Day 3 - A Flame in the Darkness: Finding Faith in Uncertainty
Day 4 - Standing Firm: The Courage to Endure Trials
Day 5 - Anchored in Hope: Believing in God's Promises
Day 6 - Fueling Your Faith: Drawing Strength from Scripture
Day 7 - Prayer-Fed Fires: Seeking the Lord's Guidance Daily
Day 8 - Quiet Confidence: Listening for God's Whisper
Day 9 - Battling Doubt: Choosing Truth Over Lies
Day 10 - Rise Up, Servant: Embracing Holy Boldness
Day 11 - From Fear to Faith: Releasing What Holds You Back
Day 12 - Wells of Encouragement: Finding Strength in Fellowship
Day 13 - Love as a Torch: Serving Through Compassion
Day 14 - Obedience in Action: Stepping Out With Purpose
Day 15 - Small Steps, Big Faith: Courage in the Everyday
Day 16 - Forged by Trials: Transforming Weakness into Strength
Day 17 - Conquering Giants: Courage in Confrontation
Day 18 - Humble Hearts, Strong Service: Leading by Example
Day 19 - Invisible Battles: Trusting God in the Unseen
Day 20 - Through the Fire: Growing in Perseverance
Day 21 - Laying Down Self: Sacrificial Service in God's Name
Day 22 - The Power of Yes: Surrendering to God's Will
Day 23 - Hope in Hardship: Finding Joy Amid Challenges
Day 24 - Carriers of Light: Reflecting Christ in a Dark World
Day 25 - Ready for the Harvest: Preparing to Serve Others
Day 26 - Lifted by Grace: Standing on Unshakable Ground
Day 27 - A Flame That Spreads: Inspiring Courage in Others
Day 28 - Redeemed for a Purpose: Embracing Your Kingdom Role
Day 29 - In the Shadow of His Wings: Security in God's Presence
Day 30 - Pressing Onward: Fueling Endurance for the Journey
Day 31 - Ignited and Unstoppable: Living Courageously for the Lord
Conclusion

Introduction

Imagine standing at the dawn of a quiet morning, the air still and waiting, as if nature itself anticipates something profound about to unfold within you—something that has long been dormant, yearning to awaken and shine a guiding light into the corners of your heart where fear once held sway. In that gentle hush before the world stirs, when the sky is tinted with the soft colors of hope, you realize that a new journey beckons: a path where courage is not merely an abstract idea but a living force that kindles warmth and strength within your soul. This is not about steeling yourself behind a stiff mask of false bravado or pretending you never tremble when uncertainty rises; rather, it's about discovering that courage, true courage, is sparked by the love and grace of the Lord who calls you by name, who sees every trembling moment and still chooses to equip you with the ability to step forward. Think of it like a small ember glowing quietly in the ashes of your doubts and worries—an ember placed there by God Himself, waiting for you to breathe life into it, to fan it into a bright flame that fuels your heart to serve Him with all that you are. As you consider what lies ahead, you might remember times you felt too weak, too broken, or too ordinary to matter much, times when your voice shook, when your resolve waned, when you wondered if God could truly use someone like you. Yet here, as you stand on this threshold, the Lord gently reminds you that He has chosen the humble and the hesitant before, that He never expects you to serve Him by your own limited strength, but promises to walk beside you, steadying your heart when storms threaten to overwhelm you. In the stillness, you sense His presence and begin to grasp a precious truth: you were never meant to gather courage alone, to summon it from empty wells of self-reliance. No, courage finds its deepest roots in the unshakable love of God, in His unwavering commitment to guide, protect, and carry you through every valley of doubt, every dark night of the soul, every challenge that insists you are not enough. There is comfort in knowing that the courage you seek is not a distant prize to be earned by heroics, but a gift God longs to give, one that flourishes as you learn to trust Him step by step. This book you hold in your hands is an invitation, an outstretched hand guiding you toward understanding how your life—right now, in all its imperfections—can become a vessel of God's courage, setting you ablaze with purpose and determination. Within these pages, you will discover that courage is not reserved for those with grand titles or dramatic destinies; it is meant for you, in your everyday life, among the people you love, in the ordinary tasks that fill your days, and in the silent struggles you face alone in the depth of your heart. The Lord can ignite a boldness inside you that transforms how you view your own limitations, enabling you to embrace challenges as opportunities to grow closer to Him, to rely more fully on His grace, and to extend His compassion to a world sorely in need of healing and hope. As you immerse yourself in this journey, imagine that you are being drawn into a circle of believers who over centuries have wrestled with the same insecurities, the same questions about worth and ability, yet emerged as bright lights shining across history. Their stories show that courage often grows in the fertile soil of surrender, where we acknowledge our need for God and find that He meets us there, turning our weaknesses into channels of His strength. It is in letting go of the desperate need to appear strong by ourselves that we discover true resilience—the kind that endures trials not by pretending they don't hurt, but by leaning into God's promises of presence and power. This book will guide you through reflections and insights that help you draw nearer to the Lord's heart, where fear loses its power under the steady gaze of His love. You will learn how to face internal battles that whisper lies of unworthiness and doubt, and how to counter them with the truth of who God says you are: His beloved child, chosen, forgiven, equipped with gifts that matter for His kingdom. Together, we will explore how courage is nurtured not in isolation, but in community, where brothers and sisters in faith can support each other, pray for each other, and celebrate each small victory as a precious stepping stone. You will see that courage does not always wear a fearless grin; sometimes it wears tears as it stands firm, sometimes it struggles to rise from its knees but manages to stand anyway. Courage is honesty in the face of uncertainty, compassion when hatred would be easier, forgiveness when bitterness begs to linger, and perseverance when circumstances tempt you to abandon all hope. Through stories, principles, and practical steps, this book will show you that your heart can become a sanctuary of courage, an inner chamber where God's Spirit whispers steady encouragement, reminding you that no challenge is too great for the One who conquered the grave. And as your courage grows, you will not only find the strength to serve the Lord in ways you once thought impossible, but also inspire courage in others. Imagine the ripple effect: your flame lighting theirs, creating a chain of emboldened hearts shining across families, communities, even nations. Your decision to trust God's strength rather than cower before your limitations can spark hope in someone who watches from the sidelines, wondering if they, too, can make a difference. Courage is contagious, and when fueled by your love for God and love for His people, it becomes a force that can soften hardened hearts, heal wounded souls, and transform despair into vibrant expectancy. Yes, the road ahead may be winding and sometimes shadowed, but remember that the same Spirit who hovered over the chaotic waters at the dawn of creation now hovers over the landscape of your life, ready to shape and renew it. Your courage is not a fragile flicker that can be easily snuffed out; it is anchored in the everlasting reality that God is faithful, and He is for you. No fear, no failure, no external power can sever the bond of love that Christ secured for you, and this truth is the bedrock beneath your feet, the shield that guards your heart when doubts assail. So step forward with heart aflame, eyes fixed not on your own strength, but on the limitless resources of God's grace. Let this book serve as a companion on your journey, reminding you that courage, once ignited, can become unstoppable, that your life, however humble or broken you fear it may be, can shine as a beacon of God's transforming love. Together, we will discover the keys to fueling your heart to serve the Lord with courage that transcends human logic, courage that defies despair and triumphs over fear. As you turn the page, know that you embark on an adventure where the Lord Himself beckons you onward, whispering, "Do not fear, for I am with you," and as you respond to that voice, you will find that no force can extinguish the flame that God ignites in a willing, trusting soul.

Day 1 - The First Spark: Embracing God's Call to Courage

Imagine standing at the edge of a quiet field at dawn, feeling the cool morning air on your face and seeing the faint glow of the rising sun stretch across the sky, and in that stillness, you begin to sense something deep within you, like a tiny spark waiting to catch fire in your heart, something urging you to step forward with faith and boldness, something gently whispering that now is the time to embrace God's call to courage, not because you feel strong or certain, but because you know deep inside that He is asking you to trust Him more than you trust your own fears; as you stand there, you might feel nervous, unsure, and even a bit unworthy, wondering if courage is meant only for great leaders or famous heroes, but the truth is that God calls every one of us—no matter how ordinary we feel—to rise up and serve Him with a heart full of faith, and in doing so, we discover that courage is not some rare quality reserved for a special few, but a precious gift that God plants like a tiny seed in every willing soul, a gift that can grow into something beautiful and life-changing when we nurture it with prayer, hope, and trust; perhaps you have had moments when you stood at the edge of making a hard decision, speaking a kind word when you were afraid others might mock you, standing up for someone who was hurting, or sharing your faith with a friend who did not understand God's love, and in those moments you felt your heart beat a little faster and your voice shake just a bit, but you also felt something else, a gentle push that said, "Go ahead, I am with you," and that was the Lord encouraging you to take the first step, to let that spark of courage find the air it needs to burst into flame; courage, after all, does not mean you never feel scared or uncertain, it means you choose to move forward and trust God, even when your knees are trembling, and when you do that, you discover that true courage is not about never feeling fear, it is about following God's call in spite of the fear, believing that He will never leave you alone, that He will strengthen you and carry you through moments you never imagined you could face, because what matters most is not your own strength, but God's strength working through you; think about some of the people in the Bible who faced huge challenges yet found courage not in their own abilities, but in God's promises—Moses, who was afraid to speak to Pharaoh, learned to trust that God would give him the words he needed; David, just a young shepherd, stepped forward to face a giant warrior named Goliath, not because David was taller or stronger, but because he trusted that God would guide his hand; Esther, who risked her life to speak to a king and save her people, prayed and believed that God was with her even when everything seemed uncertain; the disciples of Jesus, who were just regular people—fishermen, tax collectors, and others—found courage after Jesus rose from the dead and filled them with the Holy Spirit, and even though they once ran away in fear, they later stood up to powerful rulers, spreading the message of the Gospel boldly; when we read stories like these, we realize that courage does not start with having no fear at all, it starts with a willingness to let God guide you, to trust that He knows you better than you know yourself, and that He sees in you a strength and purpose you might not see yet; the first spark of courage often appears when we decide to listen more closely to God's voice than to the voices of our doubts, when we stop saying "I can't" and start praying "Lord, help me to try," and that shift in thinking comes from understanding that God is greater than any challenge or fear we will face; at times, we may stand before new opportunities with our hearts pounding, wondering if we can handle what God is placing before us—maybe it's helping someone in need when we feel too shy to approach them, maybe it's speaking kindly to a person who has been cruel to us, maybe it's volunteering at church when we feel we are not good enough, or sharing our testimony with someone who does not believe in God, and in those moments, courage means saying to yourself, "If God is calling me to do this, then He must believe I can, not by my own power, but by His, so I will trust Him"; each time you take even a small step of faith, you are giving that spark of courage a chance to catch and grow brighter, and as it grows, you begin to notice changes in the way you think and feel about serving God—what once seemed scary starts to feel more natural, and what once seemed impossible begins to feel like something you and God can handle together; you may find yourself drawn to praying more often, reading the Bible more carefully, and listening more closely to the Holy Spirit, because as you grow in courage, you also grow in your desire to stay close to the One who gives it; you might find new strength in simply remembering that God loves you and has good plans for you, that He knows every detail of your life, every fear, every worry, every hidden hope, and that He wants to use you to shine His light into this world; imagine that your heart is like a candle's wick, and courage is like a flame that the Holy Spirit brings close, ready to set it aglow, but for that flame to take hold, you must be willing to let it, to say, "Yes, Lord, I will trust You, I will step forward, even if I don't feel ready, because I know You will go before me," and when that flame catches, your heart begins to glow with a new sense of purpose, and it is not about showing off or proving how brave you are to others, it's about showing God that you trust Him enough to obey; it might help to remember that even Jesus, who was perfectly obedient and loving, faced moments that required tremendous courage—when He prayed in the Garden of Gethsemane, knowing He would soon suffer and die, He was in such deep pain that He sweated drops of blood, yet He still said, "Not my will, but Yours be done," embracing God's plan with courage beyond anything we can fully understand; Jesus showed us that courage can be quiet and steady, full of trust in God's goodness, even when the road ahead is hard, and when we think about how Jesus faced the cross for our sake, we can find the courage to face the much smaller challenges in our own lives; God does not ask us to find courage on our own, like trying to lift ourselves into the air without wings, rather, He offers courage as a gift we can accept by faith, and He strengthens us as we practice using it; just like a musician must play notes over and over to get better, or an athlete must train hard before feeling confident in a game, courage often grows through practice—each time you step out in faith to serve God, you practice courage, and it becomes a little easier the next time; at first, you might only dare to take very small steps, like praying out loud for a friend who is struggling, or offering to help with a small task at church, or sharing a Bible verse with someone who needs encouragement, and that might feel huge to you, but God sees your heart and delights in your willingness; as you take these small steps, you begin to realize that God truly does stand by you, that He holds you up, and that He never leaves you alone, and from that realization comes a greater courage, a fire burning a bit brighter, pushing you forward to take on bigger challenges, to love more deeply, to speak truth more boldly, to give more freely, and to show kindness in places where kindness is rare; this is how the first spark of courage becomes a steady flame, lighting your path as you strive to follow

God's will; it helps to understand that courage often involves facing things that are uncomfortable—maybe it's admitting you have made a mistake and asking for forgiveness, maybe it's forgiving someone who hurt you deeply, maybe it's sharing the message of God's love in a place where people resist it, or standing up for someone who is being treated unfairly when staying quiet would be safer; but as you face these situations, you learn that your true security is not found in staying safe or liked by everyone, but in doing what pleases God, knowing that He cares for you and will bless your obedience; over time, you begin to see how courage can change not only your own heart, but the lives of those around you—your example might encourage a timid friend to speak up when they see someone in need, your acts of service might inspire another believer to trust God more, your willingness to take risks for God's kingdom might plant a seed of faith in someone who has never known God's love before, and in this way, courage multiplies, setting other hearts on fire, spreading light in a world that often feels dark; remember that the first spark of courage comes when you choose to embrace God's call, and that call may not be flashy or dramatic, it might be a gentle prompting in your heart, a subtle nudge in your mind, an idea that does not seem to go away, encouraging you to do something good and right in God's name, and when you sense that call, you have a choice: you can ignore it and remain where you feel safe, or you can lean into it and watch as God empowers you to do more than you thought possible; God understands that we are weak, that we get scared, that we doubt ourselves, and that is why His Word is filled with reminders to "fear not," to "be strong and courageous," to trust Him with all our hearts—because He knows that without His help, we would shrink back, but with His help, we can move forward; think about the feeling you get when you accomplish something you never thought you could, like learning to ride a bike without training wheels, or giving a speech in front of your class, or asking forgiveness from a friend you hurt, and how once you finish, you realize it was not as scary as you imagined, and you feel proud and relieved that you found the courage to try; serving the Lord can feel like that, too, only the joy and peace you feel afterward is even deeper, because you know it mattered to God, it mattered to others, and it mattered to your own growth as a follower of Christ; embracing God's call to courage also means understanding that you will have to rely on Him daily, not just once, not just when you feel like it, but day after day, asking Him to guide your steps and show you where and how you can serve; when we rely on God continually, we realize that courage does not run out like a battery or disappear like a passing shadow, but instead is renewed as we spend time in prayer, meditate on His promises, and lean on supportive believers who encourage and uplift us; if you are not sure where to start, begin by asking God in prayer to help you recognize the places in your life where He is calling you to be brave, and trust that He will answer, that He will make it clearer as you pay attention to the opportunities and needs around you—maybe your community needs volunteers to help feed the hungry, maybe your neighbor needs a kind word, maybe your church needs someone to organize a prayer group, maybe a friend at school needs someone to stand by them when they are picked on, or maybe God is calling you to share your own testimony of faith with someone who is curious about Jesus; any of these moments, and countless others, can be the spark that ignites your courage, the point where you step out of your comfort zone and say "yes" to the Lord; keep in mind that courage also grows when we remember that God forgives us when we stumble, because serving the Lord with courage does not mean we never fail, we will sometimes feel afraid and turn away, or try to serve and not do our best, but even then, God's grace is there, ready to pick us up, dust us off, and help us try again; this takes the pressure off us to be perfect and reminds us that courage is about continuing to follow God despite our weaknesses, knowing that He can use even our most uncertain steps for His glory; as you embrace this first spark of courage, you will notice something else happening in your heart—a growing sense of purpose and peace that comes from putting your trust in the One who created you, the One who gave you unique gifts and talents, and the One who knows exactly what role you can play in making the world a brighter, kinder place; serving the Lord is not about earning His love (He already loves you more than you can understand) or trying to be better than anyone else, it is about living out the love He has poured into you, sharing it with others, and bringing hope to those who need it; the more you say "yes" to God's call, the more you embrace the courage He offers, the more you will see that your life has a meaning and direction that goes far beyond your own comfort or desires; think of it like lighting a campfire on a cool evening—at first, you strike a match and hold it against kindling, watching a tiny flame dance on a single twig, and it doesn't look like much, it might even go out if you are not careful, but if you add a little more dry grass, a few more twigs, gently shielding it from the wind, soon the flame catches more pieces of wood, and before long, you have a bright, warm fire that lights up the darkness and draws people near; that is what courage can do in your heart when you allow God to strike the match, and your willingness to trust Him acts like the kindling that helps the flame grow stronger, so that what started as a faint spark becomes a guiding light for your life and a blessing to others; the first spark of embracing God's call to courage, then, is not just a small event or a single moment, but the beginning of a journey that leads you toward greater faith, greater love, and greater impact on the people around you, because when you decide to trust God enough to be brave, you open the door for Him to use you in amazing ways, ways that you cannot even imagine now; you do not have to be rich, famous, or perfect to be courageous in God's service, you just have to be willing, and that willingness will carry you further than you ever dreamed; as you walk this path, remember that the Lord is always with you—He goes before you, preparing the way; He stands beside you, holding your hand; He dwells within you, giving you strength and comfort; and He watches over you with love, guiding you step by step; no challenge is too big for Him, no fear too strong, no doubt too deep, and by embracing the courage He offers, you say to your fears, "My God is bigger than you, and I will trust Him no matter what"; in time, you may look back on these early moments and smile at how small your courage once seemed compared to what God grew it into, and you will thank Him for teaching you that the first spark of courage was all He needed to start a roaring fire of faith and love in your heart; so take that step, say that prayer, trust that nudge, and watch how the Lord transforms your trembling "I can't" into a confident "I will, by God's help," and as you do this, let your heart be filled with hope, knowing that God never calls you to courage without walking beside you, and that when you serve Him, you are part of a greater story of goodness, mercy, and grace that can change the world, one spark at a time.

Day 2 - Overcoming Fear: Trusting the One Who Leads You

Picture yourself standing at the edge of a great forest just before dusk, with the sky painted in shades of gold and purple, and as the sun slowly sinks, you feel a flutter inside your chest, a nervous tension that creeps into your mind when you think about stepping into those dark and silent trees, unsure what lies beyond the first row of trunks, and this feeling, this quiet trembling that makes your heart beat faster, is a lot like the fear you sometimes face when you sense that God is leading you somewhere new, calling you forward to serve Him in ways that stretch beyond your comfort, and yet, in the middle of that uncertainty, He whispers gently that you are not alone, that He is going before you to guide and protect you, and if only you will trust Him, you will find the strength to overcome the fear that tries to hold you back; we all know what fear feels like—our stomachs twist, our thoughts race, our hands tremble, and our hearts worry about all the things that could go wrong if we dare to step forward, and as we stand on the brink of doing something we believe God wants us to do, we often find ourselves asking questions like, "What if I fail?" or "What if others laugh at me?" or "What if I just can't handle this?" and these questions, swirling in our minds like fallen leaves in the wind, can make us hesitate, can make us think it might be safer to just stay where we are, but the Lord does not want us trapped by fear, He wants us to know that trusting Him is the key to moving past those doubts and following wherever He leads; imagine for a moment that God is a shepherd and we are the sheep of His pasture, and though sheep can be easily frightened—by strange sounds, by new paths, by anything that seems unfamiliar—they learn to trust the voice of their shepherd, because the shepherd knows where the green grass grows, where the cool water flows, and how to keep them safe from wolves hidden in the shadows, and as long as the sheep keep their eyes and ears open to the shepherd's voice, they can move forward even when the way seems uncertain, and in the same way, when we learn to trust God's voice, when we listen closely to what He says in His Word and through prayer, we find that fear loses some of its power over us, because we know we are in the care of One who is strong, wise, and loving beyond measure; think about some of the people in the Bible who faced great fear yet chose to trust God's guidance rather than run away—consider Moses, trembling at the thought of confronting Pharaoh, the most powerful ruler in the world at that time, because he felt weak and worried about his ability to speak well, but God reminded Moses that He would go before him, that He had heard the cries of His people, and that through Moses, He would bring about their freedom, so despite his trembling heart, Moses obeyed, and over time, he watched God send mighty signs, split seas, and feed multitudes, proving again and again that when you trust Him, He makes a way; think also of Gideon, hiding in a winepress, trying to stay safe from his enemies, but the Lord called him a "mighty man of valor" and told him to lead His people to victory, and even though Gideon felt small and afraid, he chose to trust, and by following God's instructions, even when they seemed strange—like reducing the size of his army—he overcame fear and watched God deliver Israel; or consider Esther, a young woman who knew that speaking up for her people might cost her life, who knew the king could refuse her request, but she trusted God enough to face that fear, to go before the king, and to act with courage, and through her faith, God saved her people from destruction; and remember the disciples of Jesus, who often felt afraid—afraid of storms at sea, afraid of the angry crowds, afraid when Jesus spoke of His coming death—but over time, as they watched Jesus calm the waves, feed the hungry, heal the sick, and rise from the grave, their trust in Him grew stronger, and their fear began to fade, so that after Jesus returned to heaven, these once timid disciples traveled far and wide, boldly preaching the Gospel even though they risked persecution, proving that trusting God's leading can turn the weakest heart into a courageous instrument of His love; it is important to see that fear itself is not a sin or a weakness that must be hidden, it is a natural human feeling that can protect us from harm, but it can also hold us back from doing what is right and good when we give it too much control, and God understands that we feel afraid sometimes—He created our minds and hearts, and He knows the worries that swirl inside us—but He wants us to remember that He is bigger than any fear we face, that no matter how tall the mountain or how deep the valley, He is with us, holding our hand and guiding our steps; when fear stirs within you, try turning your eyes to the Lord instead of focusing on whatever frightens you, if you are nervous about speaking up in class, or praying out loud, or sharing your faith with a friend, remember that God is the One who gave you a voice and a message worth sharing, and He can give you the courage to use it for good; if you are afraid of taking on a new role in your church, or helping someone in need when you are not sure how, remember that God is the One who equips you, who provides the resources and the wisdom you need, and as you trust Him, you will find that what once seemed impossible now feels like a natural step forward; another helpful thing is to fill your mind and heart with God's promises, because when fear tries to convince you that you are alone, or that you will surely fail, or that everything will go terribly wrong, God's Word reminds you that He is faithful and good, that He never leaves nor forsakes those who love Him, that He can bring beauty out of ashes, and hope out of despair, and even if things do not go exactly as you planned, He can still use your efforts for His glory and your growth; reading the Bible, especially stories of people who faced great challenges, can encourage you to see that fear does not have the final say, and memorizing verses that speak of God's strength can help you fight back when fearful thoughts try to take over—verses like "Fear not, for I am with thee" and "Be strong and of a good courage" remind us that we are never truly alone, and that God's presence is the ultimate source of comfort and bravery; prayer is another powerful weapon against fear, because when we pray, we speak directly to the One who holds our future, the One who sees the whole picture when we see only a tiny piece, and by laying our fears before God, we can ask for His peace, His guidance, and the calm assurance that He is in control; sometimes, simply saying, "Lord, I am scared right now, but I trust You," can bring a sense of calm that was missing before, because admitting our fear does not make us weaker, it opens the door for God's strength to enter our hearts; have you ever watched a small child clinging to a parent's hand while crossing a busy street? The child might be frightened by the cars rushing by, by the noise, by the unfamiliar scene, but the parent's hand is steady and strong, leading the child safely across, and in a way, we are all children in need of our Heavenly Father's hand—when we trust that He will not let us stumble, that He knows the way and can see the danger we cannot see, we can move forward even when our hearts feel uncertain, because our trust in His love and wisdom becomes greater than our fear;

trusting God also means accepting that His plan is sometimes different from ours, that overcoming fear is not about making sure everything turns out exactly how we expect, but about believing that whatever happens, God can use it for good—maybe you attempt something brave for the Lord's sake and you do not succeed in the way you imagined, maybe fear tries to say, "See, I told you so, you should have stayed back," but if you trust God, you know that He can use even what looks like failure to teach you patience, humility, or to open a new door you never considered; over time, as you make a habit of trusting the One who leads you, you find that fear does not vanish altogether, but it loses its power to stop you, you begin to see it as just one of many feelings passing through your mind, not as a chain that binds you, and you realize that courage is not the absence of fear, but the decision to follow God in spite of it; and as your trust grows, you discover a remarkable joy in serving the Lord, because when you step out in faith, guided by His hand, you get to witness His miracles—maybe not always miracles like splitting a sea or moving a mountain, but miracles of changed hearts, of people finding hope, of friendships strengthened, of communities blessed, and knowing that God used you, even when you felt afraid, reminds you that He is truly the One in control; think of the apostle Peter, who at first was so afraid of the stormy sea that he began to sink when he tried to walk on water, but when Jesus reached out and caught him, Peter realized that even in the midst of fear, if he kept his eyes on the Lord, he could do what seemed impossible, and later, after Jesus rose from the dead, Peter would stand boldly before crowds and leaders, preaching the Gospel without flinching, because his trust in Jesus had grown to overshadow his fear; in your own life, you might face storms that make you feel small and helpless—maybe it's dealing with rejection, worrying about the future, standing up for someone who is bullied, or defending your faith in a conversation with someone who does not believe, and fear will whisper that you should keep quiet, that you should back down, that you are not strong enough, but trust reminds you that it does not depend on your strength alone, that the Lord Himself stands beside you like a mighty warrior, and that He can do far more through you than you ever expected; some people try to overcome fear by becoming tougher or by ignoring their feelings, but these methods never truly solve the problem, because deep down, fear remains like a shadow, ready to appear again when the next challenge comes along; true victory over fear comes from resting in God's presence and knowing that He is faithful, patient, and kind, and that He understands our hearts better than we do—He will never push you beyond what you can bear without giving you the strength to face it, never call you without equipping you, never send you forth without walking beside you; trusting God who leads you also means learning to be patient with yourself, because growing in courage does not happen overnight, and it's okay to take small steps at first; maybe at the start, you are only brave enough to share a kind word with a neighbor, to pray quietly for someone in need, or to sign up for a small act of service at church, and fear still nags at you, making you nervous and uncertain—but as you keep trusting, keep praying, keep listening to God's voice, you find those small steps become easier, and before long, you are willing to take bigger steps, to speak to larger groups, to stand firm in your beliefs when others disagree, to love more openly and give more generously, because you have seen over and over that the One who leads you has never let you down; in moments when you feel your courage begin to waver, remember that Jesus Himself knew what it felt like to face something scary—in the Garden of Gethsemane, He prayed, "If it be possible, let this cup pass from me," because He knew the suffering He would endure, and yet He trusted His Father's will above all else, saying, "Nevertheless, not as I will, but as thou wilt," and by overcoming His own human fears and submitting fully to God's plan, Jesus opened the door to salvation for all of us, showing that trust, not fear, should guide our steps; if the Son of God chose trust over fear, then we, who are His followers, can ask God to fill our hearts with that same trust, to help us believe that even when we are afraid, He can use our willingness to do great things; part of this process involves surrounding ourselves with other believers who encourage us to trust God, who remind us of His promises when we forget, who lift us up in prayer when we feel weak, and as we walk together in faith, we realize we are not facing our fears alone—we have a spiritual family that stands beside us, cheering us on, reminding us that we serve a mighty God; imagine the warmth of a campfire surrounded by friends on a cool evening, each person holding a marshmallow or telling a story, feeling safe, supported, and joyful in each other's presence—trusting God in the face of fear is a lot like sitting around that fire, where the warmth of His love and the encouragement of fellow believers helps drive the cold fear away, helping us move forward with smiles on our faces and hope in our hearts; remember, too, that God's timing might be different from yours, and sometimes what feels frightening today becomes a source of strength tomorrow, when you look back and see how God brought you through it; fear might say, "Don't even try, you'll only get hurt," but trust says, "God will never waste my efforts, He will use even my struggles to teach me and bless others"; fear might say, "You are all alone in this," but trust replies, "God is with me always, I am never alone"; fear might insist, "This is too hard, you can't handle it," but trust answers, "With God all things are possible, and He will give me all I need"; by choosing to listen to the voice of trust instead of fear, you train your heart to follow the light instead of the darkness, and each time you do this, you grow stronger in faith, until you reach a point where fear, while still present, feels much smaller compared to the greatness of your Lord; think about how trust in God can help you see challenges as chances to grow, rather than threats to run from—when you trust the One who leads you, you understand that He might use difficult moments to shape you, to teach you patience, compassion, or resilience, just as a blacksmith uses fire and hammer blows to make a sword strong; fear wants you to stay as you are, but trust invites you to become the person God designed you to be, someone who can face life's storms without losing hope, who can meet hardship with faith, who can love boldly even when love is risky, who can speak truth even when truth is unpopular; as you learn to overcome fear by trusting the One who leads you, you also draw closer to God's heart, discovering more of His character—His gentleness, His mercy, His strength, His faithfulness; this closer relationship with Him is not just a side benefit, it is the very core of why trusting Him matters, because the more you know Him, the more you see that He is worthy of your trust, and the less reason you have to let fear rule your life; it's like walking through a dark tunnel holding onto a trustworthy friend's hand—at first, you feel nervous because you can't see clearly, but as you sense the friend's firm grip, hear their reassuring voice, and feel them guiding you forward, you realize that you will reach the other end safely, and the darkness no longer frightens you as much, because you trust the one leading you; at the end of the day, overcoming fear is not about pretending you are never afraid, it's about choosing to follow God's call in spite of that fear, trusting that He will give you what you need, that He knows more than you do, and that He loves you too much to let fear keep you from the purpose He has for your life; whether it's a small step or a giant leap, each time you trust Him, you shine a little brighter, you spread a little more hope, and you become a living testimony that fear cannot stop a heart fueled by faith in the Lord; so, the next time you feel fear creeping in, remember to lift your eyes to the One who leads you—pray, read His Word, remind yourself of His promises, talk to other believers, and take that step forward, even if it's just one step at a time, because with each step, fear loses its grip, and courage, ignited by trust in the Lord, grows like a warm flame in your heart, lighting the way forward, showing you that you can overcome fear not by your own might, but by holding onto the hand of the One who knows your path, loves you deeply, and promises never to abandon you.

Day 3 - A Flame in the Darkness: Finding Faith in Uncertainty

Imagine standing alone in the quiet stillness of a moonless night, with no lamp in your hand and only the whisper of a gentle breeze to remind you that you are not lost in empty space, and as you gaze into the inky darkness stretching before you, you feel a steady ache of uncertainty growing in your chest, the sense that you do not know what lies ahead, where the path will lead, or how you will find your way forward; this feeling, the heavy weight of not knowing what tomorrow brings, can press down on your heart and make you want to shrink back into a corner of safety, to stay where you can see what is around you, and yet the Lord calls us to walk forward by faith, even when the path seems hidden beneath shadows, and so we must discover how to let faith become a flame in the darkness, a small but steady light that guides our steps and warms our hearts, helping us move forward without fear, because we know that God is with us; it is in these moments of uncertainty that our faith is tested and shaped, much like a lump of clay that becomes a beautiful vessel when pressed and molded under the potter's skilled hands, and though at times we wish we could see the whole picture, to know exactly what will happen and how things will turn out, the Lord often asks us to trust Him in the mystery, reminding us that His wisdom is far above our own, that His understanding is like a mighty ocean while ours is like a single drop of water, and if we learn to trust Him in the darkness, we will find our courage ignited and our hearts fueled to serve Him more fully; think of how a small flame dances within a lantern, its glow limited at first, yet enough to show you where to place your feet, enough to keep you moving along a path that, without it, would be impossible to follow—this is what faith does in times of uncertainty: it does not make the darkness vanish all at once, nor does it suddenly show you every bend and twist in the road, but it gives you enough light to take one step and then another, trusting that God holds your future in His hands, and that what is unseen to you is perfectly known to Him; consider Abraham, who left his homeland and family, guided only by a promise from God that He would make him the father of a great nation, yet Abraham could not see the end of the journey, he could not know exactly how God would fulfill His words, and still he walked forward, trusting the One who led him; think of Mary and Joseph, told that they would raise the Son of God, yet forced to travel to Bethlehem under difficult conditions, to flee to Egypt to protect their child, and to navigate countless unknowns as they raised Jesus in a world that did not fully understand who He was—though they could not see every detail of the future, they believed that God had a plan, and they moved forward step by step, holding onto faith like a flame in the night; time and again, God's people have faced times of great uncertainty—Noah building an ark before the rain began, the Israelites wandering in the wilderness without seeing the Promised Land right away, the prophets speaking God's truth not knowing how many years would pass before their words came true, the disciples leaving their old lives behind to follow Jesus, not knowing where their Lord would lead them next—and in each case, faith acted like a beam of light breaking through the darkness, making it possible to keep going, to trust that even when they could not see, God could, and that was enough; when we face uncertainty, it often reveals what we truly believe about God—do we trust that He is good even when life feels confusing and scary, do we believe He is strong enough to handle whatever we will face, do we believe that He knows us better than we know ourselves and wants good things for us in the end, do we believe that He can bring light from the darkness, hope from despair, and clarity from confusion? If we answer yes, then that belief becomes the flame that brightens our darkest nights, and as that flame burns brighter, it kindles courage within us, reminding us that we do not stand alone in the shadows but walk side by side with the One who created light itself; if you have ever watched a single candle burning in a dark room, you might notice how your eyes adjust, how that tiny flame chases away more darkness than you thought possible, and how as you draw closer to the candle, you feel the gentle warmth of its glow on your skin, and in the same way, as we draw closer to God during uncertain times, focusing on His promises rather than our fears, His character rather than our doubts, we begin to feel the warmth of His presence, the comfort of His love, and the steadying peace that comes from knowing that He does not abandon us, and suddenly, uncertainty becomes less frightening, more like a chance to see God's faithfulness in action, to watch Him carry us through when we are not sure how to move on our own; of course, this is easier said than done, for uncertainty can feel like a thick fog that wraps around us, making it hard to breathe, tempting us to panic, and pushing us to grasp for anything that will give us a sense of control, but what if, instead of panicking, we choose to pray, to lift our eyes to heaven and say, "Lord, I do not know what is coming next, I do not see the way forward, but I trust that You do, and I believe You can guide me," and in that prayer, we open a door for the Holy Spirit to breathe peace into our hearts, to remind us that God is faithful not just in bright times, but especially when shadows fall; remember that faith is not about pretending we have no questions or doubts, it is about bringing those doubts and questions to God, laying them at His feet, and saying, "I choose to trust You anyway," and when we do that, our hearts begin to change, we learn to rest in the knowledge that God's goodness does not depend on our ability to understand all His ways, that He can see around every corner, over every hill, and into every hidden valley where we cannot see, and if we believe that He is guiding us like a loving shepherd, then we can take the next step without fear, because the One who leads us does not grow weary or confused; faith in uncertainty also teaches us patience, for we live in a world that craves instant answers, quick solutions, and fast results, and when we do not see a clear path forward, we might feel frustrated or scared, but in these moments, God invites us to slow down, to trust His timing, to understand that He may be working behind the scenes in ways we cannot imagine, and that sometimes, waiting in the darkness is exactly what we need to grow stronger, wiser, and more compassionate toward others who struggle; think of a seed buried in the soil—at first, it must push through the dark earth, reaching upward even though it cannot see the sun, trusting that the warmth and moisture will help it grow, and in time, it breaks through the surface, feeling the sunlight for the first time, but if it had refused to grow in the darkness, it would never have reached the light, and so it is with our faith: as we learn to trust God in uncertain times, we stretch our spiritual roots deeper, drawing nearer to the source of life, and when we finally see the outcome of what He is doing, we will realize that the darkness helped us grow in ways we never knew we needed; uncertainty can also teach us empathy, because as we struggle to find faith when we cannot see what lies ahead, we learn how hard it can be, and this understanding makes us more gentle and kind when we meet others in their own dark valleys, reminding us that everyone wrestles with questions, everyone faces moments when their future feels unclear, and by extending love, encouragement, and support, we help each other keep going, like travelers who share a lantern on a dark road, taking turns to carry the light so no one stumbles alone; as we practice holding onto faith in uncertain times, we discover that courage begins to rise within us, not because we suddenly gain control over every part of our lives, but because we trust that God holds all things together, and courage born in darkness is often stronger than courage born in comfort, because it relies fully on God and not on our own strengths or plans; this courage then fuels our desire to serve the Lord more boldly, because we see that He can guide us through any unknown situation, that He can use even our confusion and struggle for His glory, and that as we take steps of faith in the darkness, He can shine through our lives, helping others find their way as well; when we think about Jesus, we realize He knew what it meant to walk in uncertainty from a human point of view—He knew hunger, thirst, rejection, and pain, and though He was fully God, He experienced the limitations of human life, including moments when He prayed with deep sorrow, seeking the Father's will, trusting in His plan even when facing suffering and death, and Jesus shows us that true faith does not mean we are never afraid or unsure, but that we hold fast to our Father's hand even when the darkness presses in, believing that God's love will prevail and that His purposes cannot be thwarted; in following Christ's example, we learn to keep our eyes on God rather than on the uncertainty itself, for if we stare too long into the darkness, we might convince ourselves that we are lost, but if we lift our gaze and fix it on the One who is the Light of the World, we find reason to hope, reason to believe that no matter how confusing the present seems, God's light will guide us, one step at a time, until we reach a place of greater understanding, peace, and purpose; this does not mean that the road will always be easy, or that we will never stumble, but it does mean that when we do stumble, God's grace will catch us, lift us, and help us stand again, and each time we rise after a fall, each time we choose faith in uncertainty, our courage grows like a flame fed by fresh air, shining brighter than before; if you find yourself in a season of life where everything feels uncertain—maybe you are unsure about your future, your career, your relationships, your health, or how you can serve God when you do not know what tomorrow holds—remember that you are not alone, that countless believers have stood where you stand, peering into the unknown and feeling their hearts tremble, and yet they chose to trust, and by trusting, they discovered a deeper faith, a sturdier hope, and a more vibrant courage than they ever thought possible; you can do the same by turning your fears over to God, asking Him to help you see the good He is working even in the darkness, seeking comfort in His Word, and surrounding yourself with others who will encourage you to keep believing; as you continue on this path, you will realize that uncertainty, rather than being an enemy to your faith, can be the very thing that strengthens it, forcing you to rely not on your own limited understanding, but on God's infinite wisdom, and in doing so, you will find that the darkness cannot extinguish the flame of faith that God has placed within you; instead, that flame will burn brighter, guiding your steps and allowing you to stand as a beacon to others who wander in their own valleys of doubt and confusion, for when they see you pressing forward with hope, they may find the courage to seek God's light for themselves; remember that faith is not a once-and-done decision, but a daily choice, especially in uncertain times, and some days you will feel strong, ready to face the unknown with confidence in God's goodness, while other days you may feel weak, struggling to believe that there is a purpose in what you cannot understand, but through it all, God remains the same—loving, faithful, patient, and present; He never grows tired of our questions, never scolds us for feeling unsure, never turns away when we reach for His hand in the dark; His promise is that if we seek Him, we will find Him, and if we trust Him, He will guide us, for He is the Good Shepherd, the Light of the World, the Rock on which we stand, and no darkness, no uncertainty, can ever change that; let this truth be the warmth in your soul as you face the unknown, as you feel the wind of doubt try to blow out your small flame, protect it by feeding on God's Word, by remembering His past faithfulness in your life, by listening to testimonies of how He has guided others through uncertain times, and by praying for the Holy Spirit to strengthen your heart; the more you protect and feed this flame of faith, the stronger it becomes, and soon it will not only light your own path, but also serve as a guiding star for those who look up to you, those who see how you hold onto God when nothing seems clear, and wonder how they too can find that kind of steady peace; when uncertainty tempts you to give up or turn back, remember that

God can use the darkness itself to show you the brightness of His love, that He can bring treasures out of trials, growth out of waiting, and clarity out of confusion; sometimes what we learn in the darkness can never be learned in the light, because it is in the unknown that we truly discover what we believe, what we value, and who we trust, and when we see God's hand guiding us through the night, we appreciate His presence in a new and deeper way, our hearts grow more devoted, and our courage more genuine; as you continue to live out your faith, think of uncertainty as an invitation rather than a threat, an invitation to walk closer to God, to lean not on your own understanding, but on the everlasting arms that hold you, to let go of the need for complete control and instead find freedom in trusting that the Lord, who has proven Himself faithful from the dawn of creation to this very moment, will not fail you now; this kind of faith transforms fear into courage, doubt into determination, and confusion into an opportunity for God's wisdom to shine; in the end, when you look back at these times of uncertainty, you may see that it was here, in the darkness, that your faith truly took shape, that you learned to rely on God in a way you never had before, that you discovered a wellspring of strength within you, placed there by a loving Creator who knew you would need it; you may also realize that this courage, forged in the darkness, has made you more effective in serving the Lord, because now you can stand firm even when you cannot see the whole path, now you can listen to His whisper and trust He will provide what you need, now you can step out in love and service without demanding a map of every detail ahead; and as you serve, others will see that your courage is not rooted in human confidence, but in divine faithfulness, and they may find themselves drawn to that light, eager to know the God who can lead His people through shadowed valleys to green pastures on the other side; so let the flame of faith burn brightly in your heart, a tiny spark at first that grows stronger as you trust it, as you guard it against the winds of fear, and feed it with prayer and Scripture, until it becomes a steady glow that accompanies you wherever you go; do not be discouraged if you stumble, if you have days when you feel lost or overwhelmed, because even in those moments, God is near, ready to guide you if you will only lift your voice to Him, ready to show you that His goodness is not dependent on clear skies and easy paths, but is proven most when the clouds gather and the road seems unclear; as you learn to find faith in uncertainty, you will discover a deep well of courage that can never be taken from you, because it does not depend on circumstances or feelings, but on the unchanging nature of God, who promises to be your light in the darkest night, your refuge in the storm, and your guide through the unknown; this realization changes everything, filling you with peace, determination, and a newfound desire to serve the Lord, because now you understand that wherever He leads, He will also provide, and that no darkness is so deep that His light cannot pierce it, no uncertainty so great that His wisdom cannot overcome it; in embracing this truth, you become a bearer of that flame to others, a messenger of hope who can say, "Yes, I have walked through darkness, I have faced times of uncertainty, I have had no clear answers, yet I trusted, and God led me through," and by sharing this testimony, you fan the flames in other hearts, helping them find their own courage to trust God when the path grows dim; thus, the darkness becomes not an end, but a place where faith flourishes, where courage grows strong, and where God's glory shines brighter against the shadows, proving that He alone is our rock and our salvation, and as you continue to walk by faith, remember that you are never truly alone, for God's hand holds yours, guiding you step by step, and this flame of faith within you will keep burning as long as you keep trusting, lighting your way until dawn breaks, uncertainty fades, and you find yourself standing in the fullness of His perfect light.

Day 4 - Standing Firm: The Courage to Endure Trials

Imagine yourself standing in the middle of a stormy field, rain pounding down, thunder rolling in the distance, and wind sweeping across your face so hard that it stings, and even though you can barely see through the sheets of water, you keep your feet planted firmly in the mud, refusing to run away or collapse into a trembling heap, because deep in your heart, you know you are not alone, and there is a strength in you that was placed there by the One who created all things, a strength that grows when you face trials instead of fleeing from them, and this strength is called courage, the kind of courage that does not just shine in sunny moments of hope or simple acts of kindness, but the kind that endures when everything around you seems to be shaking, threatening to knock you down; this is the courage to endure trials, to keep standing firm when the world seems to press in on every side, to hold tight to your faith when doubts buzz around like angry bees, and to trust that the God who called you to serve Him is also the One who will see you through the hardest times, even when the clouds hang low and the path ahead looks impossible to walk; the truth is that everyone who wants to serve the Lord will face trials of some kind—these trials might come in many forms, maybe you struggle with a painful loss, or face a sickness that does not go away, or deal with people who mock your faith or try to silence your voice, or you find yourself surrounded by temptations that tug at you to give up on the right path, or maybe you simply run into disappointment after disappointment, feeling as though every plan you make falls apart, every dream crumbles, and every effort leads to a dead end, and it is in moments like these that the spark of courage inside your heart must be fanned into flame, so that you can stand firm, pressing your feet deeper into the ground, holding your head up and facing whatever comes, knowing that God is bigger than your trials, and that He can turn even the toughest experiences into something meaningful, something that shapes you into a stronger, wiser, and more faithful servant; think of a mighty tree, its roots digging deep underground, clinging to the soil even as the strongest winds howl around it, bending its branches but never snapping its trunk, and remember that the courage to endure is like those deep roots, not something you show off on the surface, but something that holds you steady from within, something built over time, nurtured by trust in God's promises and strengthened by the examples of those who have gone before you; the Bible is filled with people who stood firm in the face of trials—Joseph, sold into slavery by his own brothers, thrown into prison for a crime he did not commit, yet he held onto his faith, and in time God raised him up to save his family and many others from famine; Job, who lost almost everything he had, from his children to his wealth to his health, yet he refused to curse God, even when he did not understand why he was suffering, and in the end, God restored him and taught him lessons he would have never learned without enduring hardship; Daniel, who prayed faithfully to God even when it meant being thrown into a den of hungry lions, stood firm in his belief, and God kept him safe through the night; the early disciples, who continued to preach about Jesus even when they were arrested, beaten, and threatened, trusted that God would use their trials for good, and their courage helped spread the Gospel far and wide; and of course, think of Jesus Himself, who endured the agony of the cross, not because it was easy, but because He knew it was the will of His Father, and through His suffering, He brought salvation to the world; these examples remind us that standing firm does not mean never feeling pain or fear, it means refusing to let that pain or fear make you give up, choosing instead to lean on God's strength and trusting that He will carry you through; when you face trials, you might be tempted to think that God has abandoned you or that you are too weak to handle what is happening, but the truth is that God never leaves His children, and it is often in the darkest moments that He draws closest, waiting for you to lift your eyes and reach out to Him in prayer, for when you pray, you invite His presence to comfort your spirit, guide your choices, and remind you that He is still in control, and just as a sailor learns to navigate by the stars when the sun sets, so you can learn to navigate by God's promises when the light of your understanding grows dim; it is in these times that you discover how strong God can be in you, helping you stand when you feel too weak to stand on your own, and as you grow older, you will look back on these trials and see how they shaped you, how they taught you endurance, patience, compassion, and humility, how they helped you understand that your worth is not measured by ease or success, but by faithfulness, and this understanding will fill you with a quiet confidence that cannot be shaken by every gust of trouble, a confidence that rests not in your own ability but in God's unfailing love and power; remember that standing firm in trials does not mean you must do it all alone, for God has given you other believers, a spiritual family that can help lift you up when your knees grow weak, and when you share your burdens with those who love the Lord, you find that they too have faced hard times, that they know how it feels to struggle and doubt and fight to remain faithful, and together, you can encourage one another, pray for one another, and speak words of hope that remind you that no matter how fierce the storm, God's grace is like a shelter you can run into, and when one of you grows weary, others can step in with a helping hand, a kind word, or a timely reminder that God is good; sometimes courage means holding your ground while tears roll down your cheeks, or your hands shake from the effort of holding on, and that is okay, for the Lord understands your weakness, He knows that you are human, that you feel pain and fear deeply, and He does not scold you for these feelings, but rather invites you to lean on Him, to let Him carry your burdens, and as you do, you may find that your trials, while never enjoyable, can become stepping-stones to a deeper and richer faith, a faith that grows more resilient each time it is tested; standing firm also involves trusting that God can bring good even from your hardest moments, that He can use suffering and struggle to shape your character, draw you closer to Him, and prepare you for future tasks that will require even greater courage, just like an athlete trains by pushing through challenging exercises that build muscle and endurance, so your faith muscles grow stronger when tested by trials, and in time, you may find yourself able to face even greater challenges with a calm assurance that you did not have before; think about how fire refines gold, burning away the impurities so that the metal becomes pure and bright, and in the same way, trials can refine your heart, helping you see what truly matters, what you truly believe, and what you are willing to stand for; without trials, your courage might remain shallow, untested, like a seed that never sprouts because it never faced the strain of pushing through the soil, but when hardships come, they give you a chance to put your faith into action, to show that you believe God's words not just when it is easy, but when it is costly; this kind of courage shines like a beacon in a dark world, giving hope to others who watch you endure with grace and faith, helping them see that God is indeed real and faithful, that He can hold His children steady even when the ground seems to quake beneath their feet; if you find yourself in the midst of a trial right now, know that you are not alone—countless believers across time and space have stood where you stand, faced what you face, and found God faithful; cry out to Him, express your hurt and confusion, tell Him how hard it is to keep going, and then listen, listen for that still, small voice that assures you He is near, that He sees you, that He treasures your trust even when you do not understand, and as you lift your prayer heavenward, you may feel a quiet peace settle over your weary soul, like a gentle hand wiping tears from your eyes, reminding you that this struggle, though painful, can serve a divine purpose; often we think that courage is about doing something huge and dramatic—charging into battle, standing before a crowd to speak boldly—but sometimes courage is simply refusing to give up when everything in you wants to quit, sometimes it is dragging yourself out of bed each morning and doing what is right even though it feels pointless, or continuing to be kind when others are cruel, or holding onto honesty when everyone else around you cheats, or keeping your faith when the world mocks it; these quiet acts of endurance, these choices to stand firm in the face of discouragement, are just as noble and heroic as any grand gesture, and they show that your heart is fixed on something higher than your own comfort, that you trust that God's way is worth following even when it hurts; as you endure trials, remember that you have a Savior who understands what it means to suffer, Jesus was betrayed by a friend, mocked by enemies, abandoned by followers, beaten, and nailed to a cross—all while being completely innocent, and He did it out of love for us, willingly suffering so that we could be saved; when you feel that no one understands your pain, remember that Jesus does, and that He invites you to find comfort in His presence, to know that He will never leave you, and that the same power that raised Him from the dead is at work in your life, helping you stand firm through every difficulty; lean on His words, for He said, "In this world you will have trouble, but take heart, I have overcome the world," and let that promise bring you strength, because if Jesus overcame the darkest trial of all, then no trial you face is beyond His reach; standing firm also means being careful not to let bitterness or anger take root in your heart, for trials can tempt us to grow resentful, to blame God or others for our pain, to let our hearts harden and shut out any hope, but courage means rejecting this path, choosing instead to remain open to God's love, trusting that He can heal your hurts and even use your suffering to bring compassion and wisdom into your life; it means reminding yourself that you do not have the whole picture yet, that what seems pointless now may one day make sense, and that even if it never does, you can still trust God's goodness and rest in His embrace; one powerful way to stand firm is to remember how God has helped you in the past—think back to other times when you felt scared or hurt, when you thought the situation was hopeless, yet somehow you made it through, and maybe then you can see how God provided a friend to encourage you, a verse from the Bible that comforted you, a moment of peace in the chaos, or a new opportunity that arose after the storm had passed; by recalling God's past faithfulness, you feed your courage now, reminding yourself that this God who got you through before has not changed, He is the same yesterday, today, and forever, and He is with you just as surely now as He was then; another way to stand firm is to fill your mind with truth rather than lies—when trials come, it is easy to believe that you are worthless, that your faith is meaningless, that God does not care, but these are lies that the enemy uses to break your resolve, to knock you off your feet, so fight back by holding fast to what God says in His Word: that you are His beloved child, that He has a purpose for your life, that He will never forsake you, that He can bring good out of even the worst situations, and that nothing in all creation can separate you from His love; letting these truths soak into your heart is like building a solid foundation of rock beneath your feet, so that when trials try to push you down, you stand secure and unshaken; it is also good to serve others even in your struggles, because focusing on the needs of others can help keep your own hardships in perspective, and often, when we reach out to help someone else, we discover that God uses our pain to comfort those who are going through something similar, making our struggles not a waste, but a tool for bringing hope and encouragement to another soul; think of how a wounded healer is sometimes more understanding and gentle than one who never knew pain, and how your own trials might equip you to listen with empathy, to speak with honesty, to care with depth, and thus your endurance is not only for your own growth but can also become a blessing to others; in all these things, remember that standing firm is not about never feeling weak, but about choosing to rely on God's strength when you are weak, choosing to plant your feet in faith when the ground trembles, choosing to keep your eyes on the One who holds the universe together even when your own world feels like it is falling apart, and in doing so, you become a testimony that lights up the darkness, showing others that there is a God who sustains His people, that faith can survive the fiercest storms, and that courage is born not from a lack of trials, but from holding onto God through those trials; as time passes and you continue to stand firm, you will notice changes in your own heart—you will become more patient, more compassionate, more able to withstand disappointments and difficulties without losing hope, and you will realize that your courage does not depend on feeling strong, but on trusting the Strong One, the Lord who never fails; you will begin to see that trials, though painful, can be like a sculptor's chisel, carving away what is weak and shaping you into something more solid and true, and you may even find yourself thanking God for teaching you lessons that you could not have learned any other way, for showing you that you are capable of enduring more than you thought, and that He is faithful every step of the journey; one day, when you face a new challenge, you might remember how you stood firm in the past, and that memory will give you courage to do it again, reminding you that the God who stood with you then stands with you now, that the spirit of endurance He planted in you will not wither but grow stronger, and that as long as you remain in His care, no trial can destroy your faith; and as others watch you hold steady through hardships, they may be inspired to seek the Source of your courage, to ask how you can remain calm and hopeful when the world rages around you, and in answering them, you have the chance to point them to Jesus, to share the good news of a God who overcame the world, who understands our pain, who gives us strength to endure, and who promises a future without tears or suffering; this is the power of standing firm—the power to turn trials into testimonies, suffering into seeds of faith, and endurance into a beacon of hope for all who struggle; so when the storms rage, when trials knock at your door, when you feel your legs shaking and your heart pounding, remember that God is with you, that He invites you to dig your roots deep into His love, to trust Him more than your fears, to focus on His truth rather than your doubts, and to pray for the strength to endure; if you do this, you will find that, little by little, your courage grows not weaker but stronger, shining brighter like a candle in a dark night, guiding you forward, one step at a time, and reminding you that though the trials may be hard, you serve a Lord who is greater than them all, a Lord who will never let you stand alone, and as you hold onto Him, you will endure, you will overcome, and you will emerge from the storm with a faith that is deeper, a hope that is steadier, and a courage that is ready to serve Him wherever He leads.

Day 5 - Anchored in Hope: Believing in God's Promises

Imagine yourself standing on the deck of a small boat out in the middle of a wide, deep ocean, the waves gently rocking the wooden planks beneath your feet, and the horizon stretching in every direction so far that you cannot see where the water ends and the sky begins, and though you feel a hint of unease at being so far from shore, a quiet comfort settles inside you as you remember that beneath the boat's hull, an anchor rests on the ocean floor, holding you in place, preventing the current from carrying you away, and in that moment, you understand that hope is like this anchor, a steady presence that keeps you from drifting into despair or surrendering to fear, especially when you place your hope in something unshakable and true, and the most unshakable and true thing in the entire universe is God's Word, for God's promises are like unbreakable chains linking your heart to His goodness, no matter how hard the winds blow or how dark the skies grow; when we speak of hope, we often think of a gentle feeling, a wish that things might get better, a soft candle flame flickering in a dark room, yet hope in God's promises is so much more than a fragile dream, it is a powerful certainty rooted in the very nature of the One who made all things, because God does not lie, He does not change His mind the way people do, He does not forget what He has pledged, and He does not abandon those who trust in Him, so when He gives us promises—promises of His presence, His guidance, His love, His forgiveness, and His ultimate victory over evil—we can stake our lives on those words, knowing that they will hold firm no matter what storms arise in our path; think about the stories in the Bible where God's promises played a key role: imagine Noah building the ark under a sky that had never witnessed such a worldwide flood, trusting God's word that rain would come and that God would rescue him, his family, and the animals, and how that promise became a beacon of hope through long days of hammering wood and facing the scorn of neighbors who did not believe; remember Abraham, an old man with no children, yet hearing God promise him descendants as numerous as the stars, and how he clung to that promise year after year, even when his eyes could not see how it could ever happen, until at last, God blessed him with Isaac, proving that what He says, He does; consider Joseph, a young man who received dreams from God that he would one day rise to a position of great authority, only to find himself sold into slavery and later thrown into prison, and yet even in the darkness of that cell, Joseph held onto hope, trusting that God's promises were not empty words, and indeed, God lifted him up to a place of influence and power that saved many lives; think also of the Israelites enslaved in Egypt, crying out for freedom, and how God sent Moses to deliver them, assuring them that He would lead them to a promised land flowing with milk and honey, though the journey seemed hard and filled with uncertainty, God kept every promise, guiding them with a pillar of cloud by day and a pillar of fire by night, parting the Red Sea, and providing manna in the wilderness; and what about David, anointed as a young shepherd to be the king of Israel, yet spending years running from Saul, hiding in caves, waiting for God's promise to come true, and at last, God's word stood firm, and David took his rightful place on the throne; time and again, we see that when God makes a promise, He keeps it, though we often must wait longer than we would like, though the road might twist and turn in ways that puzzle us, though our faith might be tested as we struggle to understand why certain hardships come our way, in the end, God shows Himself faithful, and this unshakable faithfulness is what allows us to anchor our hope in Him; hope anchored in God's promises changes the way we face life's challenges, instead of being tossed about by every new difficulty, instead of losing heart when we do not see immediate answers to our prayers, we learn to lean into God's promises as a stable foundation, a reason to keep believing, keep striving, keep loving, and keep serving, even when the world tries to convince us that it is pointless, because we know that God is working behind the scenes, weaving together strands of joy and sorrow, triumph and struggle, to create a tapestry of purpose and redemption that we can only partially glimpse at now; it is not always easy to hold onto hope, and God understands this—He knows that we are human, that we grow impatient, that we get discouraged, that we sometimes doubt His goodness when storms rage around us and our prayers seem to echo in silence, but part of believing in God's promises is learning that waiting does not mean God's absence, and delay does not mean He has changed His mind, sometimes He uses waiting to teach us patience, to deepen our trust, to shape our character, and to prepare us for blessings greater than we could imagine, and if we let Him, the waiting itself can become a classroom of faith, reminding us that our timetable is not God's timetable, and that He knows best when and how to fulfill the promises He has made; consider how hope anchored in God's promises can transform your daily life: when you feel lonely, you remember God's promise that He will never leave you nor forsake you, and that knowledge becomes a comfort in the emptiness, when you feel guilty or weighed down by mistakes, you recall God's promise of forgiveness through Jesus Christ, and that forgiveness lifts the heavy burden from your heart, freeing you to move forward without shame, when you feel afraid of the future, unsure what tomorrow will bring, you hold onto God's promise that He has plans to prosper you and not to harm you, to give you a future and a hope, and that assurance allows you to rest rather than worry, when you are weak and feel incapable of handling the challenges before you, you trust God's promise that His strength is made perfect in your weakness, and you discover that leaning on Him can accomplish far more than you ever could by your own power; anchoring your hope in God's promises does not mean you will never feel pain or face hardship—Jesus Himself told us that in this world we would have trouble, but it does mean that trouble does not have the final say, it means we look beyond the immediate trial to the God who stands above it, the God who can part seas, topple giants, calm storms, and even raise the dead, and if He can do all that, then there is nothing in your life that is too big or too complicated for Him to handle, no disappointment He cannot turn around, no heartbreak He cannot heal, no confusion He cannot clarify, and no fear He cannot quiet, trusting in His promises allows you to lift your eyes from the waves and fix them on the One who walks upon the water and calls you to come to Him; have you ever watched a plant grow in a shady corner, stretching its leaves toward a beam of sunlight filtering through a window? That plant reaches and leans toward the light, longing for the warmth and energy it provides, and in the same way, when we believe in God's promises, we lean toward the light of His truth, stretching our hearts toward His goodness, allowing His words to feed our souls and strengthen our roots, so that when storms come, we stand firm, not because we are unshakable on our own, but because we are planted in the rich soil of His faithfulness; hope is not merely a feeling that everything will turn out okay, it is a confidence in the goodness and power of God, rooted in His promises and proven by His track record throughout history and in our own lives, think of all the times you worried, only to find that God provided a way through, think of the moments you cried out for help and discovered that you were not alone, think of the obstacles you overcame with strength you did not know you had until God gave it to you, and remember how each answered prayer, each unexpected kindness, each open door, and each moment of peace in chaos was a reminder that God is who He says He is, and He will never cease to be faithful; as we anchor ourselves in hope, we also learn that God's promises are not just about our personal comfort or success, they are often about a bigger picture that involves blessing others through us, spreading His love and truth, and making a difference in a world that desperately needs light, when we trust God's promises, we become more willing to take risks for His kingdom, to serve sacrificially, to love courageously, and to share our faith boldly, because we know that His word will not return void, that He can use our efforts, small as they may seem, to accomplish great and lasting purposes; in a world that often seems filled with broken promises—politicians who fail to deliver on their words, friends who let us down, products that do not live up to their advertising—God's promises stand out like a solid lighthouse on a rocky shore, no matter how big the waves or how dark the night, the beam of that lighthouse cuts through the gloom, guiding weary sailors home, and God's promises do the same for us, allowing us to find our way even when life's storms threaten to toss us off course, without such a beacon, we might give up, lose heart, or drift aimlessly, but with it, we know where to set our course; hope anchored in God's promises also teaches us humility, for to trust God's word means admitting that we do not have all the answers, that we cannot control everything, that our best plans might fail, and our limited understanding might lead us astray, it means recognizing that God sees more, knows more, and loves more deeply than we can comprehend, and so we yield to Him, placing our hopes in His trustworthy hands instead of our own limited grasp on life, and in this humility, we find peace, because we learn that we do not have to carry the weight of the world on our shoulders, God is already holding it, and us, safely in His arms; think about how, when a child feels scared at night, he might hold a parent's hand or cuddle close, feeling safe and secure not because he suddenly understands the darkness, but because he trusts the one who holds him, so it can be with us and God's promises, we may not understand why certain trials come, why prayers seem delayed, or why the world can be so harsh, but if we believe in God's promises, we can rest in the knowledge that He is with us, that He knows what He is doing, and that He will never let us slip from His care; hope anchored in God's promises does not shy away from reality, it does not pretend that life is always easy or that every problem vanishes overnight, rather, it acknowledges the struggle but insists that the struggle does not define our ultimate destiny, it understands that we live in a broken world, that people may hurt us, that we may stumble, and that tears may fall, yet it refuses to believe that pain is the end of the story, because it knows the One who writes the final chapter, and He has promised to wipe away every tear, to bring justice to the oppressed, to lift up the humble, to heal the wounded, and to restore creation to its intended glory, and if He has promised, then it will happen, though not always on our schedule or in the way we expect, and that, too, is part of believing in God's promises—trusting that His way is better, even when we cannot see the full picture right now; sometimes we must remind ourselves of God's promises by reading Scripture regularly, by surrounding ourselves with other believers who encourage us to keep hoping, and by praying for the Holy Spirit to help us trust when doubts creep in, God's promises are not meant to be tucked away in some dusty corner of our minds, they are meant to be lived out, spoken aloud, sung in praise, taught to our children, applied to our struggles, and clung to with all our might when storms rage; as we do this, we become people of hope, not just hopeful people, but people who carry hope wherever we go, like a lantern that brightens a dim corridor, people who can offer comfort to the hurting by saying, "I know it is hard right now, but God promises to be near the brokenhearted," or "I see how uncertain your future feels, but remember God's promise to guide us when we trust in Him," or "I know you feel unforgivable, but God promises that if we confess our sins, He is faithful and just to forgive us and cleanse us," and by speaking these promises into the lives of others, we spread the anchor of hope far and wide, helping others find their footing in the storms of life; another important aspect of believing in God's promises is realizing that they point us to Jesus, the ultimate fulfillment of God's love for us, Jesus is the evidence that God keeps His word, because God promised long ago to send a Savior, and He did, sending His own Son to live among us, to suffer with us and for us, to die in our place, and to rise again in victory, all the promises of Scripture find their ultimate "Yes" in Jesus, who shows us that God will stop at nothing to redeem His children and bring them home, and when we anchor our hope in Christ, we anchor it in the One who overcame sin, death, and every obstacle that could separate us from God's presence; remember that hope thrives when we hold onto God's promises during times of uncertainty, like travelers who cling to a map in a strange land, trusting that it will lead them to safety, we hold onto God's Word in unfamiliar situations, believing it will guide us even when we are unsure of the path ahead, we lean on His promises when fear tries to whisper that we are alone, that we are helpless, that there is no reason to keep going, and we answer those fears with the unchanging truth that God is for us, that He loves us with an everlasting love, that He calls us by name, and that His plans are good, not for our harm but for our ultimate good; as the anchor grips the solid seabed beneath the waves, keeping the boat from drifting, so does hope grip the solid foundation of God's character and His unchanging Word, even when our emotions waver, even when our circumstances shift, even when everything we once counted on seems to slip through our fingers, hope remains, because hope is not built on what we see or feel at this moment, hope is built on the eternal faithfulness of the Almighty, and nothing can break that foundation; when life's storms reach their fiercest point, when the wind howls and the thunder booms and the rain stings your face, remember that you have an anchor in God's promises, close your eyes and recall the times He has been faithful before, the words He has spoken, the cross He bore for your sake, and allow those truths to calm your racing heart, to steady your trembling knees, to remind you that no matter how wild the storm, it cannot change the fact that God reigns, that He is good, and that He will keep every promise He has made; and as you weather these storms, your hope will grow stronger, not weaker, each trial you face and overcome by holding onto God's promises will strengthen your spiritual muscles, teach you perseverance, fill you with empathy for others who struggle, and shape you into someone who can face even greater challenges without losing heart, and so the cycle continues:

hope anchored in God's promises fosters courage, courage leads to service, and through service and faithfulness, you see more and more evidence of God's presence and keep growing in hope; it is a beautiful cycle that becomes more powerful the longer you live it, until one day you realize that no matter what happens, your heart remains anchored in the One who never fails; also, anchoring your hope in God's promises helps you distinguish between what is temporary and what is eternal, the world is full of temporary things—money, fame, pleasure—that might make us feel secure for a while, but eventually fade away, yet God's promises are eternal, they stretch beyond our brief earthly lives and point us toward a future where all that is broken will be made whole, where all tears will be wiped away, where we will be fully united with our Creator and each other in love and peace, and by believing in these promises, we learn to hold lightly to the things of this world and hold tightly to the things of heaven, to value love, faith, kindness, justice, mercy, and truth more than any passing luxury; imagine how different life would feel if you truly believed, deep in your bones, that God's promises are true, if you woke up each morning confident that no matter what happened that day, God would not fail you, if you faced your fears with the knowledge that the One who parted seas and raised the dead is on your side, if you walked into situations of uncertainty with the calm assurance that God's guidance never runs dry, that He will light your path step by step, if you approached difficulties with the understanding that they are temporary challenges on the way to a glorious destiny that God has already planned for you, this kind of hope would transform how you see yourself and the world around you, making you both humble and bold, patient and proactive, peaceful and passionate about what matters most; as you anchor yourself in hope, you might also find that you become more grateful, because you notice God's hand at work in your life, recognizing that every good thing is a reminder of His kindness and every problem overcome is proof of His faithfulness, gratitude then reinforces your hope, making it stronger and more radiant, like a candle that never runs out of wax, continuing to burn steadily through the darkest night; and so, anchored in hope by believing in God's promises, you become someone who cannot be easily shaken, not because you are unfeeling or unaware of life's hardships, but because you have chosen to trust in the One who holds tomorrow, the One who promises to work all things together for good, the One who brings beauty from ashes, joy from mourning, and life from death itself, and this hope becomes not just a safety net, but a source of power that drives you to serve the Lord wholeheartedly, to dare great things for His kingdom, to love those who are hard to love, to speak truth gently but firmly, to stand for what is right even when it costs you, and to persevere in doing good even when it seems no one notices, because you know that the One who made the promises sees every act of love, hears every whisper of faith, and will one day reward those who stand firm in hope; so remember, as you journey through life, that you have a choice: you can let the storms of uncertainty, disappointment, and fear drive you into despair, or you can throw your anchor deep into the solid bedrock of God's promises, holding firm against every wave that tries to push you off course, by doing so, you affirm that God's Word is more real than the chaos around you, that His love is stronger than any hate, and that His future for you is brighter than any darkness the present might hold, and in that choice, you find courage, strength, peace, and purpose, you find that hope does not fail when it rests on the unchanging nature of God, and this hope, alive in your heart, fuels your desire to serve the Lord with all your might, shining as a beacon for others who long for something sure and steadfast, a promise that will never be broken.

Day 6 - Fueling Your Faith: Drawing Strength from Scripture

Imagine yourself opening a well-worn book beneath the gentle glow of a reading lamp on a quiet evening, the room hushed so that you can hear the soft turning of pages and sense the weight of centuries pressing gently against your fingertips, and as you settle into a comfortable chair, you realize that what you hold in your hands is not just any ordinary book, but the Word of God, the Holy Scriptures, a living treasure that has guided countless souls through every imaginable season of life, and in this moment, you recognize that within its pages you will find stories of faith and failure, of hope and despair, of courage and fear, all woven together to reveal the steadfast goodness of the Lord who calls you to serve Him; you may have read these passages before, or perhaps some sections feel new and unfamiliar, but each time you open the Bible, you draw closer to the endless wellspring of strength and guidance that God provides, allowing His truths to settle deep into your heart like seeds planted in rich soil, ready to grow into mighty oaks of conviction and courage; think of how a candle's flame flickers brightly when fed by fresh air, or how a traveler's spirit lifts after a cool drink of water on a hot, dusty day, and understand that reading Scripture is like breathing life into your weary soul, fueling your faith and helping you stand firm in the face of all that challenges you, because through its words, God speaks, and when God speaks, mountains move, oceans tremble, and hearts long burdened by doubt or fear find the courage to rise again; this is why fueling your faith by drawing strength from Scripture is so important—it gives you a place to turn when darkness creeps in around you, a sure and steady anchor when the waves of confusion crash against your mind, a compass that points true north when the world's voices try to mislead you, and in these sacred pages, you encounter not just rules or lessons, but the very heartbeat of God's love, recorded faithfully so that generation after generation can know Him and trust Him; perhaps you have struggled with feeling uncertain about your purpose in life, or maybe you have wondered whether you truly have what it takes to serve the Lord with courage and conviction, and while it is natural to wrestle with these doubts, remember that Scripture answers them with a resounding reminder that you are not alone, that you do not have to rely solely on your own strength, and that God is eager to empower you, to lift your chin when it droops in discouragement, and to strengthen your legs when they grow weak from standing against the pressures of this world; consider the stories of ordinary people in Scripture whom God used to accomplish extraordinary things, men and women who were not perfect, who had their fair share of fears and failures, yet found the strength to stand firm because they trusted in the One who never fails: think of Moses, trembling before Pharaoh, uncertain of his ability to speak with authority, until God's words filled his mouth and gave him the courage to confront the mightiest ruler of his time; think of Joshua, stepping into Moses' enormous shoes, facing a land full of fortified cities and war-hardened warriors, until God's promise, "Be strong and of a good courage, for I am with you," ignited a flame of bravery within his heart that could not be quenched; think of David, a young shepherd boy, looking into the eyes of a giant who towered over him, until he remembered the countless times God had delivered him from lions and bears, and trusted that the Lord who rescued him then would rescue him again; think of Ruth, who clung to her mother-in-law Naomi, leaving behind all that was familiar, trusting in the God of Israel even though she was a Moabite, because she believed that God's goodness would prevail; think of Esther, trembling at the thought of approaching the king without being summoned, yet choosing to do so for the sake of her people, believing that God, who had placed her in the palace for "such a time as this," would provide the courage she needed to speak; think of the disciples, simple fishermen and tax collectors, unsure how to preach to crowds or stand against persecution, yet strengthened by the words and example of Jesus, who showed them that real greatness is found in humble service and unwavering love; these are not just distant, ancient figures with no relevance to your life, rather, their stories are recorded so that you might see how the Lord works through weak and imperfect people, taking their mustard-seed faith and growing it into towering courage, how He strengthens the trembling, lifts the fallen, encourages the discouraged, and leads them into paths of righteousness for His name's sake; when you immerse yourself in Scripture, you absorb the very words that have comforted prophets, guided kings, steadied the feet of persecuted believers, and inspired faithful servants across millennia, its pages are soaked in the tears of those who have wept with sorrow and those who have wept with joy, its verses echo with the prayers of saints who looked to heaven and found hope in God's promises; reading the Bible faithfully, allowing its truths to shape your thoughts and inform your actions, is like building a spiritual fortress brick by brick, every verse you memorize, every parable you ponder, every promise you cling to, every command you obey, each one is a building block placed carefully into the walls of your faith, making them strong enough to withstand the fiercest storms; and make no mistake, storms will come—trials of faith, moments of pain, seasons of uncertainty, temptations that threaten to pull you off course—but when your heart is fueled by the Word of God, you will find a surprising calm within the chaos, as though a quiet voice whispers to your soul, "Be still, and know that I am God," and that voice, grounded in Scripture, can silence the roar of fear and doubt, reminding you that no matter how high the waves rise, your foundation is unshakable because it rests on eternal truth; Scripture teaches us not only who God is, but who we are in Him: you learn that you are loved deeply, chosen purposefully, and equipped with all the tools you need to serve Him well, you learn that He has called you to be a light in a dark world, and that He will never demand more from you than He provides strength to accomplish, you learn that your weaknesses are not liabilities, but opportunities for God's power to shine through, so that when you face intimidating challenges—be they speaking truth in a hostile environment, defending the oppressed, extending forgiveness to those who hurt you, or walking faithfully in a calling that seems beyond your abilities—you can draw strength from verses that remind you, "I can do all things through Christ who strengthens me," and "His grace is sufficient for you, for His power is made perfect in weakness," and these truths, tucked into your mind and heart, become a reservoir of courage you can draw from at any moment; sometimes, you might feel disconnected or weary, as if your faith's flame has dimmed to a faint glow, maybe you have not opened your Bible for a while, or maybe the words felt dry and confusing the last time you tried, know that this is not unusual or unforgivable—people throughout history have struggled with dryness of spirit, with seasons when Scripture seemed distant and hard to comprehend, but take heart, because God's Word is living and active, always ready to speak to those who return to it with open hearts, and if you persist, humbly asking the Holy Spirit to guide you, the words will begin to shine again, revealing insights you never saw before, comforting your fears, challenging your doubts, and stirring the embers of your faith until they burn bright and hot once more; try making a habit of reading Scripture regularly, not out of duty or to impress others, but out of a sincere desire to know God better and to receive His guidance, even a few verses each morning can set the tone for your entire day, reminding you who you are and Whose you are, bolstering your courage to face whatever comes next, and as you read, do not rush through as if ticking off a chore, but pause, reflect, and consider how these words apply to your life, how they encourage you to trust God more deeply, how they challenge you to love more fully, how they give you courage to serve Him more boldly; Scripture is not meant to be read only on peaceful mornings or in quiet sanctuaries, it can travel with you into the chaos of the world: let it guide your decisions at work, comfort you as you deal with family struggles, strengthen your resolve when you confront injustice, inspire you to show kindness in hostile places, and give you the right words when sharing your faith with someone who might not understand what you believe, by internalizing what you read, memorizing key verses, and meditating on them throughout the day, you can carry the sword of the Spirit, which is the Word of God, ready to fend off lies and discouragement, ready to strike down temptations, and ready to shine light into dark corners; fueling your faith with Scripture also means acknowledging that you do not walk this journey alone, you stand in a long line of believers who have depended on the Word of God for guidance and courage—people who faced persecution, imprisonment, hunger, loss, and heartbreak, yet continued to trust because they knew the One who promised never to abandon them, and as you read their stories—both the ones written in the Bible and the ones told throughout church history—you realize that the same mighty God who upheld them upholds you, and the same Word that sustained them through trials can sustain you too; this realization transforms the way you see your own struggles, reminding you that you are part of something bigger than your immediate circumstances, that your faith journey is woven into a grand tapestry of God's faithfulness and love, and with every verse you learn, every psalm you pray, every teaching of Jesus you embrace, your place in that tapestry grows stronger and clearer;

Scripture also helps you discern between truth and falsehood, between godly wisdom and the empty promises of the world, in an age when so many voices clamor for your attention, each claiming to know the right way, the best approach, the only truth, the Bible cuts through the noise like a bright beam of light, reminding you that God's values are often different from what society praises, that humility is greater than pride, that serving others is nobler than serving yourself, that forgiveness is stronger than hatred, and that love overcomes all forms of darkness; by rooting yourself in these truths, you gain the courage to go against the current, to stand for what is right even when it is not popular, to love when others choose hate, to hope when others choose despair, to speak truth when others remain silent, and to offer forgiveness where others hold grudges—this kind of courage does not come from shallow optimism or self-confidence, but from the solid ground of God's Word, which assures you that He who is in you is greater than he who is in the world; keep in mind that your understanding of Scripture will grow as you do, as you pass through different stages of life—childhood, youth, adulthood, old age—the Bible speaks to you in fresh ways, revealing layers of meaning you never noticed before, you might discover that a verse that once encouraged you in a time of sorrow now inspires you to serve more wholeheartedly, or that a passage you struggled to understand now makes perfect sense because of experiences that have shaped your perspective, this growing relationship with the Word is like tending a garden, where seeds planted long ago blossom into beautiful flowers at unexpected times, feeding your faith with vibrant color and fragrance; it is also helpful to study Scripture with other believers, for when you discuss God's Word in a small group or with a trusted friend, you gain insights from their experiences and understanding, seeing truths you might have missed on your own, and as you share how certain verses have guided you through difficulties or how a particular psalm spoke to your heart when you felt discouraged, you help others see the power of Scripture in action, building one another up, strengthening each other's faith, and forging bonds of fellowship that make you even bolder in serving the Lord; throughout your life, you will face decisions that test your resolve, struggles that threaten to rob you of joy, and fears that whisper lies into your ear, but if you have been faithfully fueling your faith by drinking deeply from the fountain of Scripture, you will discover an inner resilience you did not know you had, a steady assurance that God's presence is real and reliable, that His promises stand firm, and that no matter how high the mountains appear, He can level them with a word; Scripture helps you see beyond the temporary troubles of today to the eternal hope of tomorrow, it helps you lift your eyes from the immediate pain to the ultimate purpose, and in doing so, it gives you courage to keep going, to keep serving, to keep loving, to keep believing—even when the evidence around you seems dim, for you know that the story is not finished yet, and the One who authored it will bring it to the perfect ending He has promised; let the words of Scripture be like a melody humming in the background of your life, soft but steady, guiding the rhythm of your actions and the tone of your thoughts, when discouragement threatens to muffle that melody, sing it louder by repeating God's promises to yourself, whispering them in prayer, or writing them down where you can see them often; when fear tries to silence it altogether, shout it from the rooftops, declaring that you trust God's Word above all else, and that you will not give in to despair; over time, this habit of turning to Scripture for strength and guidance becomes second nature, you will find yourself recalling verses when faced with tough choices, leaning on biblical truths when wrestling with moral dilemmas, and rejoicing in God's promises when celebrating breakthroughs and blessings, and each of these moments reinforces the truth that your faith does not depend on fleeting feelings or shaky circumstances, but on the solid rock of God's eternal Word; it is easy to see how this shapes the way you serve the Lord, because when your heart is fueled by Scripture, you serve not out of fear or obligation, but out of love and gratitude, motivated by a deep understanding that God's commands are given for your good, and that His instructions lead to fullness of life, this gives you the courage to step outside your comfort zone, to try new ways of helping others, to share your faith more boldly, and to stand up for what is right, even if it sets you apart from the crowd; as you continue to grow in this habit, never forget that Scripture itself points to the living Word, Jesus Christ, who is the ultimate source of courage and faith, the Gospels tell the story of His life—His teachings, His miracles, His sacrifice on the cross, and His glorious resurrection—and in Christ you find the perfect example of what it means to trust the Father completely and serve Him wholeheartedly, when you feel unsure, look at Jesus, who found strength in Scripture when tempted in the wilderness, who quoted God's Word to resist the devil's lies, who fulfilled the prophecies written centuries before, and who models for you what it means to love without limit; the more you immerse yourself in the Bible, the clearer His image becomes, and the more powerfully His Spirit works within you to cultivate a heart of courage, kindness, humility, and resolve, this is not a quick fix or a one-time solution, but a lifelong journey of learning, growing, stumbling, and rising again, each time stronger than before, because each time you fall, you land on the truth of Scripture, which assures you of God's grace, each time you rise, you stand a little taller because you trust more deeply in the One who holds you up; when doubts come—and they will—do not run from them, but confront them with the Word, search the Scriptures for answers, for comfort, for reassurance, and you will find that God is not afraid of your questions, that He welcomes your honest seeking, and that His Word contains wisdom you never expected, and when you find that wisdom, it fuels your faith even more, convincing you that God is not only real, but intimately involved in your life, caring for every detail and working all things together for your good; and so, by consistently drawing strength from Scripture, you will find that your heart grows steady, like a flame that cannot be snuffed out by the winds of doubt or fear, your courage to serve the Lord will increase, not because you have become fearless in a human sense, but because you fear God in the reverent, loving way that drives out all lesser fears, and with each step you take, grounded in biblical truth, you will walk more confidently into the purpose God has prepared for you; let this understanding lead you forward, let it embolden you to face challenges that once seemed impossible, let it inspire you to care for those who are hurting, to speak truth where lies have taken root, to stand firm against temptation, to encourage others who struggle, and to reflect the character of Christ in all you do, and in this way, your life becomes a living testimony to the power of God's Word, a bright flame fueled daily by Scripture's wisdom, shining ever brighter in a world that so desperately needs the guiding light of truth and love.

Day 7 - Prayer-Fed Fires: Seeking the Lord's Guidance Daily

Picture, if you will, the early morning darkness just before dawn, when the world feels quiet and still, and you stand alone in a silent place, maybe beside a window or beneath a dimly glowing lamp, breathing slowly as if each breath could settle the uneven rhythms of your heart, and in that calm, before the demands of the day rush in and before others begin to stir, you choose to meet the Lord in prayer, like a traveler stopping at a well to draw fresh water, like a builder gathering sturdy beams to support a new house, or like a caretaker adding fresh wood to a campfire so that its warm glow might continue through the coming hours; and as you close your eyes or lift them upward, as you whisper or simply hold your thoughts out before Him, you discover that prayer, this simple and yet often mysterious act of speaking and listening to God, is the very act that can feed the fires of your courage, fueling your heart with renewed strength and guiding your steps as you seek to serve the Lord each day, for just as a fire needs oxygen and fuel to burn bright and steady against the chill of night, so your soul needs the presence of God poured in through prayer, that you might live, act, and speak with a boldness not your own; think of it this way: without prayer, your spiritual fire might dwindle to faint embers, barely glowing, offering little warmth to your heart or light to your path, but when you regularly pause to seek the Lord, to open your heart to His guidance, to listen for His still, small voice, and to bring your fears, hopes, doubts, and desires to Him, it's as though you're adding fresh logs to a campfire, each prayer another piece of wood that catches and crackles, sending sparks of faith into your soul and making the flame dance higher, casting out shadows of uncertainty, and lighting up the world around you, so that you can see where to step next, how to serve, and how to stand strong even when life's challenges surround you; in a world that often tries to pull you in countless directions, tempting you to rely on your own wisdom, to make decisions based on fear or selfish ambition, prayer is the practice that recenters you, anchoring you in God's truth and reminding you of what matters most, for in prayer you remember that life is not about following the crowd or pleasing yourself at any cost, but about aligning your will with the will of the One who created you, trusting that He knows the way far better than you ever could, and as you kneel in spirit or body, you learn to release your grip on control, placing all your dreams and struggles into God's capable hands, and discovering that true courage does not mean never feeling afraid, but means pressing forward, guided by God's voice, in spite of your fears; day by day, as you continue this practice, you will begin to notice changes, at first subtle, like the gradual warming of the air as a fire burns steadily, and then more pronounced, like the brightening sky just before sunrise, for by turning to God in prayer each morning, each midday, each evening, you set a rhythm in your life that beats in tune with God's heart, learning to pause before reacting in anger, to breathe before blurting out hurtful words, to reflect before making hasty decisions, to ask God for help before despairing that you must handle everything alone, and with time, these small shifts accumulate, weaving through your thoughts and actions until it becomes natural to call upon Him, not just when you are desperate, but whenever you long to stay close, to walk steadily on the path He has set before you; prayer teaches you humility, reminding you that you do not have all the answers, that your perspective is limited, that your strength alone may not be enough to face every trial that comes your way, and yet it also instills confidence, because you learn that you serve a God whose wisdom is boundless, whose power has no limits, whose love for you runs deeper than the ocean and taller than the highest mountains, and in prayer you tap into the eternal source of courage, the unfailing well of hope, the storehouse of grace that God so freely offers to His children, and each time you do, you walk away carrying a piece of that strength within you, glowing like a hidden ember beneath the surface of your skin, ready to flare up into bold action when challenges arise; prayer also refines your motives, because as you come before God honestly, He often reveals the true nature of your heart—those places where fear masquerades as caution, where selfishness pretends to be wisdom, where pride disguises itself as confidence, and by gently shining His light into these corners, He invites you to let go of what holds you back, to trade fear for trust, selfishness for love, pride for humility, and in making these exchanges, you find that serving the Lord with courage becomes not just an occasional brave deed, but a natural outcome of living close to His heart, for when your inner world is ordered by God's truth, your outer actions flow from a place of genuine faith and unwavering resolve; consider the examples in Scripture of those who found their strength in prayer: think of Daniel, who prayed three times a day, even when the law forbade it, trusting that God could keep him safe in a den of hungry lions, think of Nehemiah, who paused to pray before speaking to a king about rebuilding the walls of Jerusalem, receiving the courage and the right words at the right time, think of Hannah, who poured out her sorrow and longing before the Lord at the temple, and who found peace and hope in her tears as God answered her cry, think of Jesus Himself, who rose early to pray in quiet places, who sought communion with the Father before choosing His disciples, before facing the cross, and who, in that garden under the weight of the world's sin, prayed, "Not my will, but Yours be done," drawing strength to endure what lay ahead, and as you reflect on these stories, you see that prayer was never just a duty, but a lifeline, a channel through which God's servants received what they needed to stand firm and fulfill His calling, and this same lifeline is available to you right now; it is important to understand that prayer need not always be formal or complicated, for God knows your heart, He sees beyond your words, and He welcomes you as you are—sometimes your prayers might be long and careful, shaped by the words of Scripture or thought out in advance, other times they might be as simple as a whispered plea, "Lord, help me," or a word of thanks, "Thank you, God," or a sigh of surrender, "Your will be done," prayer can fill quiet mornings and also busy afternoons, it can accompany you as you walk the halls of your school, drive to work, care for children, or navigate crowded city streets, and the more you practice it, the more natural it becomes, like breathing in and out, a constant connection with the One who guides your every step; through prayer, you learn to listen as well as speak, to quiet your racing thoughts and pay attention to the gentle nudges of the Holy Spirit, who may bring to mind a verse you've read before, place on your heart the name of someone who needs encouragement, or prompt you to pause before making a rash decision, and in these still, listening moments, God can do deep work within your soul, reshaping your priorities, infusing you with courage you did not know you had, and giving you a sense of direction that no human guide could provide, though you may not always hear a loud, clear voice or see a dramatic vision, you begin to recognize the subtle ways God communicates—through peace that settles in your chest when you consider a certain path, through an idea that glows bright in your mind with unusual clarity, or through a scripture passage that suddenly resonates as though it were written just for your situation; prayer reminds you that you are part of something larger than your own ambitions, that you are a member of God's family and a soldier in His spiritual army, and as you regularly seek His guidance, you start to understand that courage is not just about personal bravery, but about fulfilling a divine purpose—loving others well, speaking truth in love, standing up for those who have no voice, giving generously even when it costs you, extending mercy to those who least deserve it, and walking faithfully through every season of life, be it joy or sorrow, victory or loss, knowing that the One who called you is faithful and will equip you for every good work; in prayer, you also learn the value of perseverance, because sometimes God's answers do not come quickly, and you must keep coming back, day after day, to present your requests and to remind yourself that you rely on Him, not on instant solutions, this waiting can test your patience and humility, but it also strengthens you, like muscles worked through steady exercise, and over time, you grow more confident that even when you cannot see God's hand at work, He is still guiding the outcome, shaping events according to His wise design, and when at last the answer arrives—perhaps in a form different from what you expected—you can look back and see how prayer kept you anchored and hopeful throughout the uncertainty; as you feed the fire of your courage with prayer, you might discover that the people around you begin to notice a change, they may see in you a steadiness they cannot explain, a kindness that does not falter under stress, a resilience that bounces back after difficulties, and an integrity that holds firm even when tested, and as they wonder where this strength comes from, you have the opportunity to point them to the source, to share that it is not your own greatness, but the grace and wisdom of God poured into your life through prayer, in this way, your prayer life not only fuels your own heart, but also becomes a witness, inspiring others to seek the Lord's guidance and discover their own courage in Him; remember that prayer is not a magic formula that guarantees an easy life, it does not shield you from all trials or remove every obstacle from your path, but it does give you the perspective, strength, and courage to face whatever comes your way, knowing that God's purposes are good and that He can bring beauty from ashes, joy from mourning, and hope from despair, and armed with this understanding, you can approach challenges with confidence, not because you feel invincible, but because you know the One who goes before you is unstoppable; day by day, as you make prayer a regular and honest conversation with God, you establish a strong foundation that can withstand storms, prayer is like the hidden roots of a tall tree, unseen but essential, drawing nourishment from the depths of God's presence, making you stable in changing winds, or like the keel of a ship, keeping you steady even when waves crash and try to tip you over, prayer keeps you connected to your true source of life and courage, so that no matter what happens on the surface, you remain secure in your relationship with the Lord; consider too that prayer can bring comfort in times of grief, perspective in times of confusion, peace in times of conflict, and courage in times of fear, it transforms your view of the world, because when you regularly lift your eyes above your immediate circumstances, you remember that your story is part of a much greater narrative, a story where God is the author, directing the course of history toward a good and just ending, and this realization can dispel the darkness of despair, remind you that your labor in the Lord is never in vain, and encourage you to keep loving and serving even when you do not see immediate results; think about how a blacksmith repeatedly heats iron in the fire, hammering and shaping it, cooling it, and heating it again until it becomes a strong, useful tool, prayer is like that refining process, each encounter with God's presence in prayer softens the hardened areas of your heart, shapes your character, and strengthens your resolve, over time, what began as a timid flicker of faith grows into a steady flame of courage, ready to shine out in service to the Lord and to others, prayer prepares you to meet the demands of the day ahead, not with shrinking fear, but with bold confidence, trusting that God's wisdom and power flow through you; consider Jesus' example once more: even though He was the Son of God, He spent quiet hours in prayer, slipping away from the crowds, rising early in the morning, seeking the Father's guidance before making important decisions and drawing strength from their communion before facing the cross, if Jesus, who was without sin, needed to pray, how much more do we need it, with all our weaknesses, distractions, and limitations, by following His example, we learn that prayer is not optional, but essential, the very breath of spiritual life, the channel through which courage, guidance, and love flow into our hearts; as you continue on this path, you may find it helpful to keep a simple journal of your prayers, noting the times you brought specific requests to God and how, over weeks or months, you see changes in your own heart or in circumstances around you, sometimes you may realize that while you were praying for a certain outcome, God was changing your desires, helping you appreciate what truly matters, or giving you the strength to accept a different answer than you wanted, other times you will look back and see that God's timing was perfect, that what felt like a delay was actually preparation, that what seemed like a closed door was protection or redirection, these insights deepen your trust in God's faithfulness and encourage you to pray more boldly and consistently, knowing that every prayer is heard and that none are wasted; prayer also helps you extend grace to others, because as you bring people's names and situations before the Lord, as you pour out your frustrations and hurts, He works in your heart to grow compassion, understanding, and forgiveness, over time, you may find your anger softening, your bitterness melting, and your perspective shifting, so that you begin to see others as God sees them—precious, loved, and in need of His mercy—and this new perspective fuels your courage to serve even those who have wounded you, to stand by those who are marginalized, to show kindness in the face of cruelty, for now you know that love, backed by prayer and guided by God's hand, can break through barriers and change lives; prayer, in essence, keeps the fires of your courage burning bright, for even when you feel tired, confused, or discouraged, prayer invites you back into God's light, where He warms your heart, strengthens your soul, and reminds you that you are never alone, that He walks with you through every valley and celebrates with you on every mountaintop, that your value does not rest on achievements but on His love, and that your weaknesses are not failings, but places where He can show His strength; therefore, do not hesitate to approach God's throne of grace boldly, as Scripture encourages, knowing that you are welcomed there as a beloved child, and as you kneel or stand or sit in prayer, as you lift your thoughts to Him in the stillness of morning or the weariness of evening, in the rush of midday or the quiet of midnight, remember that every word you speak, every sigh, every tear, every silent longing, is noticed and cherished by the One who knows your heart better than you know it yourself, He will not turn you away, nor will He leave you unchanged, for His Spirit uses prayer to shape you into a person of steady faith, radiant hope, and fearless love; as the days turn into weeks, weeks into months, and months into years, you will see how prayer has guided your steps more than you ever realized at the time, how it saved you from rash decisions, encouraged you to take leaps of faith you might have otherwise avoided, equipped you to comfort others with the comfort you received from God, and spurred you on to acts of service that reflect His glory, and looking back, you will marvel at how a regular pattern of seeking God's guidance each day in prayer produced a legacy of courage and faithfulness in your life, a testimony not to your strength, but to God's, and this will inspire you to keep praying, keep listening, keep trusting, and keep igniting that fire of courage, for as long as you have breath, you have the privilege of communing with the Creator of the universe, and through that communion, you become a beacon of His light in a world that needs hope, truth, and love; so let these prayer-fed fires keep burning, keep fueling your heart to serve the Lord with a courage that does not fade, and know that as you do, you are helping to carry out His purposes, spreading His compassion, extending His kingdom, and showing others that the strength they seek can be found, just as you found it, in daily conversations with the God who loves them beyond measure—after all, prayer is not just a spiritual practice, it is the open door to the heart of the Almighty, the channel through which your courage and His guidance become one, and in that holy meeting place, all fear, doubt, and weakness yield to the power of faith, hope, and love.

Day 8 - Quiet Confidence: Listening for God's Whisper

Imagine yourself standing at the edge of a quiet forest, just as the last light of day slips beneath the horizon, and the world around you seems to fall silent, no longer buzzing with the hurried voices of people or the ceaseless hum of traffic, but settling into a gentle hush that invites you to listen more closely than you ever have before, and as the daylight fades, shadows stretch across the soft mossy ground, and the breeze that whispers through the branches carries a sense of calm, causing you to slow your breathing and open your heart to something deeper than the noise that usually surrounds your life; in this subtle, almost hidden silence, you begin to realize that courage does not always roar like a lion or announce itself with the blast of trumpets, sometimes it comes as a quiet confidence, a steady inner strength that grows in the stillness when you learn to listen for God's whisper, and as you stand there, you recall how often you've chased after loud answers and dramatic signs, hoping that God would send lightning bolts of clarity or shout His instructions from the mountaintops, but now you sense that He wants you to lean in closer, to tune out the clamor of the world, and to pay attention to the gentle voice He uses to guide those who trust Him; it is easy to overlook the power of a whisper, to assume that if something is truly important, it will arrive with grandeur and force, but think about how a whisper can carry more weight than a scream when it comes from someone you love and respect—a friend leaning close to offer words of understanding, a parent quietly reminding you of your worth, or a teacher softly encouraging you to try again, and now imagine the Creator of the universe doing the same, leaning near to your soul, not to startle you or force your hand, but to nudge you gently toward a better path, to remind you that you belong to Him, and that He has good plans for you that require not the clamor of the crowd, but the courage to trust in what you cannot always see; this quiet confidence does not mean you will never feel fear or uncertainty, it means that even when the wind outside howls and the storms of life threaten your footing, you have learned to remain still enough inside to hear God's guiding words, and in hearing them, to trust them more than the noisy doubts rattling around your mind; think of the prophet Elijah in the Bible, who had witnessed great wonders—fire falling from heaven, mighty displays of God's power—yet still found himself discouraged, hiding in a cave, desperate to hear from God again, and when God came, He did not appear in the roaring wind, nor in the earthquake, nor in the blazing fire, but in a gentle whisper, reminding Elijah that true strength and guidance often come wrapped in quietness, requiring a listening ear and a humble heart, and so Elijah learned that the God who can shake the mountains can also choose to speak softly, guiding His servant with tenderness rather than thunder; this is what quiet confidence looks like in your own life: learning to slow down, to step away from the noise and endless demands of daily living, and to find a moment—no matter how brief—to focus your heart on God's presence, it might be early morning, before the world wakes up, or late at night when the stars shimmer above a sleeping town, or even a stolen pause in the middle of a busy afternoon, when you close your eyes and breathe, and let the layers of worry and hurry peel away so you can hear something deeper, something truer, something that comes not from your own anxious thoughts but from the Spirit of God who dwells within you; through this practice, you learn that courage is not always about charging forward into battle with loud cries, but about standing firm in stillness, unshaken, because you know Whose hand holds you, and when everyone else might be rushing around, making decisions out of fear, you remain calm, listening for God's whisper, waiting for His gentle promptings that say, "This is the way, walk in it," and in doing so, you discover that His whisper can open doors you never noticed, can guide you to speak words of kindness you never would have chosen on your own, can help you step out in faith to serve others even when it feels risky, and can give you the courage to hold onto hope when circumstances suggest giving up; this quiet confidence grows when you fill your heart with God's truth, reading His Word and letting it soak into your mind so that His promises and instructions become familiar, like the voice of a dear friend, because the more you know His heart from Scripture, the easier it is to recognize His whisper amid the world's clamor, you begin to sense His promptings when you feel a sudden peace about a decision, or a gentle conviction that leads you away from something harmful, or a warmth in your chest that encourages you to speak life to someone who is hurting, and as you follow these subtle nudges, you build a track record with God, seeing over time how faithfully He leads you, never misleading or failing you, always working things together for good, even if it's not the path you would have chosen on your own; and this record of faithfulness fuels your courage, because you know that even if you stumble, He will be there to catch you, that even if you misunderstand or miss His whisper at times, He will patiently guide you back, that even if you face challenges or opposition, His gentle voice will remind you that you are not alone, that He is with you, and that His strength is enough to carry you through; there is something profoundly freeing about this approach to life, instead of straining your ears for shouts and dramatic signs, you learn to trust that God does not need to raise His voice to lead you well—He can speak softly because He is close, because He resides within you through His Spirit, and when you accept this closeness, you realize that the peace and courage you seek do not have to be chased or wrestled from life's grip, but simply received by waiting in quiet expectation, by believing that God's voice is real, available, and active, and by approaching Him with an open heart, willing to listen and obey; this quiet confidence stands in stark contrast to the world's idea of strength, which often celebrates the loudest voice, the strongest arm, the biggest display of power, but as you learn from God's whisper, true courage can be measured not by how loudly you shout, but by how patiently and faithfully you follow the soft guidance of the Almighty, how you trust His words more than the world's advice, how you remain calm in crises because you know He has never failed you, and how you dare to do good in places where others remain silent or fearful, confident that God is with you, whispering, "Be not afraid, for I am your God," into the very center of your being; of course, learning to listen for God's whisper is not always easy, it takes practice, patience, and a willingness to let go of distractions, just as a musician trains their ear to recognize subtle notes or a naturalist trains their senses to detect quiet movements in the forest, you train your soul to sense God's presence, turning off the blaring noise of constant entertainment, setting aside moments from busy schedules, and humbly admitting that you need His guidance more than your own clever ideas, and at first, you might struggle, feeling awkward in the silence, uncertain whether you're really hearing anything at all, but over time, you begin to recognize patterns, you sense the fruit of the Spirit—love, joy, peace, patience, kindness, goodness, faithfulness, gentleness, and self-control—rising up within you whenever you pay attention to that gentle inner voice, and you know that these qualities do not arise from your own anxious mind, but from the One who promised to be with you always; think about Jesus, who often withdrew to quiet places to pray, even though He was the Son of God, He still valued silence and solitude as a way to commune with His Father, to renew His strength, and to prepare His heart for the work ahead, and if Jesus needed these quiet moments, how much more do we, who are so easily swayed by the noise and opinions around us, need to pause and listen for that still, small voice, to trust that real courage is formed not in chaos, but in calm trust, to understand that God does not compete with the world's volume, but instead invites us to step away from it, to enter His presence and find our direction in whispers rather than shouts; as you embrace this way of living, you might find that courage emerges in unexpected places, maybe it's in having a gentle but honest conversation with someone you disagree with, rather than arguing loudly to prove a point, maybe it's in choosing to stand by a friend who's facing rejection, offering quiet support and love even if it doesn't make headlines, maybe it's in holding your tongue when tempted to gossip, or showing kindness to a stranger without expecting any applause, these acts of courage often happen beneath the radar, fueled by an inner assurance that comes from staying close to God's heart, from hearing His whispers say, "This is right," or "Love them anyway," or "Hold onto hope," and by following that voice, you discover that courage can be both gentle and mighty, capable of changing lives one quiet act at a time; over time, your sense of identity shifts, too, because listening for God's whisper reminds you that you are more than just another face in the crowd, you are a child of the King, known and loved personally, guided by a voice that calls you beloved, chosen, and equipped, and this knowledge frees you from the need to prove yourself through noise or showy deeds, because your worth is found not in what the world values, but in what God whispers to your soul, telling you that you are His, that He has created you with purpose, and that He delights in the quiet moments where you simply listen and trust; in these quiet moments, your vision clears, you see more clearly the path set before you, not because it's free of obstacles, but because you trust the One who guides you to lead you around them or through them, and as you move forward, step by step, you carry within you a peaceful strength that does not falter when opposition arises, because it's not based on your own courage alone, but on the courage God grows within you through His soft-spoken guidance, and when fear tries to creep in, you know to return to that quiet place in your heart, to listen again, to let His whisper dispel your doubts, refill your courage, and send you back out with renewed determination to love, serve, and stand for what is right; this kind of quiet confidence also helps you weather seasons of uncertainty, when you don't know what tomorrow holds, or when your long-held plans crumble at your feet, or when the future seems hazy and confusing, in those times, you remember that God never promised a life without challenges, but He did promise to be with you always, and listening for His whisper reminds you that He is right there, still speaking, still guiding, even when you can't see the outcome clearly, and so you hold onto His whisper as a lifeline, trusting that He will lead you through the valley and onto higher ground, and that even the waiting can teach you patience, resilience, and a deeper faith than you had before; as this pattern becomes a way of life, you find that quiet confidence shapes how you approach relationships, work, and service, you no longer feel the need to force your opinions loudly to be heard, because you know your worth is not tied to winning every argument, you become more compassionate, because when you slow down to listen for God's voice, you also become more attentive to the needs and pains of others, more willing to let God use you as an instrument of peace, comfort, and understanding, and this gentle courage allows you to step into difficult situations where anger or fear might dominate, carrying instead an atmosphere of calm that can soothe tensions and invite people to consider a new perspective; in your service to the Lord, this quiet confidence means you show up faithfully, not always seeking the spotlight, but content to do the work He places before you, whether it's volunteering in a soup kitchen, teaching a Sunday school class, mentoring a teenager, praying for your neighbors, or simply being kind to someone who looks lonely, it might not make headlines, but you know that a whisper can change a heart if it's guided by God's love, that a small act of faithfulness can ripple outward and affect lives you never even meet, and so you keep listening, keep trusting, keep moving forward with the assurance that God's whisper speaks truth over your life, and that truth is enough to give you all the courage you need; sometimes you may wonder if this quiet confidence is real courage at all, because we're so used to thinking of courage as loud and grand, but remember the heroes of faith who trusted God in the stillness: Mary, who pondered all these things in her heart, Joseph, who quietly followed the angel's instructions, Simeon and Anna, who waited patiently in the temple for God's promise to be revealed, or the disciples who learned to listen to their risen Lord's gentle instructions before they went out and changed the world, their power did not come from shouting louder than others, but from holding onto the quiet conviction that God's words would guide them, no matter what they faced; this is the heart of quiet confidence: knowing that you don't have to push your way forward by force, that you don't have to manufacture courage by pumping yourself up with shallow affirmations, instead, you can rest in the presence of the One who shaped galaxies, who knows every thought in your head and every beat of your heart, and who chooses to speak softly, inviting you closer rather than pushing you away, you can trust that His whisper holds more authority than the world's screams, that His subtle guidance can outsmart the most cunning schemes of darkness, and that as you learn to listen, your heart will overflow with the courage to serve Him faithfully; ultimately, quiet confidence teaches you that peace and strength are not enemies but partners, that you can be both calm and brave, both gentle and unyielding, both patient and determined, and as you embrace this truth, you will find yourself standing firm in places where you once felt too weak to stand, loving people you once found too difficult to love, and daring to hope when the world tries to drown you in despair, and all the while, that whisper remains, constant and reassuring, reminding you that the One who formed you for this purpose has never stopped speaking, never stopped guiding, never stopped believing in what He can accomplish through a humble heart that's willing to listen; so let this be your prayer: to become quiet enough inside to hear God's whisper, to cherish those moments when His voice cuts through your confusion with simple clarity, to treasure the stillness that gives birth to courage, and to let this quiet confidence fuel your heart to serve the Lord, not just in the grand arenas of life, but in the small corners where kindness and compassion are needed most, and as you walk this path, know that you are not alone, that countless believers have found strength in God's gentle voice, and that as you trust Him more, the flame of courage within you will burn steadily, guided not by noise or chaos, but by the sure and steady whisper of a loving God who delights in leading His children one soft word at a time.

Day 9 - Battling Doubt: Choosing Truth Over Lies

Imagine yourself standing at the edge of a vast field beneath a heavy gray sky, with the wind sighing low in the tall grass around your ankles, and in your heart, there is a battlefield no one else can see, a place where whispers swirl like dust motes caught in a beam of pale light, each whisper trying to shape what you believe about yourself, your purpose, and your ability to serve the Lord, and as you stand there, you can feel the weight of doubt pressing against your mind, carrying voices that sound like your own thoughts, but are twisted just enough to make you question everything good and true, these voices might say that you are not strong enough, not holy enough, not smart enough, not brave enough, that your past mistakes are too big, your weaknesses too deep, your fears too fierce, that you have nothing worthwhile to offer, and if you let them, these doubts can spread like creeping vines, wrapping around your hope, squeezing the life out of your faith until you feel too small, too broken, too uncertain to move forward; this is what doubt does, it thrives in the hidden corners of your heart, feeding on insecurities and fears, whispering lies that sound so convincing that you might start to believe them, and it does not matter how much you have accomplished in the past, or how many times you have seen God's faithfulness, doubt tries to erase those memories, painting your future in gray shadows, telling you that this time God won't come through, this time your courage will fail, this time the giants are too big and the mountains too high, it wants you to forget the truth you know, to trade it for a handful of lies that leave your spirit trembling, but you must remember that you have a choice, that faith is not just a feeling, but a decision to trust what God says over what your fears say, and that choosing truth over lies is like lighting a candle in a dark room—suddenly everything looks different, suddenly what seemed impossible looks possible, suddenly what felt hopeless feels charged with the promise that God's Word never fails; think about the nature of these lies: they often come disguised as your own reasoning, your own voice, your own critical thoughts, they might show up when you look in the mirror, telling you that you are not beautiful in God's eyes, even though He created you in His image, they might slip in when you consider a calling that God placed on your heart, telling you that you could never accomplish such a thing, that you don't have the gifts or the strength, even though Scripture clearly states that you can do all things through Christ who strengthens you, or maybe they arise when you think about sharing your faith with a friend or standing up for what is right in a difficult situation, whispering that you will fail, that your words will fall flat, that everyone will laugh or turn away, even though God says He is with you, that He will never leave you nor forsake you, that His Spirit will give you words to speak when you need them; these lies are not just random thoughts, they are part of a spiritual battle, for the enemy of your soul knows that if he can make you doubt, he can slow you down, rob you of courage, and keep you from walking boldly in God's calling, he understands that a fearful, uncertain believer is far less effective than a believer who stands confidently on the truth, so he shoots arrows of doubt at your heart, hoping they will stick, hoping you will listen to them instead of the voice of your Heavenly Father, but you do not have to stand there and take it, you do not have to accept every thought that crosses your mind as truth, you can learn to recognize these lies for what they are—cheap imitations of truth that cannot hold up under the weight of God's Word—and then you can choose to cast them aside, to replace them with the firm promises found in Scripture, to say, "No, I will not believe this lie, because God's truth says something different, and I trust God more than my own feelings or the enemy's sneaky voice"; choosing truth over lies is not always easy, because lies can feel so familiar, and sometimes the truth might seem too good to be true, or too distant to grasp, but remember that truth is anchored in who God is, and God is unchanging, faithful, and perfect in love, He does not make mistakes, He does not mislead, He does not forget what He has promised, and His words have the power to shape reality, to create galaxies with a single breath, to calm storms with a whisper, so when He tells you that you are loved, that you are chosen, that you are equipped to do His will, that He works all things together for the good of those who love Him, these are not empty phrases, they are rock-solid truths that you can stand on when everything else feels shaky, and when you compare these truths to the flimsy lies of doubt, you see how weak the lies truly are, how they crumble under the weight of God's authority, how they scatter like smoke in the wind when you shine the light of Scripture upon them; but what does it look like in everyday life to choose truth over lies? It means taking a proactive approach to what goes on in your mind, paying attention to the thoughts that pass through, and not allowing them to set up camp without checking them against God's Word, for example, suppose you think, "I can never do anything right, I will fail at this task God has given me," before you accept that as fact, ask yourself if it lines up with Scripture, God says that His strength is made perfect in weakness, that He can use the foolish things of the world to shame the wise, that He gives talents and gifts according to His purpose, that He does not call the equipped, but equips the called—so does your thought line up with that? No, it does not, it contradicts what God says, so you reject that thought as a lie, you do not entertain it or build your identity around it, instead you speak truth to yourself, "God has given me everything I need to do what He asks, I may feel weak, but He is strong in me, I trust that if He called me to this, He will help me succeed according to His plan," and as you affirm this truth, you feel a spark of courage ignite in your heart, a warmth that whispers, "Yes, you can trust Him," and that courage grows over time, making it easier to stand firm the next time doubt tries to creep in; another way to choose truth over lies is to fill your mind and heart with Scripture regularly, think of your mind as a garden that needs constant care, if you leave it unattended, weeds of doubt can grow quickly, but if you plant seeds of truth—verses that remind you of God's love, passages that highlight His faithfulness, stories that show how He helped ordinary people accomplish extraordinary things—then truth begins to crowd out lies, just like healthy plants crowd out weeds, and when doubts arise, you have a ready supply of truth to counter them, you can say, "Wait, I remember that David was just a shepherd boy, but with God's help he defeated Goliath," or "I recall that Gideon felt weak and afraid, but God called him a mighty warrior and led him to victory," or "I know that Peter denied Jesus three times, yet Jesus forgave him and used him mightily to build the early church," these stories are not just ancient tales, they are patterns of God's character, showing you what He can do in a willing heart, no matter how shaky it feels, and as you remember these truths, your doubt loses its power, and your courage builds; prayer also plays a key role in battling doubt, when you feel overwhelmed by lies, turn to God and ask Him to help you see the truth clearly, to guard your mind and keep it focused on His promises, and as you pray, be honest about your fears and doubts, God is not disappointed in your struggle, He understands how fragile we are, and He is more than willing to strengthen your faith, to open your eyes to the lies you've been believing, and to help you replace them with truth, in prayer you might say, "Lord, I feel so uncertain right now, I'm scared that I'm not good enough, that I'll fail, but I know your Word says that you are with me always, please help me believe that, help me hold on to your promise and reject the lies that say otherwise," and God, who hears even the quietest whispers of your heart, will respond, maybe not with thunder or lightning, but with a gentle reassurance that seeps into your soul, reminding you that He is faithful and true; sometimes you may need the help of other believers to strengthen your grip on truth, when doubt clouds your vision, lean on people who love God and know His Word, share your struggles with trusted friends or mentors who can remind you of what is real and lasting, who can gently point out when you're embracing a lie and encourage you to choose truth, none of us are meant to walk this path alone, and often God uses others to speak into our lives, to shine a light on our blind spots, to help us see what we cannot see by ourselves, and as you accept their support, you'll find that it's easier to stand firm, easier to push back against lies, and easier to let courage fill your heart, because you know you are not alone in this fight; as you learn to choose truth over lies, notice how it changes the way you approach serving the Lord, instead of holding back because you feel inadequate, you step forward, trusting that God will supply what you lack, instead of staying silent when you know you should speak up, you open your mouth, trusting that God will guide your words, instead of giving up when obstacles arise, you press on, knowing that difficulties do not mean God has abandoned you, but may be opportunities for growth, and in all these moments, your courage does not come from a puffed-up sense of your own ability, but from a steady confidence in the One who has never failed, never lied, and never broken a promise, you become someone who can stand amid uncertainty and still move forward, because your foundation is built on truths that cannot be shaken, and the world around you, which often thrives on fear and confusion, begins to see something different in you, a quiet strength that comes from knowing that the truth of God's Word is more solid than any quicksand doubt could ever produce; remember that even people we consider heroes of the faith wrestled with doubt, think of Moses, who questioned his ability to speak to Pharaoh, or Jeremiah, who felt too young and inexperienced, or Thomas, who doubted the resurrection until he saw Jesus with his own eyes, God did not discard them because of their doubts, He patiently showed them truth, helped them trust, and used them anyway, and this should give you hope, for if giants of faith struggled with doubt and still accomplished great things for God's kingdom, then you are not doomed by your moments of uncertainty either, as you consistently choose truth, you grow stronger, and your doubts lose their grip, becoming smaller in the face of God's eternal promises; it is also important to recognize that sometimes doubt arises because of wounds and pain in your past, maybe someone spoke hurtful words over you when you were younger, and those words left scars that make it hard for you to believe the truth about your worth in God's eyes, maybe you faced a significant failure that makes you fear trying again, or maybe you've encountered disappointment that made you wonder if God cares, these experiences can give lies a foothold in your heart, but remember that God is a healer, He desires not only to strengthen you against future doubts, but also to heal the hurts that allowed those doubts to root, by bringing your wounds to Him, by allowing Him to reveal truth about how He sees you, how He forgives, how He redeems, how He brings beauty from ashes, you can find freedom from the lies that have haunted you for too long, you can move forward unburdened by shame or regret, and that freedom fuels even more courage, because you know that if God can heal your broken places, He can certainly equip you to serve Him with a bold, trusting heart; there will be times when choosing truth feels like swimming upstream, when the world around you scoffs at the idea of trusting in God's Word, when circumstances seem to contradict what you believe, when your emotions tell you to give up, but this is when your decision matters most, faith is believing what God says is true even when it's hard to see with your physical eyes, it's trusting that He is at work behind the scenes, lining up circumstances, preparing you for future tasks, even when everything seems messy and uncertain, and as you persevere through these tough seasons, refusing to give the microphone to doubt, you develop a resilience that will serve you well in your journey, because the more you practice choosing truth, the more natural it becomes, until one day you realize that what used to shake you now barely stirs a ripple in your soul, because your anchor sinks deep into the ocean floor of God's faithfulness; consider the outcome of a life lived by choosing truth over lies: you become a person who can walk into challenging situations with steady eyes and an untroubled heart, not because you are naive or in denial, but because you understand that God's Word outranks your fears, you become someone who can be a source of hope and encouragement to others, pointing them back to God's promises when they are lost in their own doubts, you become a living testimony that truth really does set people free, that it breaks the chains of insecurity and timidity, releasing you to serve the Lord boldly, and your service, touched by the glow of God's truth, shines brighter, influencing others to wonder about the source of your courage, the steady hand that guides you, and this opens doors to share your faith, to say, "I can stand firm because I choose to believe what God says about me, about the world, and about His plan, rather than the lies that try to tear me down," and who knows how many hearts might be softened, how many doubters might be inspired to explore God's Word for themselves, how many lives might be changed because you decided that truth matters more than fear, more than failure, more than uncertainty; the process of battling doubt and choosing truth is ongoing, you won't master it overnight, and you may have days when the lies seem louder than usual, days when your heart feels heavy and you struggle to find the courage you seek, but do not lose heart, remember that God's mercies are new every morning, that His grace is sufficient for you, and that He has begun a good work in you that He will bring to completion, each time you choose truth, each time you stand against a lie and say, "No, I will not believe this because God's Word says otherwise," you are strengthening your spiritual muscles, becoming more and more the person God designed you to be—a courageous servant who walks by faith, not by sight, and in the end, that kind of courage will help you face challenges with a peace that confounds understanding, a confidence that does not depend on circumstances, and a love that can overcome even the darkest moments; so as you stand in that imagined field beneath the gray sky, remember that you hold a shield in your hand—the shield of faith—able to extinguish the flaming arrows of doubt, you hold the sword of the Spirit—the Word of God—able to cut through the lies and stand firm in truth, and your feet are planted on solid ground, not sinking sand, because you have chosen to believe what the Lord says about who He is and who you are, let your heart rest in this reality: though doubt will try to make you waver, you have the power, by God's grace, to resist it, to turn your gaze to what is true, noble, right, pure, lovely, and admirable, to think on these things, to let them fill your mind and strengthen your soul, and as you do, you ignite courage that fuels your heart to serve the Lord, moving forward in faith and not fear, trusting that the One who calls you is faithful, and that truth will always prevail over lies.

Day 10 - Rise Up, Servant: Embracing Holy Boldness

Imagine the moment when dawn first touches the horizon, painting the sky with pale yellows and gentle pinks, and how the quiet world slowly awakens from darkness to face the coming day, and in that stillness, you feel a stirring in your soul, a call that whispers through the gentle rustling of leaves and the distant hum of waking birds—"Rise up, servant," it says, "embrace holy boldness." If you stand very still and listen, you can sense God's Spirit nudging you forward, urging you to break free from the chains of fear and self-doubt that have held you back for too long. Perhaps you have spent years tiptoeing around your calling, shrinking from opportunities to speak truth, hesitating to offer your gifts, holding back your love, or delaying acts of kindness because you felt uncertain, weak, or unworthy, but now is the time to stand up straighter, lift your eyes, and recognize that the God who formed the stars and shaped the mountains has placed something precious and powerful inside you—a spark of courage, a glimmer of purpose, a calling to serve Him boldly, to shine His light into dark places, and to touch hearts that need hope. Holy boldness is not about showing off or making yourself look important; it is not the same as pride or arrogance, for those come from a place of selfishness. Holy boldness is about stepping forward with a heart surrendered to God's will, believing that He can do mighty works through anyone who trusts Him, even through someone as imperfect and unsure as you. It is about the quiet but firm decision to let God's strength flow through your weaknesses, to let His truth guide your words, and to let His love shape your actions. Instead of focusing on what you cannot do, holy boldness fixes your eyes on the One who can do all things, who parted seas, calmed storms, raised the dead, and still works miracles in human hearts. Picture what might happen if you choose this path: instead of keeping silent when someone needs encouragement, you open your mouth and speak words of life; instead of ignoring the hungry, you share your bread with them; instead of fearing ridicule when sharing your faith, you speak gently but firmly of God's goodness; instead of hiding your talents, you use them to serve others, trusting that God can multiply even the smallest offering. When you embrace holy boldness, you refuse to let fear rule your decisions. Fear whispers that you are too small, too clumsy, too young, too old, too broken, too untrained, too ordinary to make a difference. But holy boldness answers back that God delights in using the humble and the weak, that He perfects His strength in your weakness. Fear warns you that you will fail, but holy boldness says that the outcome belongs to God, and your task is merely to obey. Fear tries to convince you that your voice won't matter, that speaking truth will only lead to conflict, that standing up for what's right will get you hurt or laughed at. Holy boldness reminds you that prophets, apostles, and heroes of faith throughout the ages dared to stand with God, often against fierce odds, and through them, God changed the world. They were not fearless, but they trusted God more than their fears, and that is the secret—trusting God more than your fears. Embracing holy boldness does not mean you never tremble inside or that your heart never beats fast before you act. It means you move forward anyway, knowing that the Holy Spirit who lives in you is greater than the voices that try to hold you back. Think of David running toward Goliath, a shepherd boy facing a giant; think of Esther entering the king's court uninvited, risking her life to save her people; think of Daniel calmly praying even though it meant a night in the lion's den; think of Peter stepping out of the boat onto the waves, trusting Jesus to hold him up. Each of these servants faced a moment where they could have played it safe, retreated into the shadows, but instead they embraced holy boldness, and God did wonders through them. When you rise up and step forward in faith, you learn something marvelous: that God is faithful to guide your steps. He does not push you into battle without armor; He provides the armor of truth, righteousness, faith, salvation, and His Word. He does not send you into a storm without a lifeline; He holds you by the hand, whispering, "Fear not, for I am with you." He does not call you to a mission without giving you the gifts you need; He equips you with talents, opportunities, and spiritual strength, often beyond what you imagined. But He will not force you to use these gifts. He waits for you to choose, to say "yes" to His invitation. Holy boldness is born in the secret place where you meet God in prayer, where you pour out your fears and uncertainties, and He pours in His peace and assurance. It grows as you meditate on Scripture, letting its truth soak into your heart until you are so filled with God's promises that lies and doubts cannot take root. It is nurtured by remembering past victories, times when God carried you through difficult seasons, answered your prayers, or gave you courage when you felt you had none. Each memory becomes a stepping stone, lifting you higher so that you can see beyond today's challenges into the vast landscape of God's faithfulness. Holy boldness also thrives in community, among fellow believers who cheer you on, pray for you, share their own stories of overcoming fear, and remind you that you're not alone. When you see how God works through others who also struggle, who also wrestle with doubts and insecurities, but press on anyway, you realize that courage is not reserved for a special few. It is available to anyone who follows Jesus, anyone willing to say, "Lord, I cannot do this on my own, but I believe You can work through me." Embracing holy boldness involves seeing the world through God's eyes. When you look at people, do you see their pain, their longing for meaning, their hunger for love and acceptance? When you look at the broken systems and injustices around you, do you sense God's sadness and His desire to set things right? Holy boldness dares you to become part of His solution, to reach out a hand, to speak a word, to take action that might upset the status quo but brings healing, justice, and truth. This kind of boldness does not tear others down to prove a point; it lifts them up. It seeks God's will, not personal glory. It stands firm in truth but always cloaks that truth in compassion and grace. Perhaps you have been feeling that stirring within you for a while, a sense that there must be more to your walk of faith than just going through the motions. Maybe you've known deep down that God wants to use you in ways that stretch your comfort zone, ways that might cost you time, energy, popularity, or security. Instead of running from that call, what if you stepped toward it? Instead of giving your doubts the final say, what if you let holy boldness speak louder? Imagine how it would feel to wake up each morning knowing that fear does not control you, that today you can say "yes" to divine opportunities that appear in subtle or dramatic ways. Picture offering a kind word to a stranger who looks lonely, trusting that the Holy Spirit can turn simple kindness into profound change. Picture advocating for someone who has no voice, believing that God hears and sees the powerless and calls His people to stand on their behalf. Picture praying with someone who is hurting, even though you feel awkward or unsure what to say, trusting that God's presence matters more than perfect words. Picture using your God-given abilities—whether in art, teaching, music, science, business, or any field—to reflect God's character, striving for excellence not to earn praise, but to honor the One who created you to shine as a light in this world. When you rise up, servant of God, you inspire others to rise as well. Holy boldness is contagious. It encourages those around you to reconsider their own fears, to remember that God is just as present for them. In a world where negativity, cynicism, and despair often seem to have the loudest voices, your willingness to serve courageously stands out like a bright flame in the night. And that's exactly what Jesus called His followers to be—lights in the darkness, a city on a hill, salt that flavors and preserves. It takes boldness to be salt and light, because it means you must be different, not for the sake of being rebellious, but because you follow a different King and a different kingdom. You carry a hope that is not based on human promises but on God's eternal Word. You measure success not by worldly standards, but by obedience to His will. You find strength not in your own might, but in the Spirit who lives within you. Embracing holy boldness means being ready to take risks for the sake of the Gospel. It might mean confronting harmful patterns in your own life or in your community. It might mean forgiving someone who hurt you deeply, trusting that God's grace can restore what was broken. It might mean offering truth where lies have been embraced, knowing that people may resist or misunderstand you. It might mean sharing your testimony of how God's love rescued you from hopelessness, even if you fear people's judgment. Each act of holy boldness is a seed planted in faith, watered by prayer, and cultivated by God's power. Not every seed will sprout immediately, not every effort will produce visible fruit right away, but you trust that God is at work, weaving your acts of obedience into His larger plan. Over time, you see that courage is not about being fearless, but about loving God and others enough to do what needs to be done despite fear. You learn that boldness does not mean never making mistakes, but being willing to learn, grow, and try again. And with each new step of faith, your heart expands to hold more compassion, more determination, and more trust in God's sovereignty. There is a quiet confidence that comes with holy boldness, a sense of purpose that does not rise and fall with your moods or circumstances. You know who you serve and why. You understand that your life is part of something bigger than your own comfort or ambitions. You are connected to believers around the world and across time who have also taken their place, stood their ground, and let God use them to make His love known. When trials come, and they will, you do not crumble easily, because you know that your courage is not built on shaky ground. It is anchored in the character of God, in His unchanging promises, and in the example of Jesus, who showed us what true holy boldness looks like—laying down His life to save us, speaking truth in love, challenging hypocrisy, comforting the broken, and rising from the grave to prove that nothing can stand against God's plan. If Jesus, the Son of God, lived and breathed holy boldness, facing opposition, rejection, and suffering out of love for humanity, how can we not follow in His footsteps with at least a fraction of that courage? How can we remain hidden in our small fears when He calls us to stand with Him, to carry His message of hope, to serve those who are hurting, and to do so with confidence, knowing that He is alive and with us even now? Imagine reaching the end of your life and looking back, seeing that while you felt afraid at times, you stepped out in faith anyway, that you dared to be bold, not because you believed in yourself more than anyone else, but because you believed in the God who called you. Imagine the joy of knowing that your efforts, no matter how small, contributed to God's kingdom, that someone found comfort, learned the truth, or drew closer to Christ because you said "yes" to holy boldness. That joy outweighs any discomfort you might face in the moment. So rise up, servant of God. The day is breaking, the fields are ready for laborers, and your Lord stands ready to empower you. Embrace holy boldness not as a passing feeling, but as a way of life grounded in humility, sustained by prayer, sharpened by Scripture, and shared in community. You will find that even on days when you stumble or hesitate, God's grace is there to lift you again. Remember that boldness is not about shouting louder than others, but about standing firm when it counts, loving fiercely when it's needed, speaking truth when silence would be easier, and trusting that God can use even your trembling voice to declare His goodness. As you move forward with holy boldness, the fears that once held you captive lose their grip. The doubts that kept you small fade as you see God's faithfulness show up again and again. Your heart grows braver, your spirit steadier, and your service more effective. You understand that this boldness was never meant to magnify you—it magnifies God's power working through you. The world is waiting for servants who will not be paralyzed by fear, who will not be lulled into quiet resignation, but who will rise up and shine light into darkness. May you be one of them. May you lift your head, straighten your shoulders, and say, "Here I am, Lord, send me." May holy boldness fill your heart to overflowing, fueling your courage to serve the Lord so that your life becomes a beacon of hope, truth, and love in a world desperately needing all three. And as you do, remember that He who called you is faithful and true, and will surely equip you to stand boldly in every moment He has planned for you.

Day 11 - From Fear to Faith: Releasing What Holds You Back

Imagine yourself standing at the edge of a quiet lake just before sunrise, the water so still it almost looks like glass, the sky brushed with soft shades of gray and violet, and a light mist hovering over the surface, hiding what lies beneath; in this hush, you sense that you are not alone, for there is a gentle stirring inside your heart, a voice that speaks with neither sound nor shape, but a message that comes through as clearly as if someone were standing right beside you, whispering in your ear: it is time to release what holds you back, it is time to let go of fear and embrace faith, it is time to learn that courage comes not from denying the presence of fear, but from facing it head-on and choosing to trust God's plan over your trembling. You stand there, knowing that you have carried certain fears with you for a long time—fears of failure and disappointment, fears of rejection and loss, fears that if you step out and try something new for the Lord, you might stumble and prove yourself unworthy; maybe these fears were planted long ago, by words spoken in anger or neglect, by painful experiences that made you question your abilities, or by the bitter taste of defeat when something you tried just didn't work out. Over time, these fears might have grown roots in your heart, digging in and making themselves at home, until you started believing they were simply part of who you are. But they are not who you are. They are chains holding you back from living the life God intends, a life of stepping forward in faith, of loving boldly, of serving fearlessly, of trusting that His strength will carry you where your own courage falters. As you stand by this quiet lake, imagine dropping those fears into the still waters, watching them sink into the depths, and realizing that, like pebbles tossed into a pond, their ripples fade away, leaving the surface calm again. For this to happen, you must face the truth that fear has held too much power over your choices—maybe it has kept you from speaking up when God nudged you to share an encouraging word with someone who was hurting, or maybe it has made you say "no" to opportunities that would have stretched your faith, or convinced you to hide your talents, staying safe in the shadows rather than shining as a light in a dark world. Perhaps fear has even tried to tell you that God cannot use you, that you are too broken, too flawed, too ordinary. If you listen closely, you recognize that these fearful whispers are simply not in line with what Scripture tells you. The Bible is filled with stories of men and women who struggled with doubt and fear, who felt weak and small, yet God delighted in using them mightily. Moses trembled at the thought of confronting Pharaoh, Gideon hid in a winepress, Elijah fled from a wicked queen, and the disciples locked themselves in a room after Jesus died—yet God met each one in their fear, nudged them forward, and turned their hesitant steps into actions that changed history. These stories serve to remind you that fear does not disqualify you, that feeling afraid does not mean you are unfit for the Lord's work. Instead, these stories reveal that God works powerfully through those who admit their weakness and trust Him anyway. It's as if, when fear tries to close in on you, God says, "Give me that fear, watch what I can do with a heart that surrenders," and then He takes your trembling faith and grows it like a seed planted in fertile soil, transforming it into courage that can weather any storm. Releasing what holds you back is not an act of denying your fear or pretending it doesn't exist; it is, rather, acknowledging it—naming it, seeing how it has shaped your life—and then choosing, step by step, to move forward despite it. When you choose faith over fear, you are telling God, "I believe You are bigger than this. I believe Your promises outweigh my worries. I believe that I am safe in Your hands, even if I feel unsteady." Fear thrives on uncertainty, on focusing your attention on what might go wrong, but faith invites you to look at who God is and what He has done. Has He not been faithful in the past? Has He not guided you through hard seasons, providing exactly what you needed at the right time? Has He not shown, through the testimonies of countless believers before you, that He can bring beauty from ashes and purpose from pain? When you remember these truths, fear loses some of its power, becoming smaller in the light of God's goodness and strength. Consider that fear often tells you stories—stories of failure, stories of shame, stories that end in disaster. Faith, on the other hand, tells God's story—one of redemption, grace, victory, and love that never fails. When you embrace faith, you embrace this larger story, realizing that your life is not defined by the sum of your anxieties, but by the fingerprints of a Creator who knows you inside and out, who calls you by name, who prepared good works in advance for you to do. He does not expect you to perform them flawlessly on your own strength; He longs to walk with you through every moment, giving you what you need as you need it, not before. This is where trust comes in: letting go of the need to see the entire path ahead, to control every outcome, and instead trusting that God sees the end from the beginning, that He knows the steps that will lead you where you need to go, and that even if you stumble, He will pick you up and continue to lead. Imagine taking one small step away from fear. Maybe it's agreeing to pray aloud for someone who needs comfort, even though your voice shakes. Maybe it's signing up to help with a ministry that intimidates you, or learning a new skill to serve in a way you never imagined you could. Maybe it's sharing your story with someone who doubts God's love, even though you worry they won't understand. Each of these steps feels risky because fear wants to keep you silent, keep you hidden, keep you locked in a familiar corner where nothing changes. But faith beckons you forward, reminding you that you don't grow by staying safe. You grow when you stretch, when you try, when you trust. Over time, as you continue choosing faith, those once terrifying steps become a little easier, not because you have magically become fearless, but because you have learned that fear does not have the last word. You have seen that God is faithful when you step out on the waters of uncertainty. Just like Peter, who walked on the water toward Jesus, you may still feel the wind and see the waves, and at times you might even begin to sink, but also like Peter, you can cry out to Jesus, and He will reach out and catch you, proving once again that He is present, He is strong, and He will not let you drown in your fears. Another crucial part of releasing what holds you back is understanding that fear often disguises itself as wisdom or caution. Sometimes it's wise to be careful, but there is a difference between being prudent and being paralyzed. You must discern when fear's warnings are stopping you from moving forward entirely. Are you saying "no" to opportunities because it genuinely is not God's timing, or because you are scared you will fail? Are you withholding love or kindness from someone because you believe God wants you to keep your distance, or because you fear rejection or betrayal? Praying for discernment in these areas can help you identify when fear is masquerading as something harmless. If you find that fear is the root of your hesitations, ask God to replace it with faith, to help you trust His voice more than the whisper of doubt. Another trick of fear is to make you believe that if you fail, it will define you forever. But consider that failure, in God's hands, becomes a stepping stone rather than a verdict. God does not look at your attempts to serve Him and scold you for not achieving perfect results. He looks at your heart, sees your willingness, your effort, your desire to please Him, and He can use even the times you stumble for good. Every failure can teach you something valuable—humility, perseverance, empathy for others' struggles, a clearer sense of your true calling. When you release the fear of failure and embrace the faith that God can work all things together for good, you find freedom in trying, in stepping forward, in giving your best effort without the crushing burden of perfection. Releasing what holds you back also means releasing the fear of what others might think. Far too often, we keep our faith quiet or our service minimal because we worry about people's opinions. We fear they will judge us, mock us, or misunderstand us. Yet, as followers of Christ, our main concern should be what pleases Him. People's opinions can shift like the wind, but God's truth is steady. He knows your heart better than anyone else. If you live to honor Him, you are building on a foundation that cannot be shaken. Fear of others' judgment only holds you back from fully expressing the love and truth God placed in you. Choose faith that God is the ultimate judge, that His delight in you matters more than fleeting human approval, and you will find fresh courage to serve boldly. Sometimes, what holds you back is not just fear for yourself, but fear for others—fear that if you step out in faith, you might disappoint loved ones who expect you to walk a certain path, or fear that if you say what God has placed on your heart, people you care about will reject you. While it's painful to think of losing relationships or approval, consider that true obedience to God never leads to ultimate loss. It may lead to temporary conflicts or painful separations, but in the long run, trust that God can bring healing, understanding, or new relationships that fit who He is shaping you to be. Faith does not guarantee that life will be easy, but it assures you that life will be purposeful, guided by His hand. As you begin this journey from fear to faith, you might find it helpful to remember times in your past when you overcame something you once feared. Perhaps as a child, you were afraid to ride a bike without training wheels, but eventually you tried, fell, got up, tried again, and one day you discovered you could balance, pedal, and move forward freely. Now you don't even think twice about it. This simple example shows a pattern: facing fear, trying, failing, trying again, and finally breaking through. Apply this pattern to spiritual matters—serving the Lord, sharing His message, acting in love, standing for truth. You might fumble at first, feel awkward or uncertain, but each time you choose faith over fear, you gain a bit more confidence, a bit more skill, until one day you realize that what once terrified you now feels natural. The Holy Spirit's role in this transformation cannot be ignored. You are not battling fear on your own strength. The Spirit lives within you, guiding your thoughts, reminding you of Scripture, prompting you to action. When fear whispers, "You can't do this," the Spirit can remind you, "With God, all things are possible." When fear says, "You're all alone," the Spirit whispers, "I am with you always." When fear tries to paint a grim picture of the future, the Spirit can show you a vision of God's promises fulfilled, of souls touched by your obedience, of growth and blessing that come from stepping out in faith. Pray for the Holy Spirit's help as you move forward, and expect that help to come—not always in dramatic ways, but often through a sense of peace, a timely verse, a word of encouragement from a friend, or a calm assurance that nudges you forward when all seems uncertain. Releasing what holds you back also involves forgiveness. Sometimes fear is tied to resentment or anger, perhaps you fear reaching out because someone hurt you in the past, and you do not want to risk being hurt again. Forgiveness does not mean excusing wrong behavior, but it does mean freeing yourself from the grip of bitterness. When you choose to forgive, you are choosing to say that the past will not dictate your future. You are letting go of another chain that fear uses to keep you from loving courageously. Forgiveness releases you to trust God with justice, healing, and reconciliation, allowing you to move forward unburdened, more willing to extend kindness, more able to risk love again. Another aspect is understanding the difference between fear and reverence. The Bible speaks of a "fear of the Lord" which is a holy respect, awe, and acknowledgment of God's greatness. This is not the kind of fear that holds you back; this reverence actually propels you forward, because it puts everything else in perspective. When you truly grasp God's power, wisdom, and love, all other fears shrink in comparison. If God is for you, who can stand against you? If He holds the universe together, can He not hold your life securely? Embracing a reverent awe of God helps displace the petty fears that try to limit your obedience. Also, remember that no one else can release what holds you back for you. People can encourage you, offer wisdom, and cheer you on, but ultimately, you must make the choice to surrender your fears to God. It might help to do something symbolic—maybe you write down your fears on a piece of paper and then tear it up, praying as you do, "Lord, I give these fears to You. Replace them with trust in Your goodness." Or maybe you find a quiet place to speak aloud your decision: "I choose faith over fear. I choose to trust God's promises. I will not let these doubts rule my life any longer." Such a gesture can help solidify your commitment, giving you a memorable moment to look back on when fear tries to sneak in again. As time passes, you will likely find that you need to repeat this process. Fear can be persistent, and growth in faith is an ongoing journey, not a one-time event. But each time you choose faith, you strengthen your ability to do so next time. Each victory over fear, no matter how small, builds spiritual muscle. One day you will look back and see how far you've come, how many risks you've taken for God's glory, how many lives you've touched because you refused to stay hidden. You will see that what once terrified you now seems like a small stepping stone, and you will praise God for leading you from fear to faith. By stepping out in faith, you become a reflection of God's character to the world. Others may see your courage and wonder where it comes from. You can then point them to Christ, explaining that it is not your own bravery, but the faithfulness of the One who never leaves you. Your life becomes a testimony that fear does not have the last word, that with God's help, people can rise above their doubts and do incredible things—love the unlovable, serve the needy, stand up for the truth, share the Gospel, and forgive the unforgivable. These are the marks of someone who has moved beyond the chains of fear into the freedom of faith. Remember, too, that God is patient with you. He knows the areas where you struggle, He sees the fears that keep you awake at night, and He does not condemn you for feeling afraid. Instead, He gently invites you to trust Him, to test His promises, to find out for yourself that He is as good and reliable as His Word claims. He does not expect you to run a marathon of faith on your first day out; He is pleased when you take even the smallest step of obedience. Like a parent cheering on a child who takes their first wobbling steps, God rejoices over each bit of progress you make in leaving fear behind and walking in faith. If you need further encouragement, consider how fear often exaggerates risks and minimizes God's power. Faith, by contrast, sees reality more clearly—yes, life can be hard and uncertain, but God's love and strength are certain. Yes, you may fail, but God's grace is sufficient to lift you again. Yes, people may misunderstand you, but God knows your heart and will never misunderstand. Yes, the path may be unclear, but God's Word lights your way, step by step. Faith does not ignore the facts of life's challenges; it simply remembers that God is greater than them all. In moving from fear to faith, you give God room to show Himself strong on your behalf. When you cling to fear, you rely on your own limited resources, but when you choose faith, you invite God's limitless power and wisdom into the situation. You say, "Lord, I cannot do this, but You can. I trust You." Those words, spoken sincerely, unleash a force greater than any fear—God's presence working in and through you. As you keep walking this path, you will notice changes in your inner life. Anxiety will slowly loosen its grip, replaced by a sense of peace that does not depend on easy circumstances. Instead of shrinking back when facing new challenges, you begin to approach them with curiosity, wondering what God might teach you this time. Instead of dreading failure, you become open to learning and growing. Instead of fearing people's judgments, you value God's approval above all. Instead of hiding your gifts, you present them to the Lord, trusting He will use them as He sees fit. By releasing what holds you back, you become more fully yourself—the person God created you to be, not the person fear tried to force you to become. You discover freedom: freedom to love radically, to speak truthfully, to create beautifully, to serve humbly. You realize that fear was never a good master, never a truthful guide. Faith, in contrast, opens your heart to new possibilities. It shows you that courage and humility can coexist, that confidence and kindness are partners, that strength can look like quiet trust rather than loud bravado. It teaches you to look beyond yourself and see God's hand at work in every situation. In time, you find that what once held you back has lost its power. You stand at the edge of that still lake, and the fears that once weighed you down are now resting at the bottom, swallowed by God's grace. The sunrise continues, painting the sky with brighter colors—soft oranges and pinks shifting to a clear, warm light—and you realize that you are stepping into a new day, a day defined not by the ghostly voices of fear, but by the living voice of your Savior, who says, "Do not be afraid; I am with you always." You walk away from the water's edge feeling lighter, taller, more hopeful, because you have decided that faith, not fear, will guide your steps. And as you move forward, serving the Lord with heart aflame, you understand that courage is not the absence of fear, but the choice, again and again, to trust God's truth over fear's lies, to surrender your worries into His capable hands, and to embrace the journey He has set before you. This is what it means to release what holds you back and live from fear to faith.

Day 12 - Wells of Encouragement: Finding Strength in Fellowship

Imagine yourself walking along a dusty road beneath a brilliant blue sky, feeling the warmth of the sun on your shoulders, yet sensing a lingering weariness deep inside, as if your heart has traveled too far without rest, and as you continue on this path, the horizon stretches out before you, promising something new, something better, if only you keep going, but you know that courage sometimes wanes when you walk alone for too long, that the flame within your soul, meant to burn steadily and brightly, can start to flicker in the face of trials, doubts, and difficulties; you may recall how often you have tried to press on by yourself, gritting your teeth against discouragement, pushing forward with nothing but your own strained determination, yet there comes a point when your soul cries out for refreshment, for support, for voices other than your own echoing in your mind, and it is in moments like this, when you feel close to running dry, that you discover the precious gift of fellowship, wells of encouragement waiting to quench your thirst and strengthen your heart so that you can serve the Lord with renewed vigor, for in the company of fellow believers, you can find an oasis of hope and understanding that softens your burdens and lifts your spirit; picture arriving at a small clearing beside the road, where a circle of travelers has gathered around a cool, clean well, its water shimmering gently as each person takes a turn drawing it up, and here, as you approach, they greet you with warm smiles and kind words, offering not only a place to rest, but also a place to share your story, your struggles, and your dreams, and as they listen, you feel something begin to shift within you—no longer are you just one weary soul wandering through life's challenges, you are now part of a community woven together by faith and love, a fellowship that can breathe courage into your bones and remind you that you were never meant to walk this journey alone; fellowship is more than just being in the same room with people who share your beliefs, it is about opening your heart, inviting others to see the real you, trusting that their encouragement will help you rediscover your strength, and within this fellowship, you learn that everyone carries burdens, everyone faces moments of trembling knees and shaky voices, everyone has confronted fears that threatened to swallow their hopes, and as each person lays their struggles before the group, an amazing thing happens: empathy is born, understanding blossoms, and compassion lights up the faces of those who once seemed like strangers, you realize that you are not alone in your doubts, your failures, or your battles against discouragement—others have walked paths like yours, felt similar pains, questioned their worth and calling, and found comfort in being heard and supported; in this fellowship, no one has to pretend to have it all together, to hide their scars or cloak their tears in forced laughter, because this circle of believers acknowledges that we are all works in progress, all in need of God's grace, and all capable of offering grace to each other, and when you see someone else lower their guard, admit their weaknesses, and still be embraced with love, something inside you relaxes, as if a door you had bolted shut finally swings open, allowing fresh air to soothe your weary soul; fellowship teaches you that it's safe to be honest about your fears, to say, "I'm scared I'm not good enough," or "I don't know if I can serve the Lord in the way He's calling me," and instead of dismissing these worries, your brothers and sisters in faith lean in, reminding you of God's promises, His faithfulness, and the countless ways He has worked through people who once felt just as unsure; as you spend time in this kind of community, you begin to see how encouragement works like water for your heart, washing away the dust of despair, refreshing your spirit, and giving you the courage to stand up again, to try again, to believe again, and sometimes it comes through a gentle word spoken softly, sometimes through a laugh shared over a simple meal, and sometimes through a tear shed together in the quiet understanding that life is hard, but God is good; the beauty of fellowship lies in its variety—people of different ages, backgrounds, and personalities come together, each with their own stories of faith, their own encounters with God's goodness, and as they share their testimonies, you realize that courage can be contagious, that hearing about how someone overcame a struggle through prayer and perseverance can ignite a spark of hope in your own heart, and that's what happens in these wells of encouragement: as one person's courage flares up like a bright torch, others' courage begins to glow brighter too, passing the flame around so that soon the circle is bathed in a warm, steady light; you might find yourself drawn to a mentor figure in the group—someone whose steady faith and thoughtful words guide you like a compass pointing north, this person may have walked with the Lord for many years, learned how to trust Him through storms and hardships, and now willingly pours their wisdom into your life, encouraging you to press on and trust that God is working even when you cannot see the outcome, their encouragement might not come in flashy sermons or grand gestures, but in the quiet consistency of their presence, in the way they remember your prayer requests, ask how you're doing, and remind you that God is faithful; in fellowship, you also find the younger voices, the ones who come with fresh eagerness and wide-eyed wonder about what God can do, and as you see their enthusiasm, their willingness to serve, you remember the fire that once burned strong in your own heart, and it rekindles within you, making you say, "If they can dare to hope, so can I," and just as the older believers encourage the younger with wisdom, the younger encourage the older with energy, each generation feeding the other like roots and leaves of a tree, working together to draw life from the soil and reach toward the sky; think about how hard it is to stand firm in faith when you feel isolated, how doubt can seem louder in silence, how temptation grows stronger when no one knows you're struggling, how discouragement quickly multiplies in the dark corners of your mind, fellowship shines a light into those corners, reminding you that you are seen, understood, and supported, and when someone puts a hand on your shoulder and prays for you, calling out your name before God, asking for strength, guidance, and protection, you sense something shift inside—like a burden being lifted, or a cold fear being warmed by love, even if circumstances do not change immediately, you now face them knowing that others stand with you, cheering you on, believing that God will help you overcome; this encouragement does not always solve every problem overnight, but it strengthens you to keep walking, to keep trusting, to keep serving, and this is the heart of fellowship: it gives you the courage to serve the Lord because you no longer try to draw strength only from your own limited well, you dip your bucket into the wells of encouragement found in your brothers and sisters in Christ, and their faith, their experiences, their victories and lessons learned, become part of your story too, reminding you that when you grow weary, others can help carry the load, that when your voice trembles, others can speak words of faith, that when your confidence wanes, others can remind you of what is true; in these wells of encouragement, you also find accountability, a gentle but firm presence that will not let you settle for less than what God has called you to be, while encouragement lifts you up when you're down, accountability calls you higher when you're tempted to slide back or give in, and sometimes encouragement comes in the form of honest challenges, friends who love you enough to say, "I think you can do better," or "Have you considered that God might be leading you this way?" or "Let's pray about this decision together," and though it might sting at first, this kind of encouragement pushes you forward, sharpening your character, and helping you grow in wisdom and courage; it's important to remember that fellowship does not mean you will never feel lonely or that you will never face misunderstanding, after all, we are all imperfect humans, each carrying our own struggles, but the difference is that in fellowship, you have a place to bring those feelings, to talk them through, to work toward forgiveness and healing when conflicts arise, to learn patience, grace, and mercy as you deal with one another, and even in times of tension, if you are committed to fellowship, you find that honesty, humility, and prayer can restore unity, strengthening the bond of encouragement so that it becomes even more resilient; consider the image of the early church described in the Bible: they gathered often, shared their resources, broke bread together, prayed for one another, and devoted themselves to the apostles' teaching, and as a result, they grew in faith and numbers, their joy overflowed, their courage to share the Gospel spread, even in the face of persecution, they found strength in fellowship that allowed them to serve the Lord boldly, and though centuries have passed, the same principle applies today: when believers come together with open hearts, ready to love, support, and encourage, the Church becomes a force of hope and healing in the world, a family where each member's gifts and stories enrich the whole; when you find yourself discouraged, fellowship can remind you of your purpose, calling you back to the reason you chose to follow Christ in the first place, if at times the voice of God seems distant, fellowship can help you hear His whispers again, as others share verses and stories that speak directly to your heart, when you fear stepping out to serve in a new ministry or speak boldly about your faith, fellowship can remind you that God does not send you alone—He surrounds you with people who will pray for you, celebrate your victories, weep with you in your sorrows, and challenge you when you need a nudge; it's like the difference between a lone soldier and a united army: one soldier might be brave, but easily overwhelmed; an entire army, united in purpose, can accomplish far more, supporting one another, covering each other's weaknesses, and sharing resources, and in the context of serving the Lord, you are not a lone soldier, you are part of God's army—His Church—designed to work together, to lean on each other, and to find courage not only within yourself, but in the collective faith of God's people; beyond the walls of a church building, fellowship can take many forms: small groups meeting in living rooms, believers connecting over meals, prayer partners sending each other encouraging messages throughout the week, friends calling each other to share how God answered a prayer, mentors sitting in a quiet corner of a coffee shop, guiding a younger believer through tough questions, service teams traveling together to bring aid and hope to those in need, missions groups supporting each other through culture shock and language barriers, all these expressions of fellowship serve as wells of encouragement where your heart can be renewed; when your courage wavers, remember that you can draw near to these wells, you can reach out to someone and say, "I'm struggling, can we talk?" or "Would you pray with me?" and by doing so, you discover that seeking fellowship is not a sign of weakness, but a sign of wisdom, it acknowledges that God designed us to thrive in relationships, that isolation often leads to confusion and despair, but fellowship fosters clarity and determination, helping you see your gifts more clearly, understand your calling more deeply, and trust God's presence more fully; fellowship also expands your vision, showing you that your problems, while real and painful, are not the whole story, when you listen to others share how God carried them through trials, overcame obstacles, and answered prayers in surprising ways, your perspective widens, you realize that the same God who helped them can help you, the same grace that sustained them is available to you, and the same Spirit that empowered them to serve in hard places can also empower you, this growing vision of God's faithfulness instills a courage that cannot be easily shaken, because it is rooted not just in your own experience, but in the collective testimony of the entire Body of Christ; sometimes encouragement is as simple as a timely word—someone telling you, "I believe in you," or "God will make a way," at the exact moment you thought of quitting, or maybe it's an arm around your shoulder after a loss, a meal brought to your doorstep when you're too weary to cook, or a note left in your Bible that says, "You are loved," these small acts of kindness, fueled by genuine faith, remind you that you matter, that your journey matters, and that your efforts to serve the Lord are not in vain, together, these acts form a wellspring of hope, each drop of encouragement adding up until you feel ready to take another step, face another challenge, say another prayer for someone who needs God's touch; in fellowship, you learn that courage can be shared, passed around like bread, so that no one goes hungry for encouragement, when one person's courage runs low, another can lend a portion of their faith, reminding them of who God is, what He has done, and what He promises to do, and as that person regains their strength, they too can turn around and encourage someone else, creating a cycle of support that strengthens the entire community, making it more resilient, more loving, and more effective in serving the Lord; this cycle of encouragement also protects against the temptation to give up, to think that your contribution doesn't matter, or that your voice is too small to make a difference, in fellowship, you see how each person's gifts, no matter how humble, add to the whole, like threads in a tapestry, each one essential to the overall design, and as you recognize the value of your brothers and sisters, you also learn to recognize your own value, understanding that God placed you among these people for a reason, that your presence, your prayers, and your kindness could be the spark that ignites courage in another heart; of course, building deep fellowship takes time and effort, it means showing up, investing in relationships, asking questions, listening without judgment, and being willing to help carry another's burdens, it means being patient when misunderstandings arise, extending forgiveness when someone offends you, and humbly receiving correction when you stray from the path, but as you put in this effort, you begin to reap the rewards: richer friendships, a sense of belonging, and a well of encouragement so deep and abundant that you never have to face your challenges alone; think about how Jesus Himself valued fellowship: He chose twelve disciples to walk closely with Him, to share in His ministry, His struggles, and His joys, even the Son of God surrounded Himself with companions, knowing that there is strength in walking together, and after His resurrection, the early believers gathered often, supporting one another through prayers, teachings, shared meals, and collective worship, their fellowship became a powerful testimony to the world, showing that followers of Christ are not just scattered individuals, but a family bound together by love; as you find strength in fellowship, your courage to serve the Lord is fueled by the knowledge that you are part of something far greater than yourself, you are joined to a living community that spans generations and continents, a people called out of darkness into God's marvelous light, a people who encourage, uplift, and inspire one another toward greater acts of faith, hope, and love, and as you continue your journey, no longer walking alone but surrounded by these faithful companions, the road no longer feels as long or as daunting, the horizon no longer seems unreachable; you realize that what began as a lonely trek under a harsh sun has now become a shared adventure, where laughter cuts through tension, where prayers rise like incense, and where even tears are met with understanding rather than judgment, in these wells of encouragement, you find the courage not only to keep going, but to run with the purpose God has placed in your heart, knowing that if you stumble, many hands will reach out to steady you, and if your flame burns low, others will share their flame until yours burns bright again; and so, as you move forward, embrace the gift of fellowship, draw from its deep wells, and let the encouragement you find there spark fresh courage in your soul, for you are not a lone wanderer— you are a cherished member of God's family, connected by faith and guided by love, supported by those who have tasted the sweetness of His grace and long to see you flourish in service to the King, take heart, therefore, and know that through fellowship, through these wells of encouragement, your strength is renewed, your footsteps made steadier, and your heart emboldened to serve the Lord with a fiery passion that no fear or doubt can quench.

Day 13 - Love as a Torch: Serving Through Compassion

Imagine yourself deep within a quiet forest at dusk, the tall trees whispering secrets to the soft wind, their leaves glowing faintly as the last light of day fades away, and in this gentle hush, you stand holding a torch—not a torch of fiery anger or harsh judgment, but a torch fueled by the purest flame of love, a flame that offers warmth instead of scorn, light instead of confusion, hope instead of despair, and as this torch glows steadily, it reveals a path ahead, a path that leads you toward serving the Lord by serving others, not out of duty or fear, but out of compassion that flows freely from your heart, and you realize that this love, this selfless concern for the well-being of others, is the very spark that can ignite courage within you, fueling your desire to step forward, to reach out, and to become a source of comfort, healing, and strength; too often we think of courage as something roaring and fierce, like a lion's roar echoing through a canyon, but true courage, the kind that honors God, can also be found in gentle acts of kindness, in the soft-spoken words spoken to a hurting friend, in the quiet choice to put someone else's needs before your own, and it is through love that this gentle courage emerges, a love that does not boast or demand attention, but instead humbly meets people where they are, sees their pain, listens to their fears, and chooses to care, even when it might be easier to turn away; consider the example of Jesus, who could have commanded legions of angels with a word, who held all power in His grasp, yet instead walked among the broken, the sick, the rejected, healing their wounds, feeding their hunger, touching the untouchable, weeping with those who mourned, it was love that guided Him, love that moved Him to stoop low and wash His disciples' feet, love that led Him to the cross, not as a display of might, but as a sacrifice that would open the door for humanity to know forgiveness and hope, this love was not weak, it was love as a torch, blazing through the darkness, showing that true courage is found when we serve others out of compassion, laying down selfish desires and fears; when you think of serving the Lord, you might picture great deeds performed on grand stages, mighty acts that change the course of history, and yes, God sometimes calls people to such tasks, but more often, He calls you to quiet acts of compassion woven into your daily life—the warm meal you deliver to a neighbor who lost their job, the encouraging note you leave for a friend facing a tough decision, the honest apology you offer to someone you have hurt, the patient listening ear you lend when a coworker just needs someone to understand their struggles, these simple acts might not seem like much on their own, but each one burns like a small flame of love, and when combined, they create a bonfire of compassion that can brighten even the darkest corners of human sorrow; love as a torch is not about perfection or having all the right answers, rather, it's about showing up, being present, and acknowledging that every person you meet carries burdens you may not fully understand—fears, wounds, regrets, longings—and by choosing to care about them, you reflect the heart of the Savior who saw beyond people's failures and weaknesses to the precious souls created by a loving God, imagine what it would feel like to know that no matter how uncertain or afraid you feel, you can still show love, still offer kindness, still let compassion guide your steps, and in doing so, you discover a kind of courage that cannot be bought or faked, a courage that arises from knowing you are participating in God's work of healing and restoring the world; this does not mean it will always be easy to love, there are times when selfishness whispers in your ear, urging you to protect your comfort, to close your heart to the pain around you, to shrug and say it's not your problem, fear may warn you that if you reach out, you might get hurt, that your efforts might be unappreciated, misunderstood, or even rejected, but love as a torch means you shine light into these doubts, remembering that courage is not the absence of fear, but the willingness to press on despite it, trusting that God is with you, that He sees your efforts, and that He can use even the simplest act of compassion to bring hope, no matter how small it seems to you; consider the great saints and heroes of faith who came before you—many of them were not mighty conquerors or famous rulers, but humble servants who loved deeply and served faithfully, think of Mother Teresa, who cared for the poorest of the poor in the streets of Calcutta, not because she expected praise, but because she saw Jesus in the faces of the suffering, think of countless unnamed believers who have visited hospitals, fed the hungry, comforted the grieving, taught children to read and pray, gently corrected those who strayed, and welcomed strangers with open arms, their actions, guided by compassion, have lit a path for others to follow, showing that courage and love walk hand in hand; love as a torch also teaches you that sometimes words are not enough, or that the right words are hard to find, in those moments, compassion can speak louder through actions—holding someone's hand while they cry, cooking a meal for a friend too tired to stand at the stove, helping an elderly neighbor with their yard work, defending someone who has been unfairly treated, praying silently for a stranger you pass on the street, these quiet gestures, born of genuine care, can cut through the noise and confusion, reminding you and others that God's presence often shows up through ordinary people doing ordinary things with extraordinary love; it's important to remember that compassion does not mean you have to carry the weight of the world's pain on your shoulders, no single person can fix every problem or heal every wound, but love as a torch encourages you to do what you can, where you are, with the resources God has given you, sometimes this means going beyond your comfort zone, giving more time or energy than you feel you have, or standing up for someone when it would be easier to blend into the background, other times it means listening intently, letting someone vent their worries without rushing to offer advice, simply being present in their struggle so that they do not feel alone; and when you feel unsure, remember that your compassion comes from a source greater than yourself—God's love flows into you and can flow out through you, enabling you to keep loving even when you feel empty, pray for His help, ask Him to fill you with His love so that you can share it with others, and trust that He will answer this prayer, because it aligns perfectly with His heart, the more you rely on His love, the stronger your torch burns, and the more courage you find to keep serving, even when the path is rough; there may be moments when your compassion is tested, when someone you try to help responds with anger or mistrust, or when your efforts seem to make no difference at all, in those moments, it's natural to feel discouraged, to wonder if all this loving and caring is worth it, love as a torch reminds you that even if you cannot see the immediate outcome, God can use your actions in ways beyond your understanding, maybe your kind gesture plants a seed of hope in their heart that takes years to grow, maybe your calm response to their anger helps them see that not everyone in the world is against them, maybe your willingness to serve becomes part of a chain of events that leads them closer to God, trust that God can turn even the smallest spark of love into something beautiful; serving through compassion also reshapes your own heart, as you give of yourself in love, you find that your priorities shift, you become less focused on what you lack and more grateful for what you have, more aware of the needs around you, and more willing to share your time and resources with those who have less, your perspective broadens to see that life is richer and more meaningful when it's not all about you, this change in your heart builds confidence and courage, because you see yourself not as a victim of circumstances, but as an instrument of God's grace, able to make a difference in ways both large and small; love as a torch can guide you when you face decisions about your future—what career to pursue, where to live, how to spend your free time—by asking yourself how you can serve others and glorify God through these choices, you let compassion shape your direction, and as you follow that path, you may find yourself in places you never expected, meeting people you never dreamed you would meet, and discovering strengths and gifts within yourself that you never knew existed, all because you allowed love to illuminate your journey; consider the ripple effects of your compassion, imagine lighting your torch of love and carrying it into the lives of those around you, one by one, others are touched by that light and begin to shine their own small torches, passing them along to people you may never meet, and so the circle of care grows wider, spreading through families, neighborhoods, schools, churches, workplaces, and communities, suddenly courage to serve is not just your story—it becomes a shared story, a network of hearts all glowing with the same flame of love, and over time, these collective acts of compassion can bring healing, bridge divides, melt bitterness, and point people toward the God who first loved us; this is how love as a torch overcomes hate and indifference, how it breaks down walls of misunderstanding and fear, how it stands firm in the face of injustice and cruelty, how it shows that every human being, made in God's image, deserves dignity and respect, when you carry the torch of love, you refuse to let the darkness define reality, you declare that compassion, not apathy, will shape your actions, and this declaration itself is a bold act of faith, an act of courage that says you believe God's truth is stronger than any lie, His mercy deeper than any wound, His peace greater than any chaos; to keep your love burning bright, you must also care for your own relationship with God, spend time in prayer, meditate on Scripture, remember the way Jesus served others without seeking anything in return, connect with fellow believers who can encourage you when you feel worn out, compassion grows when you draw near to the source of all love, filling your heart with His grace, just as a torch must be replenished with oil or kindling, so your heart must be continually nourished by God's presence, His Word, and the fellowship of His people, the more you soak in His love, the more naturally it spills out onto others; as you journey forward, realize that serving through compassion does not always look dramatic, it can be quiet, subtle, almost hidden, like a candle flickering in a bedroom window, but even a small light shines brightly in darkness, your quiet acts of love can mean the world to someone who feels invisible, unheard, or unloved, your willingness to forgive can mend a relationship on the brink of collapse, your gentle encouragement can inspire someone to try again after a crushing failure, these small flames, seemingly insignificant on their own, gather together to form a brilliant display of God's love at work in the world; if you ever doubt that your compassion matters, think about times in your own life when someone else's kindness lifted you up, maybe it was a friend who listened without judging when you needed to talk, or a teacher who believed in your potential when you felt uncertain, or a neighbor who helped your family during a difficult season, those moments mattered, they touched you in a way that made you feel seen and valued, they likely gave you courage to keep going when you felt like giving up, now, by serving through compassion, you pass on that gift, paying forward the kindness you received, and in doing so, you weave your story into a larger tapestry of love that stretches across time and space; love as a torch challenges you to love even those who are hard to love—the ones who seem closed off, angry, or suspicious—maybe they have built walls around their hearts because of past hurts, and you are called to shine the light of compassion gently, not forcing them to open up, but showing that you care, that you will not abandon them, that you see beyond their rough exterior, this takes patience, and sometimes you must trust that God's love can soften hearts over time, your role is not to change them by force, but to offer the love that might, in God's timing, lead them toward healing and trust; in a world filled with noise, conflict, and confusion, love as a torch stands out as a quiet but undeniable force for good, it does not need a spotlight or a stage, because it glows from within, fueled by the Holy Spirit, it does not seek applause or rewards, because it finds its fulfillment in knowing that it reflects Christ's heart, it does not tremble before darkness, because it knows that even the smallest light can pierce the night, giving others a glimpse of God's everlasting goodness; as you embrace compassion, you find that your own fears of inadequacy begin to fade, replaced by a growing sense of God's ability to work through you, love does not require you to be perfect, only willing, and in being willing, you step into a courage that surprises you, a courage that comes from seeing yourself as God's instrument, carrying a torch that can guide others closer to His love, this courage builds over time, and you find yourself daring to serve in ways you never considered before—volunteering for a local shelter, mentoring a younger believer, speaking up against injustice, or simply offering a listening ear to someone everyone else has ignored; when doubts arise—am I really making a difference, or is my love too small?—remember that God's measure of success differs from the world's, He values faithfulness, even in little things, He treasures the moments when you choose compassion over convenience, love over indifference, mercy over judgment, He sees the quiet sacrifices you make, the times you swallow pride to help another, the nights you pray for someone who will never know about those prayers, and He smiles, because He knows that each act of compassion is another torch lit in the darkness, another step toward a world more aligned with His kingdom; love as a torch also teaches you gratitude, as you serve others, you become aware of your own blessings, not just material ones, but the spiritual treasures God pours into your life—hope, forgiveness, peace, direction—these gifts become the fuel that keeps your torch burning bright, fueling your heart with an endless supply of reasons to keep loving, keep giving, keep serving, even when you feel tired or discouraged, gratitude reminds you that God has been patient with your own faults, generous with His grace, gentle in guiding you toward growth, and how can you not pass this kindness along to others, allowing them to taste and see that the Lord is good?; through compassion, you also build bridges, sometimes people distrust Christians because they have only seen anger or hypocrisy, but when they encounter real love, when they see you caring for them without an agenda, seeking their good without trying to manipulate them, their hearts may open, they may begin to wonder what inspires such kindness, and you can humbly point them to Jesus, the ultimate source of love, explaining that you serve not to gain anything, but to reflect His character, you become a gentle invitation for them to consider the love that has transformed your own life, thus compassion not only comforts the hurting, but also paves the way for the Gospel to touch hearts; love as a torch can also guide you through personal storms, when you face your own struggles—illness, loss, disappointment, failure—turning outward in compassion can help lift you above your pain, not by denying it, but by reminding you that you still have something to give, still have a purpose beyond your current sorrow, serving others in the midst of your own hardship can be a powerful statement of faith that God is still good, that you still trust Him to bring something beautiful out of your brokenness, and through this process, you may find that healing flows in unexpected ways, as your compassionate acts become healing balm not just for others, but for your own wounded spirit; over time, as love becomes your guiding torch, you develop a reputation for compassion, people notice when someone consistently cares, listens, and helps, they begin to trust you, confide in you, seek your advice or your company, and while this might seem like added responsibility, it's actually a gift—an opportunity to shine your light even brighter, to model what it means to follow Christ through kindness and humility, as your influence grows, you can encourage others to carry their own torches of love, multiplying the impact of compassion until it spreads beyond your immediate circle, touching lives you may never meet; love as a torch leaves a lasting legacy, long after you are gone, the memories of your kindness remain in the hearts of those you served, your compassion can inspire future generations to choose love over hate, to solve problems with empathy rather than force, to see each person as worthy of care and attention, who knows how far the ripples of your love may travel, perhaps the child you encouraged today will grow up to mentor others, the friend you comforted in their grief will later comfort someone else, and so forth, weaving an unbroken chain of compassion that outlives your earthly journey; in all this, you remain grounded in the truth that love is not something you must generate by your own power, love comes from God, who first loved us, through prayer and reflection, you reconnect with the divine source of this flame, letting Him reignite the torch when it flickers, asking Him to guide you toward those who need your compassion most, trusting that He will supply what you lack, because if He calls you to serve with love, He will also provide the courage, strength, patience, and resources you need, He will never send you on this journey empty-handed; as you continue walking through life's forest, carrying this torch of love, you find that the darkness no longer frightens you as it once did, you see that your purpose is clearer, your heart stronger, and your steps more confident, not because you have become fearless, but because compassion has taught you that God's love is greater than your fears, that serving others is more fulfilling than living for yourself, that shining light into another's darkness lifts your own spirit as well, and this gentle, loving courage enables you to serve the Lord wholeheartedly, making your life a beacon of hope that draws others toward the warmth of His presence; so keep loving, keep caring, keep choosing compassion as your guide, for in doing so, you ignite courage in your own heart and in the hearts of those around you, transforming ordinary moments into holy encounters where God's love breaks through, and as this love spreads, like countless torches lighting the way, the world becomes brighter, warmer, and more like the place God intended it to be—one flame, one act of compassion, one heart at a time, all fueled by love as a torch, serving through compassion, and boldly following the One who showed us the meaning of true love.

Day 14 - Obedience in Action: Stepping Out With Purpose

Imagine yourself standing at the edge of a wide, open field, the grass bending gently beneath a warm breeze, the sky stretched out above you in shades of soft blue and white, and within that peaceful moment you feel a stirring in your heart, a call that invites you to take a step forward, to leave behind the familiar comfort of your hiding place, and to obey a quiet whisper that speaks of purpose, truth, and serving the Lord with all that you are; it's not always easy to obey, for obedience means not only hearing God's voice, but choosing to follow it even when you don't understand every detail, even when fear gnaws at your thoughts, even when you long to remain still and safe, yet something inside you knows that the only way to truly live as God intended is to put your faith into action, to do more than nod your head or say the right words, to let your feet, your hands, your choices, and your life reflect the truth you claim to believe, and so you stand here, heart pounding, on the edge of that field, the place where thought meets action, where intentions give birth to deeds, and you ask yourself if you have the courage to step out with purpose; obedience, after all, is not a passive thing, it is a decision to trust God's direction even if the path ahead is unclear, it is the movement of your will aligning with His greater plan, it is the difference between saying you believe and showing you believe, for you can claim faith from the safety of your comfort zone, whisper lofty prayers from the quiet corners of your mind, but without obedience—without actually moving forward—your faith may remain a gentle breeze instead of becoming a driving force that carries you into territories you never dreamed you could enter, territories where your compassion is tested, where your trust grows deeper, where your willingness to serve opens doors of blessing you never imagined; obedience in action means taking the first step even if your knees wobble, means saying yes when your voice trembles, means offering your time, your energy, your gifts to God's work even if you feel small, uncertain, or unqualified, it is not about being perfect or strong in your own right, but about surrendering your weaknesses to the One who can turn your humble efforts into something beautiful, something that can touch hearts, heal wounds, bring hope where despair once reigned, and so you must remember that you do not walk alone, that the Lord who calls you also equips you, that the Spirit who whispers within you also empowers you to move beyond your fears, to find strength in His promises, to trust that He is faithful and will not abandon you when the journey grows difficult; stepping out with purpose begins in the quiet spaces of your heart where you first recognize God's voice calling you toward something more—a greater kindness, a deeper love, a willingness to serve those in need, a boldness to speak truth in a world confused by lies, or a readiness to stand for righteousness when it costs you something dear—these whispers might start small, like a seed planted in soft soil, and over time they grow, their roots sinking deeper as you pray and seek His will, as you open your Bible and discover that God has guided countless others before you, ordinary people who became extraordinary instruments in His hands because they chose to obey rather than shrink back, because they trusted the unseen rather than clinging to what they could grasp, and these stories remind you that you are part of a long line of believers who dared to step out into the unknown, who obeyed not because it was easy, but because it was right; think of Abraham leaving his homeland behind on nothing but a promise, think of Moses standing before Pharaoh despite his own insecurities, think of Esther risking her life to speak up for her people, think of Peter stepping out of the boat onto the waves at Jesus' command, these figures did not know exactly how things would end, yet they stepped forward in obedience, and in doing so they learned that God's faithfulness far outweighed their fears, so as you stand in your own moment of decision, remember that your obedience is not just about you, it is also about what God wants to accomplish through you for the sake of others, how your willingness to move forward can bring comfort to the hurting, encouragement to the weary, guidance to the lost, and a shining example of faith to those who watch quietly from the sidelines; obedience in action also involves letting go of excuses that hold you back, telling yourself you are too young, too old, too inexperienced, too flawed, too busy, or too weak, these excuses try to keep you stuck in place, to convince you that God surely must have chosen someone else better suited to the task, but Scripture is full of examples where God chose unlikely individuals to carry out His plans, reminding us that it is not about our credentials, but about His power at work in us, if you trust that He can use you right where you are, with the gifts you have, then you open the door for Him to do amazing things, and each act of obedience becomes another brushstroke in the masterpiece God is painting in your life, a masterpiece that you may not fully appreciate until you look back and see how far you've come, how many lives have been touched, how many hearts have been warmed by the glow of your faithful service; stepping out with purpose calls you to be intentional, to stop drifting aimlessly and instead focus on what God is asking of you today, not waiting for some distant future moment when you feel more prepared or confident, but taking the small steps now—maybe it's offering a sincere apology to someone you wronged, maybe it's volunteering at a local shelter, maybe it's writing a note of encouragement to a friend who is struggling, maybe it's sharing your testimony of how God has worked in your life, even if your voice shakes, each of these steps, no matter how small they seem, adds fuel to the fire of your courage, training you to listen closely to His voice and respond swiftly and willingly, over time these smaller acts of obedience strengthen your spiritual muscles, preparing you for bigger leaps of faith that may come later, as you learn that God can be trusted with each step, you grow bolder, more certain that He will guide you, lift you, catch you if you stumble, and celebrate with you as you grow more like Christ; obedience in action does not mean you will never feel afraid or uncertain, fear may still hover at the edges of your mind, whispering that you might fail, be misunderstood, or meet resistance, but courage is not the absence of fear, it is the decision to act in spite of fear, to believe that God's love and power are greater than any obstacle, that He is on your side, that He can turn your fears into testimonies of His grace, in the face of these fears, remember that God calls you not to walk alone, but as part of a body of believers who can encourage, support, and pray for you, that fellowship can serve as a safe haven, a well of strength from which you draw courage and resilience, for when you see others stepping out in obedience, you realize you are not alone, you see that God is moving in many hearts, orchestrating a grand tapestry of faith and obedience that covers the earth, shining light into dark places, melting hearts hardened by pain, and stirring souls long trapped in hopelessness; sometimes obedience will lead you to face your own weaknesses, to confront parts of your heart that still cling to selfish desires or stubborn pride, for serving the Lord requires humility, a willingness to bend and yield to His correction, but even this process, though it can be uncomfortable, draws you closer to God's heart, as you allow Him to refine you, to shape you, to remove the rough edges, you become a more fitting instrument in His hands, better able to serve with sincerity, compassion, and understanding, it is through obedience that your character is formed, your faith tested, your motives purified, and as you grow, you find a deeper joy in giving yourself fully to His purposes, a satisfaction that no earthly reward can match, because you know you are aligned with the eternal will of the Creator who formed you; obedience in action also reminds you that serving the Lord is not just about grand missions or public ministries, it can happen in your home as you treat your family with patience and love, it can happen in your workplace when you show integrity and kindness, it can happen in your classroom when you help a struggling classmate understand a lesson, it can happen in the way you handle your finances, your leisure time, your relationships, your words, and your choices, for every area of your life can become a platform for obedience, a stage on which you demonstrate trust in God's ways rather than the world's patterns, and as you weave obedience into these everyday moments, your entire life becomes a testimony, a living sermon that points others toward the One you serve, without having to shout or force anything, your quiet, consistent obedience can be more powerful than any speech; stepping out with purpose may sometimes lead you to places you never wanted to go or never imagined going, perhaps you will be called to serve in a foreign land, learn a new language to share God's love, or step into a leadership role you never thought you could handle, perhaps you will be asked to befriend someone who seems completely different from you, to invest in a community that has been forgotten or ignored, or to stand up for justice in a situation where silence would be easier, in all these cases, obedience stretches you beyond the boundaries of what you considered safe, teaching you that your comfort is not God's highest priority, rather, He cares about your growth, your impact, your closeness to Him, and yes, He cares about the countless souls who can be reached, encouraged, and uplifted through your willingness to step forward; when you look at Jesus, the perfect model of obedience, you see that His actions were always guided by the Father's will, even when it led Him to the cross,

He obeyed not out of blind submission, but out of perfect love and trust, knowing that through His obedience, salvation would come to many, and if you are called to follow in His footsteps, know that your own obedience, while less grand, can still have ripples of blessing that extend far beyond what your eyes can see, maybe your service encourages a single person who goes on to touch many more lives, maybe your act of kindness sparks a chain of compassion that transforms a broken relationship, maybe your patient teaching shapes the character of a young mind who will one day lead others to truth, the seeds you plant in obedience can grow into mighty oaks of influence, sheltering and nourishing countless souls; obedience in action, stepping out with purpose, also grants you a sense of direction that cuts through the noise of modern life, we live in a world full of distractions, temptations, shifting values, and hollow promises, and it's easy to feel lost or aimless, yet obedience anchors you in God's eternal perspective, it helps you choose what truly matters over what simply feels good at the moment, it prevents you from drifting with the tide of popular opinion, and instead invites you to stand firmly on the solid ground of God's truth, as you continue to obey, you become more sensitive to His voice, more attuned to the Spirit's guidance, more able to discern right from wrong, essential from trivial, permanent from passing, and this clarity empowers you to spend your time, energy, and resources on the things that carry eternal significance, rather than squandering your life on empty pursuits; in the midst of challenges and obstacles that may arise as you try to obey, remember that God is not looking for flawless performance, He is looking for a willing heart, one that says "yes" even when uncertain, one that tries and, if necessary, fails and gets back up again with His grace, for God's mercy covers your shortcomings, His grace strengthens your resolve, and His love assures you that you are precious to Him regardless of how perfectly you execute the tasks He sets before you, when you understand this, you are free to act boldly, to take risks for the sake of righteousness, to move past the fear of failure and embrace the adventure of living out your calling; stepping out with purpose is not just about what you do, but also about who you become, each act of obedience shapes you a little more into the image of Christ, making you more patient, more forgiving, more generous, more empathetic, as you serve others selflessly, you learn the joy of giving without expecting anything in return, as you stand for truth, you gain the strength to resist compromise, as you show mercy, you discover that compassion heals not only those you help but also your own wounded soul, and as you persevere through hardships, trusting that God is at work, you develop resilience, hope, and an unshakable peace that can weather any storm; in time, you may begin to notice that your initial fears and doubts have less power over you, that the once-paralyzing questions—what if I fail, what if people reject me, what if I lose something dear—start to fade in the light of a bigger question: what if I obey and see God move in ways I never imagined? what if my small step of faith contributes to a far greater story God is writing? what if my obedience allows God's love to reach someone who desperately needs it, changing their life forever? as you dwell on these possibilities, courage swells within you, and you realize that your life, guided by obedience, can become a vessel for divine grace, a channel through which God's blessings flow into the world; this single focus on obeying God's call, on stepping out with purpose, can bring meaning and coherence to your entire existence, no matter your age, your background, your education, or your skills, you have a role to play in God's kingdom, a unique place in His plan, and when you embrace obedience, you say "yes" to that role, you abandon the idea that life is just a random series of events or that you must carve your own path out of sheer will, instead, you embrace the truth that the Designer of galaxies has invited you to take part in His redemptive work, that the Author of life trusts you to carry out certain tasks, speak certain words, love certain people, and walk certain roads, not for your glory, but for His, and in serving Him, you find a sense of belonging, of purpose, of destiny that no other pursuit can satisfy; let your obedience be fueled by gratitude, for you have received so much from the Lord—breath, life, opportunities, forgiveness, grace—He has lifted you from despair, offered salvation, given you hope and eternal life, so when He calls you to step out and serve, how can you not respond with a grateful heart? how can you not say, "Yes, Lord, here I am, send me"? and as you respond, your obedience itself becomes an act of worship, a living sacrifice offered up to God, pleasing in His sight, not because of its grandeur, but because of its sincerity and love; at times, you may look back and marvel at how far God has led you, how stepping out in obedience at one point led to a series of divine appointments, new relationships, unexpected blessings, and inner growth, you may see how the very things you once feared turned out to be stepping stones toward a deeper understanding of God's goodness, or how the people you served ended up blessing you in return, teaching you valuable lessons about humility, perseverance, and faith, life guided by obedience has a way of surprising you with the beauty of God's orchestration, showing you that nothing given to Him is ever wasted, no act of kindness lost, no word of encouragement forgotten; obedience in action is not a onetime event, but a daily choice, each morning you wake up to another day of possibilities, and again you face the question: will I follow where God leads me today, or will I shrink back? will I trust Him even when I don't understand, or will I rely on my limited perspective? will I invest my gifts in service, or bury them in fear? will I honor Him with my words, my time, my body, my relationships, or chase after empty promises of comfort and pleasure? these choices define the trajectory of your life, and every time you choose obedience, you ignite a spark of courage that strengthens your resolve, lifts your eyes heavenward, and propels you forward on the path of true purpose; if you find yourself uncertain right now, remember that God can handle your questions, bring them to Him in prayer, ask Him to clarify your calling, to show you the next step, to give you wisdom, to open doors that no one can shut and close doors that would lead you astray, seek counsel from mature believers who have walked this road, read Scripture to anchor your heart in truth, and watch for the gentle nudges of the Holy Spirit as He guides your thoughts and feelings, obedience does not mean you will never ask questions, it means you are willing to trust God's answers more than your own doubts, and as you do so, you find the courage you need to step out with purpose—purpose born of God's eternal plan, purpose that infuses every moment with meaning, purpose that transforms an ordinary life into a vessel of grace; so now, as you stand at the edge of that wide field, the wind tugging softly at your clothes, your heart brimming with possibility, your mind filled with the memory of God's promises, understand that obedience in action is your invitation to move forward, to let your faith show in what you do, how you live, how you love, to take that step, then another, and another, trusting that God's hand is steadying you, cheering you on, and using you to accomplish something far greater than you can imagine, when you do this, you find that your fears lose their power, your insecurities fade in the light of His greatness, and your willingness to serve the Lord becomes the very flame that ignites courage within your heart, fueling your soul to press on, to keep going, to rise above every challenge, and to shine like a beacon of hope in a world that desperately needs to see what faith in action looks like, you become a living testimony that obedience—humble, trusting, joyful obedience—is the key to stepping out with purpose and discovering the full richness of serving the Lord with all your heart.

Day 15 - Small Steps, Big Faith: Courage in the Everyday

Imagine standing in the soft light of early morning, your breath still gentle from sleep, the day ahead unrolled before you like a quiet path through a familiar landscape, and though no grand trumpet call greets you, no angelic choir sings at the window, you sense deep inside that this day holds a chance for courage, not the kind that wins medals or makes headlines, but the steady kind that grows through simple acts of faith, and you realize that serving the Lord does not always require giant leaps across mountains, but can be found in small steps taken right where you live, right in the middle of ordinary routines, tasks, and faces you know by heart; it is here, in the gentle hum of everyday life, that courage can ignite quietly, like a single spark catching on a dry leaf, then softly glowing brighter and brighter, for courage does not only bloom in moments of dramatic choice, it also appears when you dare to speak kindly to someone who seems distant, when you choose to give a bit of your time to help a neighbor, when you whisper a prayer for a friend in need, or when you decide to start the day by opening your heart to God's guidance, these are small steps, yet each one, when done with faith, becomes a brave action that shapes your heart and makes you more like the One you follow; think of how often we assume courage must be bold and loud, like a hero rushing into danger or standing up to a giant foe, yet consider that courage can also be as gentle as a quiet "yes" to God's call, as soft as forgiving someone who hurt you, or as simple as reaching out to a lonely person who sits by themselves day after day, there is a kind of strength in these small acts that can surprise you, for they show a willingness to trust God's leading without the promise of applause or praise, they remind you that the Lord sees every choice you make, even those others overlook, and He values the times you dare to act in love and truth when it would be easier to do nothing at all; maybe you remember how Jesus praised the widow who gave two small coins at the temple, not because the amount was large, but because her heart was fully engaged, she gave what little she had, and in doing so, she showed more courage than those who gave out of their wealth, this story teaches us that in God's kingdom, small steps of faith can hold great meaning, they can shine brightly not because of their size, but because they reflect trust, hope, and obedience, and that should encourage you, for it means that even when you feel unimpressive or ordinary, you can still make a real difference by offering what you have, whether it's your time, your kindness, your smile, or your patient ear; each day comes with chances to practice this kind of faith-filled courage, it might appear in how you treat a family member who irritates you, choosing patience instead of snapping back, or in how you handle disappointment, picking yourself up and trying again rather than giving into despair, it might show up when you stop to pray for direction before making a routine decision, trusting God cares about even the small corners of your life, it could emerge when you see a mess that is not yours to clean yet decide to tidy it anyway to bless someone else, or when you notice a friend struggling with worry and share a comforting word, these simple, everyday moments can become sacred ground where your faith is tested and strengthened, for it's often in these quiet spaces that God molds your character; courage in the everyday also means not waiting for perfect conditions before taking action, perhaps you think you must reach some higher level of holiness or knowledge before God can use you, but that's not what the Bible teaches, it shows that God works through people who are willing, even if they feel small or unsure, He invites you to trust Him with whatever you have today, in this moment, and as you obey in these small things, He often opens greater doors down the road, think of David, who tended sheep faithfully long before he faced Goliath, or Ruth, who stayed loyal to Naomi in ordinary, day-to-day struggles before becoming part of a grand story of redemption, they did not set out to become heroes, they simply did what was right and faithful in their present circumstances, and God wove their small acts into something beautiful and lasting; when you feel discouraged that your efforts are too tiny or too weak, remember that a mighty forest can grow from a single seed, and a raging river can start as a humble trickle of water, so too can your everyday acts of courage, guided by faith, grow into a life that bears lasting fruit, you may not see the full impact of your choices right away, or maybe not at all, but God sees the bigger picture, He knows the chain reactions your little steps can set in motion, perhaps a kind word you speak today encourages a friend to persevere through a tough time, and that friend later helps someone else in need, and on and on it goes, creating ripples of compassion and grace that spread far beyond what you can imagine; another element of courage in the everyday is learning to trust that even small steps taken in weakness can bring glory to God, you might worry that your faith feels too fragile, that doubt sometimes lurks in your mind, or that your prayers seem faint and unsteady, yet consider that courage does not mean you never feel afraid or uncertain, it means you choose to act despite those feelings, you choose to trust God more than your fears, to believe He can work through you even when you feel inadequate, this shift in perspective helps you see that the Lord cherishes sincere efforts made in faith, no matter how humble, and He can use them to accomplish more than you would think possible; think about how you spend your days, often filled with routines like going to school, working, taking care of chores, interacting with friends and family, these are not wasted hours, they are the very fabric of your life, and within these patterns lie countless opportunities to serve God and others, maybe your courage today is simply showing up for a friend who is having a hard time, not with fancy solutions, but with a listening heart, maybe it's choosing to do your best in a task you find dull, trusting that doing your work with integrity honors God, or perhaps it's being honest when it would be easier to lie, these might feel like small steps, but each one trains your heart to obey God's call in bigger things later on; as you walk this path of small steps and everyday courage, you learn that growth often comes slowly, like a seedling pushing through the soil, it takes time, patience, and persistence, you might have days when you feel strong and days when you feel weak, days when you serve with joy and days when you struggle just to keep going, but do not underestimate the value of pressing forward, each time you act in love, speak truth, stand for what is right, or show grace instead of anger, you are adding a drop of courage to your soul, over time these drops accumulate, gradually filling you with a steady reservoir of faith that helps you face larger challenges with confidence and peace; sometimes you may think that serving the Lord requires a grand, dramatic calling, like becoming a missionary in a distant land or preaching to crowds, but God's work often unfolds in much quieter ways, He might call you to care for an elderly relative, to mentor a younger student, to bake bread for a neighbor going through a loss, to write a heartfelt letter of encouragement to someone who feels forgotten, to pray daily for people you have never met, each of these acts, small and unassuming, can reflect the character of God's kingdom, showing that love, kindness, and mercy matter deeply, and that you can make a difference right where you stand; a key part of finding courage in the everyday is staying connected to the source of your strength, you cannot rely solely on your own willpower or determination to keep taking these small steps, you need to tap into God's presence, His Word, and His Spirit, spending time in prayer and Scripture can refresh you, remind you of His promises, and renew your resolve to live faithfully, gathering with other believers and sharing stories of how God is working in daily life can inspire you as well, seeing that you are not alone in your journey, that others also strive to honor God in ordinary moments, gives you encouragement to keep going; it's helpful to remember that Jesus Himself found meaning in small moments of connection, consider how He stopped to talk with a Samaritan woman at a well, how He noticed a tax collector named Zacchaeus perched in a tree, how He healed individuals one by one, or taught lessons using simple examples from nature, though He was the Son of God, He did not rush past these everyday encounters, He embraced them, showing that real change often happens in personal, face-to-face moments of compassion, if Jesus valued the small and the ordinary, how much more can we trust that our seemingly minor acts of obedience count in His sight; courage in the everyday might also mean standing firm against temptations that arise quietly, temptations to gossip, to cheat on a test, to treat someone unfairly, to give in to bitterness or envy, resisting these temptations may not earn applause, but it builds spiritual strength and aligns your life more closely with God's standards, choosing honesty when no one would know if you lied, choosing generosity when selfishness would be easier, choosing purity when the world says it does not matter, these are all ways of showing God that you value His truth above all else, and though they might seem small, they fortify your heart, making you braver and more stable in your faith over time; think of each day as a field where you have a chance to plant seeds of faith through small acts of courage, these seeds might not sprout instantly, but as you water them with prayer, kindness, perseverance, and faith, they will grow into something fruitful, and one day, looking back, you will see that your field is full of good things—relationships built on trust, a character shaped by godly principles, a soul at peace because it has learned to rely on God's strength rather than human recognition, this kind of rich harvest comes from daily choosing to follow Christ in the little things, the hidden corners, the quiet moments that seem unimportant; sometimes you may feel invisible, as if no one notices your choices to be kind or your efforts to do the right thing, but remember that God sees what others do not, He sees the courage it takes to stand alone in your convictions, He sees the patience you show when no one else is around, He sees the tears you shed in private as you pray for guidance, He sees the decision to say "yes" to His nudging, even if it leads you into uncertain territory, knowing that He watches and cares can give you the strength to continue, fueling your heart with the courage needed to keep going, even on days when your faith feels small and your strength feels thin; another aspect of courage in the everyday is learning to be gentle with yourself, not every attempt will go perfectly, you might try to comfort someone and stumble over your words, or attempt a kind act that is misunderstood, or falter when temptation sneaks up on you unexpectedly, in these moments, do not give up, but lean into God's grace, He knows your heart and your intentions, and His forgiveness covers your mistakes, pick yourself up, learn from the experience, and keep moving forward, this resilience is part of building true courage, understanding that failures are not final, but can become stepping stones to a stronger, wiser you, one who trusts God more deeply because of what you have learned; we live in a world that often celebrates big achievements, loud announcements, and flashy accomplishments, it's easy to feel small or unimportant when you measure your worth by such standards, but in God's economy, the currency is different, He values faithfulness over fame, sincerity over show, humility over hype, and perseverance over perfection, knowing this frees you to serve Him wholeheartedly in whatever circumstances He places you, no matter how ordinary or routine they may seem, it assures you that your small steps of obedience are significant, that your steady acts of love are noticed, and that your faithful choices are building a legacy of spiritual strength that no one can take away; finding courage in the everyday also involves being present, truly paying attention to the opportunities God gives you moment by moment, slow down enough to notice the person who looks sad in the hallway, the coworker overwhelmed with work, the stranger who might need a friendly smile, the family member who could use a reassuring hug, by focusing on the present, you open your eyes to places where you can bring hope and light, and as you respond to these needs, you discover that courage doesn't always roar like a lion, sometimes it whispers in your ear, "Go ahead, help them, say a kind word, don't be afraid," and as you listen to that whisper, you grow more confident in your ability to be God's hands and feet in the world; consider how small steps taken consistently can lead to big changes over time, just as a long journey is completed by placing one foot in front of the other, a life of strong faith is built through daily decisions that honor God, when you discipline yourself to pray each morning, to read Scripture regularly, to speak truthfully, to treat others with respect, you shape your character into a reflection of Christ's love, and though you might not feel different overnight, one day you realize that your responses to challenges are calmer, your patience deeper, your generosity more natural, that is the power of courage in the everyday—transforming you from the inside out, one small choice at a time; as your faith deepens and your heart grows bolder, you may find that God leads you into slightly bigger steps, perhaps prompting you to share your faith story with someone curious, or to take on a role in your church's outreach, or to support a mission that speaks to your heart, the small steps you took quietly in your daily life have prepared you for these moments, giving you the foundation of trust and obedience you need to embrace new challenges without being paralyzed by fear, and as you obey in these more visible ways, you see that courage is not just a trait for a select few, but a gift God nurtures in all His children who are willing to follow Him faithfully, even in the smallest of tasks; remember that every saint who achieved great things for God started out with small steps of faith, they were once beginners too, unsure of themselves, learning to listen for God's voice and respond in simple ways, over time, as they remained faithful in the little things, God entrusted them with bigger responsibilities, and their stories became legends of faith that inspire us today, you too can be part of this great story, not necessarily by doing something dramatic, but by living each day with a heart surrendered to God, letting Him shape your desires, guide your actions, and fill you with a love that casts out fear; courage in the everyday is not dull or boring, though it may feel routine, it is infused with a quiet excitement, knowing that you are cooperating with God's plan, even if you do not fully see the results yet, like a gardener planting seeds without seeing the harvest immediately, you trust that God will bring growth in due season, your job is to keep planting those seeds through acts of kindness, honesty, mercy, and service, trusting that He will water them with His grace and cause them to bear fruit at the right time; keep your eyes on Jesus as you walk this path, He understands what it means to live among ordinary people and face daily challenges, He knows how it feels to be tired, to be misunderstood, to be surrounded by the mundane tasks of life, yet He always acted with love, wisdom, and courage, drawing strength from His relationship with the Father, you can do the same, resting in the knowledge that the same Spirit who empowered Him can empower you as well, that the same Father who guided Him through each day's events will guide you, that the same love that filled His heart can fill yours too, giving you courage you never knew you had; when your soul grows weary and you wonder if these small steps matter, pause and remember that God's kingdom often grows in quiet ways, a mustard seed is tiny, yet it grows into a large tree that provides shelter, a bit of yeast can affect a whole batch of dough, making it rise, so your small, faithful actions can influence the lives of others in ways you cannot foresee, a gentle word today might prepare someone's heart to receive truth tomorrow, a small act of forgiveness now might heal a broken friendship that goes on to bless many others, your everyday courage can create ripples of goodness that spread far beyond your line of sight; courage in the everyday also means resisting the urge to compare your life to others, you might see someone else's grand achievements and feel small by comparison, but remember that your call is unique, God might have placed you in your particular situation for reasons only He knows, and He calls you to faithfulness, not to envy or self-pity, celebrate the victories of others and trust that your own small victories are precious to God, each time you choose to do the right thing, to extend love, to seek justice, to show mercy, to stand for truth, you honor God and fulfill a part of the purpose He designed you for; as the seasons of your life change, so will the shape of your everyday courage, at times you might be caring for young children, showing patience and love through countless small routines, at other times you might be a student, facing tests of integrity and diligence, or you might be older, guiding younger believers with your experience and gentle counsel, in each stage, the small steps differ, but the principle remains: your daily choices to trust and obey build a legacy of faith that no one can take from you, and through these choices, you discover that courage is not an unreachable dream, but something you practice and grow into day by day; so stand tall in your ordinary setting, knowing that great things can happen through small steps taken in faith, let courage guide you as you perform simple acts of kindness, honesty, loyalty, and compassion, let it guide you as you read your Bible quietly in the early dawn, or pray for your neighbor late at night, let it guide you as you speak encouraging words to a friend, or offer a helping hand to a stranger, let it guide you as you choose to forgive someone who hurt you, or as you resist a temptation to do wrong, each one of these choices, no matter how small, contributes to a bigger tapestry of God's work in your life, and as that tapestry grows, you will see that your trust in God has deepened, your character has matured, and your heart has found a steady bravery that does not depend on applause or recognition; in the end, courage in the everyday is about living out your faith where you are, with what you have, in the life you've been given, it's about believing that no moment is too small for God to use, no action too humble for Him to bless, no kind word too quiet for Him to hear, as you continue to take these small steps with big faith, you will find your heart kindled with courage, fueled by the presence of the Lord who walks alongside you, teaching you that truly serving Him is not always about moving mountains, but often about walking faithfully in their shadow, trusting that He sees, He cares, and He will make every small step count for His glory and your growth, so move forward with confidence, child of God, and let your everyday courage shine as a light that points back to Him.

Day 16 - Forged by Trials: Transforming Weakness into Strength

Imagine standing before a vast furnace, its heat radiating against your face, watching bright sparks fly as raw metal is hammered and shaped, and in that moment, you understand a truth about life that can fuel your heart with courage and resolve to serve the Lord: we are like that metal, placed into the fire of trials, pounded by challenges that test our limits, and though it may feel painful, confusing, and overwhelming, this forging process is not meant to destroy us, but to refine us, transforming our weakness into strength, teaching us that true courage often emerges not in calm, easy days but in storms where our faith is pushed to its limits; consider how a sword, smooth and shining, begins as a lump of ore, dull and without form, and it is only after being thrust into intense heat, hammered and shaped by a skilled blacksmith, quenched in water, and polished over time that it emerges as a powerful, gleaming blade, ready to serve a noble purpose, in a similar way, our hearts, marked by flaws and fears, enter the fires of hardship, challenge, disappointment, and loss, and through these fiery trials, God, the Master Craftsman, patiently works on us, not to crush us, but to mold us into people of greater faith, resilience, and courage, who can rise above their old limitations and step forward to serve Him in ways that once seemed impossible; we often wish for a path free of trouble, longing for comfort and ease, yet it is in the struggles that we grow the most, for these trials reveal who we are deep inside, showing us both our strengths and weaknesses, when things are smooth, we can easily imagine we are strong and brave, but when the ground shakes beneath our feet, when our plans crumble, when our health falters, or when loved ones disappoint us, we see the truth: that we are human, fragile, and in need of help, and though this realization may sting, it also opens the door for God's power to enter, for when we admit our weakness and turn to Him, He pours His strength into us, allowing His grace to shine most brightly in our darkest hours; think of the men and women in Scripture who faced overwhelming trials and came through them transformed: Joseph, betrayed by his own brothers, sold into slavery, wrongly accused and thrown into prison, yet through all this, he learned patience, forgiveness, and wisdom, so that when he finally rose to power in Egypt, he was ready to save many lives from famine and also reconcile with his family; or consider Moses, who once fled from Egypt in fear, spending years in the desert feeling like a failure, only to return later, guided by God's voice, to confront Pharaoh and lead the Israelites to freedom, or Ruth, a widow in a foreign land, with nothing but her loyalty and faith, who found herself woven into God's greater plan of redemption, or David, running from King Saul, hiding in caves, questioning when God's promise would be fulfilled, yet emerging from those trials as a ruler after God's own heart; these stories remind us that trials are not random punishments, but tools in God's hands, shaping us into people who can carry out His purposes, each difficulty we face can teach us perseverance, humility, compassion, empathy, and trust, as if each blow of the hammer on the anvil breaks away the brittle parts of our character, leaving something stronger and purer behind, no, trials are not pleasant, and God does not delight in our pain, but He knows that through these hardships, we can become more like Christ, who Himself endured the ultimate suffering on the cross, conquering sin and death not by avoiding pain, but by facing it with faith and love; when a storm hits your life—whether it's a loss, a betrayal, a serious illness, financial hardship, or a shattered dream—you have a choice: you can curl up in despair and curse the darkness, or you can turn your heart toward God, trusting that He can use even this painful season to refine you, you might ask, "How can any good come from this?" and sometimes the answer does not come quickly, but over time, as you cling to His promises, seek His presence, and continue doing what is right even when it's hard, you begin to see small changes in yourself—perhaps you become more patient, more aware of others' pain, more eager to pray, more sensitive to the Spirit's leading, or more courageous in standing for truth, you find yourself leaning on God's Word with new urgency, discovering that verses you once read casually now speak directly to your wounded soul, bringing comfort and strength you never knew you needed; as you push through trials, you also learn that you are not alone, that the body of believers can act as God's hands and feet, offering support, prayers, encouragement, and love during your hardest moments, and this experience can soften your heart toward others who suffer, making you want to reach out and help when their turn comes, thus, trials not only strengthen your own faith, they also create a network of empathy and understanding among God's children, drawing them closer together and painting a picture of a community shaped by compassion rather than judgment; there is another hidden blessing in being forged by trials: discovering that your worth in God's eyes is not based on your comfort or success, the world often measures value by achievements, wealth, popularity, or strength, but God values faithfulness, perseverance, and humility, and trials strip away our illusions and reveal what truly matters, showing us that God's love does not waver when we struggle, that His faithfulness does not disappear when we fail, and that His promise to be with us stands firm through every storm, knowing this frees you from the crippling fear of failure or the desperate need to impress others, because you learn to rest in the assurance that your identity is rooted in Christ's love, not in how smoothly your life flows; think of how gold is purified by fire, the intense heat burns away impurities, leaving behind a more radiant metal, in a similar manner, trials can expose and remove spiritual impurities—pride, selfishness, envy, insecurity—that block the fullness of God's work in your life, though it hurts to face these flaws, the end result is a purer heart, one that can reflect God's image more clearly and shine as a testimony of His transforming power, when you look back after enduring such refining seasons, you might marvel at how much you've changed, how burdens that once weighed you down no longer rule you, how fears that once paralyzed you have lost their hold, and how courage that once seemed out of reach now feels like a natural outflow of your faith; enduring trials also teaches you that serving the Lord is not just for the sunny days, it's about staying faithful when clouds gather, when questions go unanswered, when the world's noise drowns out easy solutions, it's about trusting that God's plan is bigger than your immediate comfort, that He sees the eternal picture while you see only a fragment, and that if you keep walking forward, step by step, He will guide you to a place of deeper purpose and greater courage, in fact, some of the greatest acts of service happen not when life is smooth, but when you choose to love, give, and share hope despite your own pain, a wounded healer can empathize with those who hurt, a broken heart can show tenderness and understanding, and a person who has survived the fire can stand firm in courage, inspiring others to persevere; think of Paul, who wrote letters of encouragement and truth while chained in a prison cell, think of Christians throughout history who sang hymns as they faced suffering, think of believers today who carry on serving the needy even as their own resources run low, their ability to do so is not born of natural strength or willpower, but from a faith forged in trials, a faith that learned to cling to God's grace in the darkest valley, and from that faith springs a courage that does not depend on circumstances, but rests on the unchanging character of God, these examples remind us that when we emerge from trials, we carry with us a story of survival and growth, a testimony that can give others hope, for if you have seen God's faithfulness in the fire, you can encourage someone else standing in the flames, showing them that weakness can become strength, that fear can become confidence, that sorrow can bloom into compassion, and that God can turn a mess into a message of courage and faith; to be forged by trials does not mean you must enjoy pain or seek hardship, it means recognizing that when hardship comes, as it inevitably will in this world, you can choose how to respond, you can let anger, bitterness, or despair take root, or you can invite God to use this experience to refine you, to reveal deeper truths, and to strengthen your spirit, it means understanding that storms can water the seeds of your faith, helping them grow into a sturdy tree whose roots run deep, able to withstand future tempests without toppling, and each time you weather a storm, you add another ring to that trunk, another layer of resilience, until you can stand tall and courageous no matter what winds blow against you; this transformation is not instant, it is a process that unfolds gradually as you cooperate with God's work in your life, at first, you might only see ashes and ruin, you might cry out in confusion and frustration, wondering why God allows such pain, but as time passes and you keep turning to Him, you begin to notice subtle changes—a greater patience, a clearer sense of direction, a newfound empathy for others' struggles, a boldness to speak truth without fear, and a deeper reliance on God's power rather than your own limited strength, these changes are the marks of metal shaped by fire, the evidence that your weaknesses are being transformed into strengths that serve His kingdom; trials also teach you about surrender, for when life spins out of your control, you must decide whom to trust, if you cling desperately to your own understanding, to your pride, to your illusion of control, you will find only frustration and exhaustion, but if you choose to let go, to place your worries, your wounds, your shattered dreams in God's hands, you discover a peace that passes understanding, you learn that giving up your agenda in favor of His plan opens the door to unexpected blessings, relationships, and opportunities for ministry that you never would have chosen on your own, and through this surrender, courage emerges, because you realize that you are not alone, that you never have to face hardship by your own limited resources, that the Lord who formed galaxies knows how to guide you through a tough season, and that His strength can fill the gaps in your own shattered heart; as you reflect on your journey, you might see that before the trials came, you depended heavily on your own skills, talents, intelligence, or charm, perhaps you believed you were doing well enough on your own, but the refining fire of difficulty revealed how flimsy that self-reliance could be, and though it was painful to learn, this lesson frees you from a burden you never should have carried, it reminds you that real strength comes from leaning on God, that your greatest potential is unlocked when you admit you cannot do everything alone, that in Him you find the wellspring of courage, perseverance, and vision that lifts you above your limitations, and this shift from self-reliance to God-dependence is one of the greatest victories trials can produce, for it places your source of strength on an immovable foundation rather than on shaky ground; consider the image of your heart as iron heated to glowing red, each blow of adversity shaping it, and when finally cooled and polished, it does not return to its original form, it emerges as something more refined, more resilient, more fitted for the role God has prepared for it, and this stronger heart can withstand future tests, serve with greater passion, and inspire others by its quiet stability, remember that people watch how you respond to hardship, they notice if your faith holds steady or crumbles, your steadfastness in the face of trials can become a lighthouse for someone drifting in darkness, a proof that faith in God is not just pretty words, but a living power that can uphold a trembling soul; when the next trial comes—and it will, for life in a broken world is full of challenges—you can face it with more confidence than before, not because you enjoy pain, but because you know that pain does not have the last word, you have seen God work through difficulty and bring about unexpected good, you have felt His presence in the valley of shadows, you have tasted the sweetness of His comfort and heard His whispered promises in the midst of your tears, this knowledge fortifies you, allowing you to walk into new storms without losing hope, to serve Him even when the path is strewn with obstacles, to offer kindness and love even when your own heart aches, and in doing so, you transform from someone who fears trials into someone who understands their purpose; from this vantage point, you can begin to appreciate the surprising gift hidden in hardship: the chance to grow beyond what you ever thought possible, the permission to put aside childish notions of faith and embrace a mature trust that holds strong in adversity, the opportunity to turn weaknesses—those habits, doubts, and frailties that once chained you—into testimonies of God's redemptive work, and as you emerge more courageous, you find a greater joy in serving the Lord, for no longer do you serve out of mere obligation or shallow excitement, now you serve with a heart tested and true, a heart that knows God is faithful in every season, and this authenticity shines through in your ministry, making your words ring with sincerity, your touch carry genuine warmth, and your presence bring hope to those who struggle; consider that without trials, many of us would remain stuck at a surface-level faith, content to remain in shallow waters where nothing challenges our beliefs, where our understanding of God's goodness is never tested, and where our capacity for compassion remains small, but trials push us into the deep end, forcing us to wrestle with tough questions, to cling to God when easy answers fail, and to emerge with a richer, fuller understanding of His character, this deeper faith produces a stronger courage, one rooted not in naive optimism, but in hard-won conviction that God is good even when life hurts, that His promises stand firm even when everything else shakes, and that His love endures far beyond the reach of sorrow; let the memory of past trials encourage you when new ones arise, recall how you survived storms you once thought would break you, how God provided what you needed at the right time, how He sent people, verses, songs, or unexpected blessings to lift your spirit, how even losses eventually led to new growth, when you remember these faith-building experiences, you remind your heart that trials can be conquered, that they cannot stop God's plans, that they cannot separate you from His love, this remembrance is like fuel for your courage, feeding the flame that burns in your soul, allowing it to grow brighter, steadier, and more effective in illuminating your path; trials also give you the humility to acknowledge that you are part of a bigger story, one God has been writing since the dawn of time, you realize that your personal comfort and agenda are not the center of the universe, and that there is meaning in serving His higher purposes, even if it costs you something, this humility lets you hold your trials in perspective, understanding that while they hurt now, they can contribute to something grander than you can currently see, you become willing to let God write your story, shaping you as He sees fit, trusting that He knows the full picture, and that the strengths He is forging in you will be used to bless others, advance His kingdom, and bring glory to His name; as you live out this understanding, your service to the Lord takes on a different flavor, no longer driven by a desire to prove yourself, impress others, or earn God's favor, but motivated by love, gratitude, and the knowledge that He can turn every weakness into a display of His power, this transforms your attitude from timid hesitation into bold willingness to try, to speak, to help, and to endure for His sake, since you know that even if you fail by human standards, God can still use your efforts to accomplish His will, your identity is not tied up in external success, but in the simple, beautiful truth that you belong to Him and that He is making you more courageous and faithful through every ordeal; remember that Jesus Himself, though sinless, was not spared suffering, He faced rejection, betrayal, and physical agony on the cross, and Hebrews 5:8 tells us that He learned obedience through what He suffered, if Christ, our perfect example, grew through trials, how can we expect to be exempt? yet His suffering led to resurrection, victory, and the redemption of countless souls, in the same way, the trials you endure can lead to greater life, purpose, and fruitfulness, not just for you, but for those whose lives you touch, this perspective encourages you to view hardship not as evidence of God's neglect, but as an opportunity for deeper union with Him, a path toward understanding the heart of our Savior who also walked through suffering, but emerged triumphant; ultimately, being forged by trials teaches you to rely on God's strength rather than your own, you discover that human courage and willpower have limits, but His grace does not, that your understanding can fail, but His wisdom endures, that your heart can break, but His love can mend it and make it stronger than before, this reliance shifts the center of your life from self to Christ, building a stable foundation that no storm can sweep away, as you stand on this foundation, you find that even when your knees tremble, you can move forward, trusting that God's hands uphold you, that He sees every tear and hears every cry, and that He will not waste the pain you've been through; when the forging is done—or at least, when you emerge from one season of forging—you may feel a quiet confidence in the face of challenges that once terrified you, you have discovered that you are not as fragile as you feared, that with God's help, you can weather trials and come out refined, this knowledge feeds your courage, allowing you to serve the Lord in new ways, to take risks for His kingdom, to stand up for truth when it's unpopular, to show kindness in hostile environments, to speak hope where despair rules, or to invest in relationships that require patience and forgiveness, your courage is now anchored in the memory of what God has already done in you, and the assurance that He can do it again if needed; perhaps the greatest gift of being forged by trials is the ability to bring comfort to others who find themselves in similar fires, having walked through your own valley of shadows, you can guide others through theirs, your empathy, born of pain and struggle, becomes a healing balm, your stories of God's faithfulness help them believe that better days lie ahead, your patience with their doubts and fears grows from understanding your own moments of weakness, and your willingness to stand by them in silence or prayer, offering presence rather than empty platitudes, shows them God's character more clearly than polished speeches ever could, in this way, your transformed weaknesses turn into strengths that bless others, further igniting courage in your heart, and spreading it to theirs; so as you face life's inevitable trials, do not be afraid of the forging process, even though it may feel harsh and merciless at times, trust that God is the skilled blacksmith shaping you with wisdom and care, He knows exactly how much heat you can endure, how many blows of the hammer are needed, and when to cool and polish you, He does not delight in your pain, but in the finished work of grace and growth He will bring forth from it, and if you let Him have His way, if you keep your eyes on Him rather than on the flames, you will see your courage bloom like a rare flower sprouting from rocky ground, strong, resilient, and ready to serve Him with a boldness that cannot be easily shaken; as you embrace the truth that trials can transform weakness into strength, you find yourself increasingly willing to enter the unknown, to say yes to the hard assignments, to love those who are difficult to love, to forgive what seems unforgivable, to hope against hope, to believe God's promises when all evidence seems to point the other way, these choices do not become easy, but they become possible, fueled by the courage that emerges from knowing God can use every test to shape you into someone better suited for His glory and your true calling, and so you walk forward, not with pride, but with humility and trust, confident that whatever trial comes next, He who began a good work in you will be faithful to carry it on to completion, forging you into a shining instrument of His love, grace, and strength.

Day 17 - Conquering Giants: Courage in Confrontation

Imagine yourself standing in a wide valley, the air still and heavy, your heart pounding as you face a giant that towers before you, its shadow stretching long across the ground, reminding you of every insecurity, every weakness, every doubt you've ever known, and as you stand there, you can almost hear a quiet voice in your soul asking if you will have the courage to move forward, to pick up a stone of faith, to trust that the Lord who called you here will not abandon you now; this is the essence of confronting giants, those seemingly impossible challenges that loom large in your life, daring you to shrink back, to run, to give up, yet deep in your heart, where your faith sparks like a flint struck against stone, you know that courage does not mean feeling no fear at all, but choosing to act despite the fear, stepping forward in obedience to God's call even when every nerve in your body trembles, and in this moment you remember how God has never failed to stand by those who trust Him, how He has always provided a way, offering grace and strength that surpass anything you could muster on your own; think of David, a young shepherd boy stepping into a battlefield to face Goliath, a giant whose roar echoed across the valley, causing armies to quake, David did not wear fancy armor or carry a soldier's sword, he had only a sling, a handful of smooth stones, and above all, a deep faith that God's power far outweighed the giant's size, and with that courage, David ran forward, not away, and let a single stone fly, guided by the hand of the Almighty, bringing the giant crashing down and changing the course of history, his victory was not because he was big or strong, but because his heart burned with the fire of trust, ignited by a knowledge of who God is and how He can work through those who believe, this story, etched into the pages of Scripture, reminds you that you too can confront the giants that stand in your path—those fears, failures, obstacles, temptations, lies, and even spiritual forces that try to hinder you from serving the Lord with all your heart, each challenge may seem overwhelming, but remember that God is greater, His arm is not too short to save, His promises are not empty words, and His presence is not a distant dream; as you face your own giants, you realize that confrontation does not always mean shouting or raising a sword, sometimes it means quietly standing your ground, refusing to be intimidated by the voices that tell you you're not good enough, not strong enough, not skilled enough, it might mean confronting a difficult person who has wounded you, choosing to meet them with truth and grace instead of bitterness and anger, it could mean speaking out against injustice when staying silent would be easier, or standing firm in your faith when others mock or misunderstand you, in each of these battles, you hold a choice: either step back and let the giant define your reality, or step forward, calling on the Lord's strength to redefine it, when you choose to move forward, you discover that courage grows with each step of faith, each decision to trust God's guidance despite the trembling in your legs; you see, giants come in many forms, not just towering enemies on a literal battlefield, they can be the inner giants of fear, anxiety, pride, insecurity, or doubt, they can be giant barriers like sickness, financial trouble, strained relationships, or cultural pressures that push you to compromise your values, sometimes your giant could be a persistent sin that seems impossible to shake, or a calling from God that scares you because it stretches you beyond your comfort zone, each giant stands there, daring you to remain small and defeated, but as you look up at its imposing figure, you also sense that the Lord is whispering to your heart, "Am I not with you? Did I not promise to strengthen you, to uphold you with My righteous right hand?" and if you listen to that voice, you find a wellspring of courage rising within, reminding you that the size of your giant does not match the size of your God; to find the courage to confront your giants, you must learn to ground yourself in the truth of who God is, He is the Creator who spoke galaxies into being, the One who parted seas, brought down mighty walls with trumpet blasts, raised the dead to life, and overcame death itself through the cross and the empty tomb, no giant, no matter how fierce, can rival His power, and what's more, He invites you to rely on Him, to cast your cares upon Him, to trust that if He leads you into a confrontation, He will also equip you to handle it, though you might feel weak and unqualified, remember that God often delights in using the humble and unexpected to accomplish great things, so that no one can boast in their own strength, this means that your trembling is not a sign of failure, but an opportunity for God to show His might through you; confronting giants requires preparation, just as David practiced his sling on wild animals while tending sheep, you too should cultivate spiritual habits that strengthen your faith, spending time in prayer, reading Scripture, worshiping wholeheartedly, and seeking fellowship with other believers can sharpen your discernment and deepen your trust, these habits fill your heart with reminders of God's faithfulness, so when the moment of confrontation arrives, you're not relying on empty bravado, but on a well-trained faith that has seen God's hand at work before, and these spiritual disciplines act like smooth stones in your pouch, ready to be slung at the right time, each prayer prayed, each verse studied, each song sung, is another resource you can draw upon when fear attempts to paralyze you; courage in confrontation is not about being reckless or unkind, it is not about crushing others to achieve your aims, rather, it is about standing firm in truth and love, guided by the principles God has given, sometimes your giant might be a situation where you must speak truth to someone who has strayed, correct an injustice, or confront a lie with honesty, in these moments, you must remember that courage also involves grace, that the end goal is not simply to win an argument or defeat an opponent, but to honor God and to lead others toward healing, redemption, and a better understanding of His will, when your heart is aligned with God's love, even confrontation can be done with humility, patience, and a desire for reconciliation, the difference between a destructive confrontation and a redemptive one often lies in the posture of your heart, so ask God to help you approach giants not with hatred or pride, but with sincere faith and compassion; you will face moments when the giant seems to roar louder, mocking your efforts, causing your knees to weaken, in those times, hold fast to God's promises, remember that David did not defeat Goliath by human might, but by invoking the name of the Lord Almighty, who was greater than any earthly threat, likewise, when the enemy of your soul tries to fill your mind with doubts—accusing you, reminding you of past failures, predicting your defeat—you can respond by declaring the truth that God is for you, not against you, that nothing can separate you from His love, that He has given you a spirit of power, love, and self-control, not a spirit of fear, and as you speak these truths to your own heart, you usher in a fresh wave of courage, enabling you to push back the shadows of intimidation; sometimes, conquering a giant takes time, it might not fall with one swift strike, you may need to persist, to stand your ground repeatedly, to endure setbacks without giving up, remember that persistence itself is a form of courage, every time you refuse to be intimidated, every time you get back up after being knocked down, you are proclaiming that the giant does not have the final say, that God's plan and purpose remain intact despite temporary obstacles, this steadfast endurance shapes your character, teaching you patience, strengthening your faith muscles, and reminding you that victory often comes to those who refuse to surrender, your tenacity becomes a witness to others, showing them that it is possible to face what seems unfaceable and to overcome through the power of Christ; consider how the world needs people who will stand up against the giants of injustice, hatred, corruption, and despair, if believers shrink back every time a giant appears, who will shine the light of truth in dark places, who will protect the innocent, defend the marginalized, speak on behalf of the voiceless, or challenge systems built on lies? God calls you to be a vessel of His justice and mercy, and doing so often means confronting giants that guard strongholds of sin, stepping into such battles can be daunting, but trust that the Lord will guide your steps, give you wisdom to know when to speak and when to be silent, and provide the resources you need to break down barriers, your courage in these confrontations becomes a channel for God's redemptive work in the world, bringing about hope and freedom where oppression once reigned; personal giants—those within your own soul—are equally important to confront, it might be fear itself, wrapping its cold fingers around your heart, making you hesitate when you know God wants you to act, or pride, whispering that you don't need anyone's help, or anger that simmers beneath the surface, waiting to explode when challenged, these internal giants can be even trickier to face because they live inside you, wearing familiar faces and justifying their presence, but if you're willing to bring them into the light, confessing them to the Lord and perhaps to a trusted friend or mentor, you can begin the process of disarming them, God's truth can cut through the lies you've believed, showing you a path toward healing and transformation, and as you confront these inner giants, you find a new level of freedom and confidence, the kind that allows you to serve God more fully and love others more sincerely, no longer held back by hidden battles; in this journey of conquering giants, do not overlook the power of prayer, prayer aligns your will with God's, inviting His wisdom, strength, and courage to flow into your life, when you stand before a giant, your prayers do not need to be eloquent or long, they can be as simple as "Lord, help me," "Give me courage," or "Show me what to do," He hears these cries and responds with the grace you need to take the next step, sometimes He may change the situation, sometimes He may change you, softening your fears, sharpening your insight, and flooding you with a peace that surpasses understanding, this divine partnership transforms confrontation from a lonely struggle into a cooperative effort with the God who holds all power; remember too that after the victory, when the giant falls, give credit where it is due, it's tempting to pat yourself on the back, to think you overcame by your own cleverness or might, but humility and gratitude are vital, thank God for His guidance, celebrate the growth in your faith, recognize that without His hand, the outcome could have been very different, and also learn from the experience—what did you discover about yourself, about God, about the nature of courage, how can you use these lessons to encourage others facing similar challenges, by humbly reflecting on the journey, you ensure that each confrontation becomes a stepping stone, lifting you higher and preparing you for future battles; it's important to note that victory may not always look like you expect, sometimes conquering a giant means changing your perspective, learning to live with certain difficulties while still maintaining faith and joy, or relinquishing a dream that God never intended for you, the giant may not always be struck down instantly, but conquering it can mean no longer being controlled by it, rising above it to continue serving the Lord with integrity and hope, recognizing that true victory lies in remaining faithful, obedient, and filled with love, regardless of whether circumstances align perfectly with your plans, this form of victory can require even more courage, because it's not about a dramatic knockout punch, but about steady perseverance and trust that God's ways are higher than your own; as you continue in your faith journey, you will likely face multiple giants at different times, each encounter reshaping your definition of courage, reminding you that fear's hold on you weakens every time you act in faith, the more giants you face down with God's help, the more natural courage becomes, not a rare surge of adrenaline, but a calm confidence rooted in understanding God's character, you start to believe that no matter what looms ahead, the One who stands beside you is greater, that nothing can separate you from His love, that the power that raised Jesus from the dead is at work in you, enabling you to face challenges that once would have seemed insurmountable; this growth in courage also affects how you serve the Lord, you might begin to notice opportunities to share the Gospel with someone who is hostile to faith, or to mentor a troubled teenager, or to speak up in a community meeting where everyone else stays quiet, your willingness to confront these giants—be they in conversations, relationships, or larger social issues—opens doors to ministry you never would have dared walk through before, and as you trust God in these moments, He works through you, bringing light, truth, and healing into places long overshadowed by darkness, courage in confrontation thus becomes a tool not just for your personal victory, but for advancing God's kingdom on earth; in addition, the courage you develop in confronting giants can inspire others, people watch how you handle adversity, how you stand firm in the face of insults or opposition, how you respond when your principles are tested, when they see that you rely on God's strength and not your own, that you remain respectful and caring even when challenged, they may wonder what fuels your confidence, what gives you the grace to keep going, in time, this can lead them to seek the source of your courage, to ask questions that open the door to sharing your faith, thus, your confrontation with giants becomes not just about your personal growth, but a testimony that can draw others toward the God you serve; of course, none of this is simple or automatic, real courage in confrontation must be nurtured, it requires constant prayer, reflection, and willingness to learn from mistakes, you may attempt to confront a giant and stumble, losing your temper or feeling crushed by disappointment, but even then, you can come back to God, confessing your weakness, asking Him to teach you what went wrong and how to do better next time, this process of trial, error, repentance, and perseverance gradually strengthens your ability to stand firm, reminds you that God's grace covers your failures, and encourages you to keep trying, keep growing, keep believing that He can bring victory in ways beyond your imagination; as you gain experience in facing giants, you might also learn that not every battle is yours to fight, discernment is crucial, sometimes you must step back and wait, trusting God to fight on your behalf or to send someone else better equipped for this particular confrontation, other times you realize that the giant looming before you is actually a distraction, tempting you to waste your energy on a conflict that does not align with God's priorities, learning when to engage and when to refrain is part of growing in wisdom, and this wisdom ensures that your courage is not spent foolishly, but directed towards battles that truly matter, that advance God's purposes and bring lasting fruit; with each giant you conquer, or at least stand against, you add another chapter to your personal testimony of God's faithfulness, and this testimony becomes a treasure, a reminder when new giants arise that you are not facing them empty-handed, you carry with you the memory of past victories, the lessons learned, the scars that have healed and become marks of endurance, these memories fortify your heart, making you more resilient, more confident that what God did before, He can do again, in this way, your life story, shaped by courageous confrontations, forms a tapestry of faith that can encourage future generations, showing them that no giant is too strong when God is on our side; in the end, the ultimate giant—death itself—has already been conquered by Jesus, and knowing this gives you the assurance that no matter what happens, your future is secure in Him, this eternal perspective reduces even the largest giants to a manageable size, for if the greatest enemy has been defeated, what challenge can ultimately separate you from the love and victory Christ has won, this reality should embolden you further, removing the sting of ultimate defeat, and freeing you to serve the Lord wholeheartedly, to confront giants with the calm assurance that even if outcomes differ from your expectations, God remains sovereign, good, and in control; the courage you cultivate in confronting giants thus becomes a hallmark of your faith, it shapes your character, influences your choices, and inspires others, it paves the way for acts of service that honor God and uplift those around you, and as you keep pressing forward, you find that your heart grows bolder, your trust in God deepens, your ability to navigate challenges becomes more refined, and your love for Him and for people expands, this is what it means to have courage in confrontation, to know that while giants come in many shapes and forms, each one can be faced with the confidence that arises from walking closely with the Lord, letting Him guide your steps, strengthen your arm, and steady your aim; so, as you stand once again in that valley, facing whatever giant looms large today—be it external or internal, visible or invisible—remember David's example, remember the countless believers who have gone before, remember God's faithful promises, arm yourself with truth, prayer, and humility, then take that step forward, sling in hand, stone of faith ready, trusting that the God who stands beside you is mightier than any giant you will ever meet, by doing this, you not only conquer the giant at hand, but ignite a spark of courage that fuels your heart to serve the Lord, even in the face of future battles, forging a legacy of bravery, faith, and love that will stand as a beacon for all who follow in your footsteps.

Day 18 - Humble Hearts, Strong Service: Leading by Example

Imagine a quiet morning as soft light slips through the curtains, and you stand before a mirror, heart pondering how to face the day ahead, knowing deep inside that the Lord calls you not to seek your own glory, but to lower yourself in service to others, to embrace a humility that does not draw attention to itself, but instead shines a gentle light in a world obsessed with pride and self-promotion, and in that reflective moment, you begin to understand that true courage often comes hand in hand with humility, that the bravest acts of service spring not from a desire for recognition, but from a sincere love for God and for the people He has placed in your path; as you let this truth sink in, you realize that the greatest leaders in God's kingdom are not always the ones shouting commands from a throne, but those who kneel to wash another's feet, who put aside their own ambitions to help someone else succeed, who listen more than they speak, and show through their daily actions what it means to follow Christ's example, for leading by example requires more than eloquent words or bold claims—it requires a heart that chooses kindness over personal gain, patience over impatience, gentleness over force, and respect over condescension, and when you think about courage, you might picture someone standing tall, fearless, and unshakable, but in the service of the Lord, courage can also look like a person bowing low, offering their time, their gifts, their understanding, and their resources to lift another soul higher; consider how Jesus, the very Son of God, demonstrated the perfect balance of humility and strength, how He did not force His authority on others, but invited them to follow, taught them through storytelling and patience, touched the sick and the outcast without hesitation, and even knelt to wash His disciples' feet before walking the path of suffering and sacrifice, the cross itself stands as a testament to the power found in humble obedience, for though Jesus could have summoned armies of angels, He chose instead to lay down His life that we might live, and if the One who holds all power in His hands modeled a life of humble service, how much more are we called to do the same, understanding that true leadership, true influence, is earned not by demanding loyalty, but by pouring ourselves out in love, allowing others to see that our motives are pure and our hearts attuned to the needs around us; in a world where people often shout to be heard, where success is measured by followers, fame, wealth, or achievements, choosing to lead by example with a humble heart can feel counterintuitive, yet this is precisely why doing so requires courage, it takes a brave soul to step back when everyone else is rushing forward, to put another's interests before your own when selfish ambition is praised, to refuse to cut corners, lie, or manipulate others in pursuit of personal goals, it takes strength to apologize when you are wrong, to admit you do not have all the answers, to learn from those who are younger or less experienced, and to recognize that you remain a student in God's vast classroom, no matter your age or position; when you let humility guide your leadership, you inspire others in ways that words alone cannot achieve, think about people you admire who have influenced you deeply, chances are, their impact on your life came not just from what they said, but from what they did—how they treated others with respect, kept their promises, showed patience even under stress, extended grace when mistakes were made, and remained true to their values even when it cost them dearly, these quiet examples speak volumes, teaching you that character matters more than superficial impressions, that sincerity outlasts showmanship, and that people are more likely to follow someone who truly cares about their well-being rather than someone who simply wants to wield authority over them, and as you internalize this lesson, you realize that your own life can become a beacon, drawing others to the Lord by the simple authenticity of your conduct, the gentle firmness of your convictions, and the everyday courage of choosing what is right over what is easy; such humility-driven leadership also requires trust in God's strength rather than your own cleverness, for to remain humble, you must let go of the need to control everything, to prove yourself constantly, or to always be the center of attention, you must trust that as you serve faithfully, God will open the doors that need to be opened, provide the resources that need to be provided, and orchestrate events in ways that surpass your understanding, this kind of trust frees you from the pressure to compete, to brag, to flaunt your accomplishments, instead, you can devote your energy to serving wholeheartedly, confident that God sees your efforts and is pleased by your willingness to love His children well, and though you may not receive standing ovations or front-page headlines for your humble acts, you know that God's measure of success is different from the world's, and that He values the quiet heroism of a humble servant far more than empty applause; leading by example with a humble heart also means learning to celebrate others' successes, to step aside and let someone else shine without feeling threatened or jealous, imagine how uplifting it can be to encourage someone who surpasses you in talent or knowledge, to commend a coworker, a friend, or a fellow believer for their good work, and to genuinely rejoice in their achievements, doing so requires courage because it means challenging the insecurity that whispers, "You must always be on top," "You must always outdo others," instead, you stand firm against that insecurity by recognizing that the kingdom of God thrives on cooperation, not competition, on mutual encouragement rather than personal supremacy, by making room for others, you help create an environment where everyone can flourish, where each gift and calling is appreciated, and where God's glory becomes the central focus, instead of anyone's ego; when people see you consistently leading by example in this humble way, they begin to trust you more, they sense that you have no hidden agenda or selfish motives, they feel safe opening up to you, sharing their struggles, and seeking your counsel, and as trust grows, so does your influence, not the kind of influence that demands, threatens, or manipulates, but the influence that draws others closer to truth, goodness, and the heart of God, it's the difference between a harsh spotlight that blinds and a warm glow that illuminates the path ahead, guiding others gently forward, and in doing so, you reflect the grace and patience of the Lord Himself, who does not force us to follow, but invites us, lovingly and persistently, through His Word, His Spirit, and the examples of faithful believers who have gone before; humility also teaches you to listen, leading by example often means placing more emphasis on understanding others' perspectives than on pushing your own ideas, how many conflicts could be avoided if leaders paused to truly listen before speaking, to consider that those under their guidance might have insights worth hearing, by listening first, you show respect for the people around you, valuing their thoughts, feelings, and experiences, and as they feel heard, they become more receptive to any guidance or correction you might offer, your willingness to hear them out, to empathize with their concerns, breaks down walls of suspicion or resentment, paving the way for cooperation, healing, and unity, and in an age where many shout to be heard, your quiet, attentive presence stands out like a calming refuge, inviting weary souls to find rest and understanding in the warmth of your compassion; humility in leadership also involves acknowledging your own limitations, being honest about what you know and what you don't know, about the places you have succeeded and the areas in which you continue to struggle, pretending to have all the answers or to be flawless only sets you up for disappointment and can discourage others, because no one can live up to that façade, but when you admit that you are learning too, that you make mistakes, ask questions, and rely on God's wisdom rather than your own, you give permission for others to do the same, they see that growth is a journey, that faith matures over time, and that stumbling along the way is not the end but part of the process, in this atmosphere, people feel safe to be genuine, to try new things without fear of severe judgment, to trust that if they fall, the community will help them back up, this nurtures an environment where people are inspired to take their own steps of courage in serving the Lord, knowing they are supported and loved; humility in leadership also brings you closer to Christ's heart, because serving the Lord is not about building your personal empire or making a name for yourself, it's about participating in His redemptive work, sharing His love, and glorifying Him above all, the more you focus on lifting Him high rather than yourself, the more your leadership becomes an act of worship, a way to express your gratitude for His mercy, this shift in focus reduces the stress and anxiety that often come with leadership positions, since your aim is not to prove something to the world, but to remain faithful and obedient to the One who called you, and when doubts arise, when you wonder if you have what it takes to lead, remember that God never called perfect people to accomplish His will—He called faithful ones, willing ones, humble ones who understand that their power comes from relying on Him; there is courage in this humility because it means stepping out of the spotlight, resisting the urge to perform for applause, and placing your confidence in God's unseen approval, it takes bravery to believe that the small acts of kindness you do behind the scenes, the prayers you whisper in secret, the steady support you give to a struggling friend, all matter to the Lord, it takes faith to trust that your quiet example can influence others far more deeply than a flashy speech or a showy display of strength, this courage is not loud or showy, but it is steady, faithful, and enduring, like a candle that burns warmly through a cold, dark night, offering light and comfort without demanding praise; as you lead by example with humility, you also discover that your heart grows bigger and your perspective broader, you begin to see others not as threats or obstacles, but as fellow travelers on the road of faith, each with their own gifts and challenges, and you learn to appreciate the richness of community, understanding that no single person can do it all or know it all, but that together, under Christ's guidance, we form a body that can achieve great things for the kingdom, your humility allows you to celebrate diversity, to learn from those different from you, and to recognize that God's tapestry of grace includes many colors, textures, and patterns, each weaving a unique story of redemption; in times of conflict, a humble, example-driven leader can help bring reconciliation, because they are not consumed with proving they are right, but with healing wounds and restoring relationships, courage in such moments means swallowing pride, listening to complaints, taking responsibility when necessary, and working tirelessly for peace, think of how Jesus handled those who doubted Him, questioned His motives, or betrayed Him—He could have called down fire from heaven, but He chose patience, forgiveness, and teaching, His method changed hearts in a way that force never could, and when you follow this model, you harness the power of humility to bring understanding where there is confusion, compassion where there is hardness, and unity where there is division; humility also protects you from the traps of pride that so easily ensnare leaders, pride can whisper that you deserve more recognition, that you are better than others, or that your way is always correct, but a humble heart, grounded in service, reminds you to look to Christ, who though He had every right to command angels, chose to be born in a stable, live as a carpenter's son, and die a criminal's death for our sake, this profound example deflates the balloon of arrogance and points you toward the joy and freedom of humility, where you are not weighed down by the need to impress anyone, and your service flows from a heart tuned to God's purposes rather than your own ego, this kind of leadership endures because it does not depend on external approval, it remains steady through changing seasons and shifting circumstances, anchored in the eternal truth of God's Word and the love that surpasses all understanding; as you grow in this humble, service-driven leadership, you may find people approaching you, asking for guidance, seeking counsel, drawn not by any flashy display but by the authenticity they sense in your life, and when this happens, you have the honor of pointing them back to the true Source of all wisdom and courage—the Lord Himself, your influence becomes a bridge that leads others to Christ, teaching them that true greatness is found in serving, that strength is shown in kindness, that confidence is anchored in trusting God's sovereignty, this realization enriches your own faith, for you witness firsthand the ripple effect of your humble example, how one small act of love can inspire another, how a single moment of grace can plant a seed that blossoms later into a mighty tree of faith, and this inspires you to keep living out these values, to keep choosing the harder path of humility over the easier one of self-exaltation, knowing that the reward is not fleeting applause but the Father's quiet "well done" in your heart; when discouragement comes, and it surely will, remember that the Lord never promised an easy journey, but He did promise to walk with you, to strengthen you, and to guide you, humility does not ensure a life free from challenges, misunderstandings, or setbacks, but it does ensure a heart prepared to deal with them in a way that honors God, and as you continue serving others, leading by example, and keeping your heart humble, you discover that your courage grows brighter, not dimmer, over time, what once seemed intimidating now seems manageable with God's help, what once prompted anger or defensiveness now calls forth patience and a willingness to learn, what once felt like a burden now feels like a calling—one that you can embrace joyfully because you know who empowers you, who shapes you, and who receives glory from your efforts; humble hearts, strong service—these words are like a banner over your life, reminding you that the strength of your service does not come from shouting commands or dazzling displays, but from the quiet firmness of a heart rooted in love, from the daily choices you make to put others first, from the gentle words you offer to someone in need, from the steady hand you extend to help someone who has stumbled, from the integrity you maintain even when no one is watching, and as you build these habits, your influence spreads, impacting your family, your friends, your church, your community, and beyond, each life you touch becomes a testimony that love is stronger than arrogance, that truth is mightier than deception, that kindness can break down barriers that force never could; over time, you see that leading by example in humility reflects the very heart of the Gospel, which tells the story of a God who humbled Himself to become human, who walked among us, teaching, healing, and showing mercy, and who, in the ultimate act of humility, allowed Himself to be nailed to a cross, bearing our sins to restore our relationship with Him, this is the pattern we follow: to love like Jesus loved, to serve like He served, to lay down our lives for others in big and small ways, confident that such a life is not wasted but invested in eternity, it takes courage to live this way in a world that prizes self over sacrifice, it takes courage to believe that by going lower, we actually rise higher in God's eyes, it takes courage to trust that influencing people through genuine care and quiet consistency is more powerful than forcing your will upon them; in the end, humble hearts, strong service, and leading by example are about reflecting Christ's character to a watching world, showing that strength is not always loud, that leadership is not always about being first, that courage can wear a gentle smile and work tirelessly behind the scenes, if you can embrace this vision, if you can step forward with a heart willing to serve without seeking spotlight, you will find yourself igniting courage in others, fueling their hearts to serve the Lord as well, creating a ripple effect that can stretch far beyond what you imagine, your life becomes a gift placed in God's hands, ready for Him to use in ways that bring hope, healing, and glory to His name, and as you do, you discover a deeper purpose, a richer joy, a steadier courage that endures through trials and triumphs alike, rooted in humility and blossoming into service that honors the Lord, leads others closer to Him, and reshapes the world with gentle, relentless love.

Day 19 - Invisible Battles: Trusting God in the Unseen

Imagine waking before dawn when the world is still quiet, a faint gray light slipping into your room, and as you sit there, your heart feels heavy with worries that have no clear shape, no visible enemy you can name, only a sense that something unseen presses down on your spirit, stirring fears you cannot fully understand, and doubts that nip at the edges of your faith; it's in these silent, fragile moments, when the rest of the world still sleeps, that you realize life is filled with invisible battles, struggles that do not announce themselves with banners or battle cries, but creep quietly into your mind through anxious thoughts, whispered temptations, subtle lies that tug at your peace, and as you close your eyes and try to steady your breathing, you sense that these hidden conflicts—spiritual in nature, emotional in force—are real and significant, shaping the landscape of your heart and influencing how you move through this day and the days that follow, and though no human eye can see this warfare, its impact is felt in the choices you make, the attitudes you hold, the trust you place in the Lord who promises never to leave you; the unseen battles are not like the stories of knights and dragons you once read, where danger was obvious and the hero's path clear, these battles are fought in the quiet corners of your soul, where fear tries to convince you that you are alone, that no one understands, that God might not be as faithful as you believed, or where envy tries to poison your joy by making you focus on what others have and you do not, or where pride whispers that you must prove your worth at all costs, even if it means turning away from what is right, or where guilt and shame accuse you day and night, trying to make you think your past disqualifies you from grace, or where discouragement attempts to dim the light of hope, leaving you feeling trapped in a darkness that no one else can see, it is here, in these invisible realms, that your faith is tested more deeply than any outward trial could accomplish, because when the enemy is not flesh and blood, but rather thoughts, impulses, and spiritual forces you cannot touch, you must learn a different kind of trust—trust in a God who sees what you cannot, who understands the depth and nature of the struggle better than you ever will, and who stands ready to strengthen you if you will lean on Him; remember that Scripture speaks of these invisible battles, warning that we do not wrestle against human foes, but against spiritual powers, and urging us to put on the armor of God: truth like a belt to steady you, righteousness like a breastplate to protect your heart, faith like a shield to extinguish the fiery darts of lies, salvation like a helmet to guard your mind, and the Word of God like a sword to counter the whispers of deceit, this armor is not visible to human eyes, but it is very real in the spiritual sense, and putting it on involves choosing daily to believe God's promises, to hold onto His truth even when your feelings suggest otherwise, to remember His love when shame tries to overwhelm you, and to pray—opening your heart to His presence—so He can guide you through the confusion that often accompanies unseen conflict; imagine that you are standing in a field under a heavy sky, clouds shifting overhead, shadows moving in the corners of your vision, you know something lurks beyond what you can see clearly, and every step forward feels like walking into uncertain territory, yet you also know you are not walking alone, the Lord goes before you, even if you cannot see Him, His Spirit lives within you, offering peace, wisdom, and discernment, and though the enemy tries to remain hidden, God's Word shines a light, revealing the nature of these invisible foes—fear, temptation, lies, despair—and providing a map for navigating the terrain: "Fear not," He whispers through His Word, reminding you that He has overcome the world, "Resist the devil, and he will flee from you," says another verse, assuring you that these invisible enemies are not invincible if you stand firm in Christ's authority, "My grace is sufficient for you," He comforts, telling you that no matter how strong the attack feels, His power is made perfect in your weakness; in these unseen struggles, trust becomes both your compass and your anchor, trust that God is who He says He is—a loving, powerful Father who has already triumphed over darkness through the death and resurrection of His Son, trust that Jesus understands your battles intimately, for He, too, was tempted in the wilderness by the subtle voice of the enemy, and He, too, stood firm by clinging to the truth of Scripture, trust that the Holy Spirit within you can guide you into all truth, helping you recognize when a thought or desire does not align with God's goodness, and giving you the strength to reject it, trust that prayer is not a futile exercise but a lifeline connecting you to divine help, trust that even when your emotions run wild and doubts swirl like dust in a storm, you can still choose to believe God's promises, knowing your feelings do not change His nature; consider how often in life you have fought battles on visible fronts—overcoming a financial hurdle, dealing with a health issue, repairing a fractured relationship—yet even in those cases, beneath the surface lay invisible elements: fear that you could not handle it, anger boiling quietly inside, insecurity whispering that you were not enough, or spiritual oppression trying to steer you away from faith, by recognizing these invisible layers, you understand that victory is not just about fixing outward circumstances, it's also about allowing God to transform your heart, to strengthen your faith, so that no matter what outward challenges arise, your inner foundation remains solid, and as you learn to trust God in these unseen arenas, you become more resilient, less easily swayed by the winds of adversity, more anchored in the eternal truths that no storm can erase; it's humbling to admit that you cannot fight these battles alone, pride might urge you to pretend you have everything under control, that you don't need help, that you can outsmart temptation, outwill fear, or outmaneuver confusion, but humility acknowledges that you are finite, limited in understanding, easily deceived by appearances, and without God's guidance, lost in a maze of conflicting voices, when you humble yourself before Him, you open the door for His grace to pour in, grace that empowers you to see through the enemy's lies, grace that reminds you of who you are in Christ, chosen, redeemed, and called for a purpose, and grace that provides a way out when you feel trapped, God's strength is perfected in your weakness, meaning that the very moment you admit you need Him, He stands ready to supply what you lack; these invisible battles can be exhausting, because they often continue when no one else is watching, while you lie awake at night wrestling with guilt, or stand in a crowded room feeling strangely alone, or go about your daily tasks with a silent heaviness pressing on your soul, but remember that you're never truly alone, the Lord who never sleeps is with you, His Spirit intercedes even when your own prayers falter, the community of believers, though imperfect, can offer encouragement, a listening ear, or a comforting word from Scripture, and when you connect with others who have faced their own invisible battles, you discover you are not odd or weak for struggling this way—this is part of the human journey, part of living in a world where brokenness and darkness still exist, but also part of the redemptive story God is writing, one where He calls His children to stand firm, to persevere, to reflect His light in the very places that feel most shadowed; learning to trust God in the unseen also teaches you patience, because unlike a visible problem you can tackle with a plan or tool, invisible battles often require waiting on the Lord, letting Him work beneath the surface, sometimes the issues that trouble you stem from deep wounds that need time to heal, roots of lies embedded in your mind that need careful uprooting, or habits that must be unlearned through gradual surrender, patience means not giving up when progress seems slow, not losing hope when you have to fight the same temptation repeatedly before you see lasting victory, it means holding onto the promise that God is at work, that He who began a good work in you will carry it on to completion, even if you cannot see the changes day by day, He is faithful, and in due time, you will look back and realize how far you've come, how the chains that once held you tight have loosened, how the darkness that once terrified you has faded before His light; another aspect of trusting God in these unseen battles is learning to identify the enemy's tactics, the enemy rarely confronts you with an obvious threat, often it comes in subtle questions: "Did God really say...?" "Are you sure you're forgiven?" "Don't you deserve more than this?" recognizing these voices requires discernment, which grows as you immerse yourself in Scripture, letting its truth shape your understanding, when a thought appears that contradicts God's Word, you can hold it up like a counterfeit bill next to a genuine one, comparing its message to the truth you know, if it fails the test, you reject it, send it away, refuse to let it nest in your heart, and just as David confronted Goliath by referencing God's sovereignty rather than trusting in human armor, you confront the unseen lies by declaring God's promises, by reminding yourself that His Word stands firm, His love unshaken, His forgiveness complete, and His plan for you good, even if you cannot see the road ahead; at times, these invisible battles might intensify, coming at you from multiple angles: spiritual dryness, emotional heaviness, moral temptations, intellectual doubts, and relational tensions all swirling at once, in these seasons, stand even closer to God, draw near through prayer, honest prayer where you share your fears, disappointments, and confusion, and also times of silence, listening for His voice, or reading Psalms that express the raw cries of the human heart, through these practices, you learn that trust in the unseen is not a one-time decision, but a posture you maintain, a daily choice to lean into God's presence rather than lean away, to believe that He is good when circumstances are not, to trust His invisible hand guiding you when all you see is uncertainty; as you grow in trusting God amidst these invisible struggles, you'll notice changes in how you approach visible challenges too, the resilience, peace, and hope you gain by standing firm in spiritual battles equip you to face life's visible problems with greater calm and wisdom, you understand that not everything is as it appears on the surface, that behind every conflict might be a deeper spiritual reality, that every setback could hide a lesson God wants to teach you, or an opportunity to draw closer to Him, and by applying the same trust you learned in the invisible realms, you become a more stable, compassionate, and clear-sighted person in all areas of life, no longer easily rattled by shifting circumstances or rattled by others' opinions, because your anchor lies in something deeper and eternal; another blessing of these unseen battles is that they deepen your empathy for others who struggle, when you know what it's like to wrestle with silent fears, to fight temptations no one else sees, to carry doubts you feel ashamed to admit, you become more gracious and gentle with those around you, you begin to see that everyone carries invisible burdens, and this recognition urges you to offer kindness, a listening ear, or a simple gesture of support, instead of judging others for their behavior, you wonder about the unseen battles they might be fighting, and you pray for them, ask God to help them, and maybe share a word of comfort or understanding, in this way, your own invisible struggles become a source of compassion, widening your heart and making you a vessel of God's love; trusting God in the unseen also cultivates humility, because you realize how limited your perspective is, how little you actually know, you become aware that you need God's wisdom and guidance just to navigate your own thoughts and feelings, let alone the complexities of relationships, decisions, and moral dilemmas, humility steers you away from the arrogance of thinking you have all the answers, and toward a quiet reliance on God's direction, and this humble posture positions you to receive His grace more fully, for Scripture says God opposes the proud but gives grace to the humble, as you bend low, acknowledging your need, you find yourself lifted by His gentle hand, comforted by His Spirit, and enlightened by the revelation that He remains active, working all things for good, even when you do not see how; over time, as you continue trusting God in these invisible battles, you will gather testimonies of His faithfulness, moments when a night of anxiety ended in morning peace, when a season of temptation gave way to victory, when a persistent doubt was resolved by a Scripture verse arriving at just the right moment, or when the encouragement of a friend reminded you that God had not forgotten you, these memories become like stones stacked together in your mind, forming a monument to His reliability, so that when a new unseen struggle arises, you can look back and say, "He helped me before, He will help me again," and with each testimony, your faith matures, your courage grows, and your trust deepens, igniting a flame that not only warms your own heart, but can light the way for others walking a similar path; remember, as well, that no invisible battle lasts forever, God is always at work, and there are seasons of rest and refreshment too, times when He grants you a sweet sense of His presence, a clarity of mind, a breakthrough that lets you breathe more freely, these seasons are gifts to restore your soul, to remind you that He is indeed a God of hope and consolation, and while you may face more unseen struggles in the future, the comfort and strength gained in these restful periods prepare you for the next challenge, just as a runner trains steadily between competitions, building endurance for the race ahead, you too cultivate spiritual endurance in times of peace, so when invisible battles arise again, you are not caught off guard, but ready to face them with renewed confidence; leaning on God in the unseen also aligns your heart with the eternal perspective He wants you to hold, it teaches you that there is more to life than what meets the eye, that the spiritual dimension is real and significant, and that your ultimate destiny goes beyond the troubles of this present world, as you trust God in battles no one else can see, you become increasingly aware that your life is hidden with Christ, that your identity is secure in Him, and that no power of darkness can snatch you from His hand, this perspective helps you prioritize what truly matters—growing in love, faith, hope, and righteousness—over the fleeting pursuits of power, pleasure, or fame, and with each decision to stand firm in these invisible skirmishes, you store up treasures in heaven that moth and rust cannot destroy, proving that you serve a higher King and strive for a greater kingdom; as you embrace this reality, you also become more patient with God's timing, understanding that some battles are resolved not with a dramatic flourish, but gradually, step by step, decision by decision, moment by moment, trusting God means walking in faithfulness even when you can't sense immediate progress, continuing to pray even when answers seem delayed, continuing to choose righteousness even when temptation whispers "just this once," continuing to hope when despair wants to set in, and in this persistence, you discover that perseverance itself is a precious virtue, one that makes your character more robust, your faith more authentic, and your service to the Lord more effective, for people around you will see that your trust in God is not just a fair-weather faith, but a deep-rooted conviction that stands firm come what may; invisible battles also highlight the value of community, though no one can fully know the invisible struggles you face, having brothers and sisters in Christ who care, pray, and walk alongside you can provide remarkable support, they may not solve your internal conflicts, but their presence, love, and shared devotion to God can lessen the loneliness of the fight, hearing their stories of God's faithfulness, learning how they overcame their own unseen challenges, can strengthen your resolve, and praying together can open channels of grace that bring new clarity, new comfort, and a renewed sense that you are part of a people who stand under God's banner, not isolated soldiers but a united army, each carrying their own burdens but committed to bearing one another's loads, as Scripture encourages; by trusting God through these invisible battles, you gradually learn that what seemed at first like a disadvantage—fighting enemies you cannot see, grappling with doubts you cannot name, wrestling with fears that have no physical form—is in fact an opportunity for greater intimacy with the Lord, He invites you to rely on Him like never before, to discover that He truly is enough, and to taste and see that He is good, even in darkness, even in uncertainty, even when you feel your way forward by faith rather than sight, and as you lean into Him, He teaches you to discern His voice amidst the cacophony of inner and outer noise, to distinguish His gentle nudge from the harsh commands of fear or pride, to feel His presence like a warm embrace that holds you steady when all else trembles; ultimately, trusting God in the unseen transforms your relationship with Him, moving it from a theory to a lived reality, you no longer say you trust Him simply because it's the right thing to say, but because you have experienced His sustaining grace in the hidden places of your heart, you have seen Him guide you through doubts that no one else knew about, calm storms that no one else saw brewing, and heal wounds that no one else recognized as wounds, and this personal knowledge births a courage that is not flashy or arrogant, but quiet, steady, and resilient, a courage that fuels your heart to serve the Lord even more faithfully, knowing that He will always meet you in the dark valleys as well as on the bright mountaintops, that He will never abandon you in the invisible battles that shape your soul; so when you rise tomorrow and face another dawn, another day filled with challenges both visible and hidden, remember these truths, hold fast to the knowledge that your Lord is near, that He is not baffled by what confuses you, not discouraged by what discourages you, not afraid of what frightens you, but walks beside you as a faithful companion and mighty protector, trust Him enough to bring your unseen struggles into His light, to ask Him for help, to rely on His wisdom and strength, and to believe that as you do, He will equip you with everything you need, strengthening your faith, refining your character, and enabling you to stand firm, serving Him with a courage ignited in the secret places of your heart, a courage that grows steadily stronger with each invisible battle you overcome through His power and love.

Day 20 - Through the Fire: Growing in Perseverance

Imagine yourself standing at the edge of a scorching desert at midday, the heat shimmering in waves before your eyes, and though your throat is dry and your legs feel heavy, something inside you urges you onward, deeper into this unforgiving landscape, for you have set your heart on following where the Lord leads, and even if the path runs straight through the fire of hardship, testing every fiber of your being, you choose to press forward, determined to grow in perseverance, igniting a courage that does not vanish when life grows hard, but instead finds its truest form amidst the struggle; at first, the challenges you face might seem like cruel obstacles thrown in your way, unfair twists of fate that drain your strength and shake your confidence, and you might wonder why God does not simply clear the path, allowing you to serve Him without such strain, but as you continue placing one foot in front of the other, stumbling at times, pushing through thorns and shifting sands, you begin to realize that God is using these trials to shape you, forging perseverance within your soul, much like a blacksmith wields hammer and flame to transform raw iron into a solid, unbreakable blade, and though it is not pleasant to feel the heat, to experience weariness that makes your muscles tremble, to feel doubts nip at the edges of your faith, you know deep down that through this process, you are becoming stronger, more resilient, more committed to the cause that inspires you—to serve the Lord with all your heart, regardless of what stands against you; think back to when your journey first began, when you embraced a calling or a dream God placed in your heart, how excited and determined you were, how sure that the road would be fairly smooth, how enthusiastic you felt about blessing others, speaking truth, shining light in darkness, perhaps you imagined that stepping onto this path of obedience and service would bring immediate joy and fruit, and in some ways it did, for a while, but over time, reality set in: not everyone welcomed your help, not every effort bore visible fruit, not every prayer received a quick answer, and you discovered that the noble task of serving the Lord is not always met with applause, at times, it brings misunderstandings, disappointments, even spiritual resistance that leaves you feeling drained, and in these moments, you could have turned back, chosen an easier route, shelved your dreams and decided that maybe this calling wasn't for you after all, yet something sparked inside you—an ember of courage and persistence that refused to be snuffed out by adversity, and you found yourself pressing on, not because it was easy, but because you believed in what God had placed in your heart, and because deep within, you sensed that perseverance was part of the growth He intended for you; imagine walking through this desert, the sweat trickling down your neck, dust coating your tongue, and every few steps, doubts flare like hot coals under your feet, telling you to quit, to rest in the shade of mediocrity, to stop dreaming so big, after all, who do you think you are to attempt something so difficult? Why keep striving when results remain unseen, when your efforts seem to vanish into thin air with no one noticing, no one praising, but the quiet voice of the Holy Spirit stirs within your soul, reminding you of the One who endured all things for the sake of love, reminding you that the path to glory often runs through valleys of shadow, reminding you that nothing truly valuable is forged without pressure and heat, and as you cling to this truth, your perseverance takes root and begins to grow stronger, like a plant's roots digging deeper into the soil searching for water; perseverance is not a glamorous virtue, it does not dazzle like talent or charm like charisma, it is often unseen by others and uncelebrated, a quiet decision you make in your heart day after day, and yet it is perseverance that makes greatness possible, that transforms fleeting passion into lasting impact, that ensures your service to God does not wilt at the first sign of hardship, but matures into a steady, life-giving force, when you persevere, you declare to God, to yourself, and even to the unseen spiritual realm, that your faith is not a passing fancy, but a firm conviction, that you trust God's goodness and wisdom enough to keep going, even when logic screams that you have nothing left to give, and in doing so, you align yourself with countless saints who walked this path before you, men and women who faced persecution, isolation, confusion, and pain, yet pressed on, and by their example, we learn that perseverance in trial is not the mark of a fool, but of a faithful heart that treasures God's approval above ease and comfort; consider that perseverance is not merely enduring, but growing stronger as you endure, just as muscles develop when pushed to their limits, your spiritual muscles, your character, your capacity to love, forgive, and hope, all expand as you persist through difficulties, the fire that tests you also refines you, burning away impurities like selfishness and shallow motives, leaving behind a purer desire to serve God for His sake, not for the applause of others, as you persevere, you become more patient, discovering that God's timeline does not always match your own, but that His timing is perfect, you become more compassionate, realizing how hard it can be for others to keep going too, and thus more sensitive to the struggles hidden behind their smiles, you grow in wisdom, learning to recognize which battles are worth fighting, which hills are worth climbing, and what truly matters in the long run; through perseverance, you become someone who can stand firm even when the winds of opposition blow fiercely, your roots sunk deep into the soil of God's promises, His Word acting as nourishment that sustains you, His presence overshadowing you like a cloud by day and a pillar of fire by night, guiding you through the wilderness, and remember that He does not expect you to be superhuman, to never feel weak or discouraged, He knows our frame, He remembers we are dust, and still He invites us to rely on Him, for in our weakness, His strength shines brightest, and perseverance is born not from human grit alone, but from the fusion of our fragile willingness with His unending might, as you learn to lean on Him, to pour out your doubts and fears in honest prayer, to listen for His comforting whisper, you find a resilience that surpasses your natural ability, a holy endurance that reflects the heart of Christ, who for the joy set before Him endured the cross, scorning its shame, and now invites you to share in His victory; sometimes perseverance feels like walking forward in a dense fog, unable to see more than a few steps ahead, yet still placing one foot in front of the other, trusting that God sees the big picture, that He knows where you are going, and that He will not let you walk off a cliff unnoticed, in these foggy seasons, you learn to cherish the daily bread of His grace, rather than demanding a full feast of explanations, you learn to say, "Lord, I don't understand, but I trust you," and in that trust, find courage to keep moving, and when, at last, the fog lifts and you look back, you marvel at how He guided you safely, how your faith grew deeper because you had to rely on Him rather than your own sight; perseverance also shapes your attitude towards setbacks and failures, rather than seeing them as final verdicts on your worth or God's favor, you start to view them as stepping stones, as opportunities to learn and refine your approach, just as a craftsman might fail many times before creating a masterpiece, you understand that your service to the Lord may involve missteps, disappointments, and projects that do not go as planned, but each time you pick yourself up and continue, you strengthen the roots of perseverance, proving that your commitment is not conditional on easy success, and this willingness to keep trying, to remain faithful even when results are slow in coming, is itself a testimony that can inspire others, showing them that perseverance is not just a personal virtue, but a gift you give to those who look up to you, needing to see that it is indeed possible to keep going when life is hard; think of a tree planted by a stream, its leaves remain green even in drought because its roots reach deep to find water below the surface, so too does perseverance allow your spirit to draw on the living water of God's presence, even when external circumstances wither and fade, even when people disappoint you, or resources seem scarce, or encouragement is nowhere to be found, your roots of faith, strengthened by perseverance, seek out God's sustaining grace in hidden places, and because of this, you can remain steady, not tossed about by every gust of trouble, and it is in this steadiness that you reflect the character of Christ to a world desperate for hope, people who see you standing strong amid hardship might wonder how you do it, and that gives you a chance to point them to the Lord who upholds you; perseverance also teaches you to take the long view, instead of demanding immediate rewards or tangible outcomes, you learn to appreciate the slow, patient work of God's Spirit shaping your heart and influencing those around you in ways unseen, just as seeds take time to sprout and bear fruit, your efforts to serve the Lord may not yield visible harvest overnight, but by continuing faithfully, you trust that in due season, you will reap if you do not give up, and when that season arrives, whether tomorrow or years from now, the joy you experience will be richer for having been tested and proven true, you will look back and see God's fingerprints all over your journey, realizing that He never wasted a tear, a struggle, or a moment of doubt you surrendered to Him; another blessing of perseverance is the empathy it cultivates in your heart, as you suffer and push through your own struggles, you become more sensitive to others who are hurting, you understand the emotional weight of discouragement, the tight grip of fear, and the hollow ache of feeling alone, and because you know these feelings firsthand, you can come alongside others with genuine understanding and encouragement, pointing them to the strength that only God can give, offering to pray with them, listen to their stories, and remind them that they are not alone, this empathy not only enriches your ministry, making you more effective in serving people who carry invisible burdens, but it also enhances your relationship with God, for you share in the compassion that He has for His children, the compassion that led Him to rescue us at great cost; perseverance, then, becomes a bridge connecting you more deeply to God's heart and to the hearts of others, it teaches you that serving the Lord is not a sprint, but a marathon, and in marathons, the real test comes when your legs burn and your lungs ache, when the initial excitement has faded and only determination remains, this is where true character emerges, where you decide that finishing is worth the discomfort, that the goal matters enough to keep going, in spiritual terms, perseverance says: "I believe in God's promises more than my temporary pain, I trust His love more than my own doubts, I value His glory above my comfort, and I will not turn back, no matter how long or hard this race feels," with each step you take, perseverance grows, weaving itself into the fabric of your identity, so that quitting no longer seems like an option; perseverance also reveals the depth of your love for God, as Jesus said, "If you love me, you will keep my commandments," and keeping His commandments often means continuing to do good, to love your neighbor, to pray, to serve, even when it's difficult or you feel unappreciated, perseverance strips away superficial reasons for obedience—such as seeking praise or reward—and leaves you with the pure motive of honoring God because He is worthy, this purity of purpose strengthens your heart, making your devotion less fragile, less dependent on outcomes, and more rooted in who God is rather than what you get out of it, in this sense, perseverance refines not only your character, but the quality of your worship and service, making it a precious offering to the Lord; through perseverance, you learn to see trials as part of God's training program, much like an athlete grows stronger by pushing muscles to work harder, your soul grows sturdier by facing and overcoming resistance, over time, challenges that once overwhelmed you now seem manageable, temptations that used to trip you up lose their grip, fears that paralyzed you fall silent in the presence of renewed confidence in God's faithfulness, this growth is not always linear or fast, but steady and sure, and as you recognize your own progress, you can thank God for guiding you through the fire, turning what might have harmed you into a means of strengthening you, forging a resilience that will serve you well throughout your life; imagine reaching a point where, even when life throws its worst at you—unexpected loss, crushing disappointment, painful betrayal—you can still say, "Though I walk through the valley of the shadow of death, I will fear no evil, for you are with me," not as a hollow slogan, but as a lived reality, perseverance makes that possible, it gives you the inner ballast to remain upright in storms that would have capsized you before, and in doing so, you become a lighthouse for others, a person who can calmly testify, "I know what it's like to hurt and to struggle, but God never left me, and I stand here now, stronger in faith, because He carried me through," such testimonies carry immense power, encouraging others to keep going in their own battles; perseverance also frees you from the tyranny of immediate gratification, teaching you to appreciate the slow, steady growth that characterizes authentic spiritual maturity, just as a mighty oak tree takes years to grow from an acorn, your soul's full potential unfolds over time, nurtured by faith, watered by prayers, and pruned by trials, and though it might be frustrating to wait, perseverance transforms that waiting from a passive, resentful state into an active trust that God's timing is perfect, when you finally see the fruit of your labor, the resolution of a long-prayed-for breakthrough, or the arrival of a long-awaited blessing, the joy you experience will be sweeter because you persevered, tasted hardship, and kept the faith despite not knowing when relief would come, in this waiting, you learn patience, another virtue closely linked with perseverance, patience that allows you to handle delays, uncertainties, and complexities with grace and calmness; as you walk through the fire and grow in perseverance, you also learn to let go of fears that once held you captive, fear of failure diminishes when you realize that even when you fall, God is there to help you stand again, fear of rejection loses power when you understand that God's acceptance is unshakable, fear of suffering becomes less paralyzing when you trust that He can use even pain for good, by persevering through trials, you dismantle the strongholds of fear piece by piece, discovering that no fire is too hot for God to keep you safe within it, this fearless spirit does not imply recklessness or insensitivity, but a profound assurance that God's hand remains on you, guiding your steps, and that nothing can separate you from His love, not even the toughest furnace of adversity; perseverance also enhances your ability to recognize false shortcuts or easy escape routes that lead away from God's will, when challenges arise, the enemy might tempt you to compromise your values, to take a dishonest path to avoid suffering, to numb your pain with destructive habits, or to give up completely, but perseverance, honed by previous trials, sounds the alarm when such temptations arise, it reminds you that true strength is not found in running from hardship, but in facing it with integrity, that a slight relief purchased at the cost of disobeying God is never worth it, and as you resist these shortcuts and stand firm, you become more authentic, consistent, and whole, your character forged in the fire like precious metal, resistant to corrosion or cheap tricks; eventually, your perseverance helps you understand that the race you run is not about performing flawlessly, but about finishing faithfully, God does not measure you by how often you fall, but by whether you keep rising, He does not require you to pretend you are never tired, but invites you to lean on Him when fatigue sets in, He does not command you to be immune to pain, but to trust Him enough to walk through it without losing hope, knowing that at the end of your journey, when you stand before Him face to face, the scars and calluses earned through perseverance will not be signs of defeat, but of endurance, proof that you loved Him enough to keep serving, keep believing, keep striving for holiness, even when the fire raged high; in all of this, the courage ignited by perseverance fuels your heart to serve the Lord more effectively, with a depth and sincerity that superficial faith cannot achieve, you understand now that courage is not about never trembling, but about moving forward despite the trembling, perseverance taught you that you can do hard things through Christ who strengthens you, that your worst fears can be faced head-on, that your limitations do not define you if you trust in God's unlimited power, and so, when He calls you to tasks that seem daunting, to love people who are hard to love, to speak truth in uncomfortable settings, or to stand up for what's right when it costs you dearly, you no longer shrink back, instead, you press ahead, fueled by a courage refined in the fires of trial, certain that the same God who guided you through deserts before will do so again, and that your perseverance has equipped you to handle whatever new challenges lie ahead; when others see this courage in action, they witness not your personal strength or cleverness, but the fruit of a life surrendered to God, they see a person who, though flawed and imperfect, has learned that giving up is not an option, that through persistent faith, even the hardest battles can be won, they may ask you how you do it, and you can share the truth: that you serve a faithful Lord who never abandons His children, who meets them in the fire and walks beside them until they emerge stronger and more radiant, and in sharing this truth, you become a beacon of hope, inspiring others to trust God through their own trials, to believe that perseverance is possible, that courage can bloom even in scorched earth, and that the Lord's grace is always sufficient; ultimately, perseverance is part of God's plan to draw you closer to Him, shaping you into the person He created you to be, no hardship is wasted in His economy, no tear, no disappointment, no lonely struggle fails to produce growth if you yield it to Him, and by choosing perseverance, you participate in the grand story He is writing, one where even broken dreams, painful losses, and fearful nights find their place in a tapestry of redemption, as the years pass and you look back on your journey, you will see how each trial taught you something priceless, how each challenge contributed to your readiness to serve with a humble and resilient heart, how the fire you walked through was never meant to destroy you, but to refine and strengthen your spirit; so stand firm, hold fast, and keep moving forward through the fire, trusting that God's hand remains on you, that He will not allow you to be tested beyond what you can bear, and that He is always ready to supply the grace and courage you need at just the right moment, embrace the lessons of perseverance, knowing that they will bear fruit in time, and remember that every step you take, however small, adds to a cumulative strength that will carry you through storms you have yet to face, know that your perseverance is a precious offering to the Lord, a sign that you believe His promises more than your pain, and as you continue on this path, serving Him with a heart tempered by trials, ignited by courage, and fueled by unwavering faith, you become a living testimony to the power of God to transform weakness into strength, ashes into beauty, and fleeting struggles into eternal purpose.

Day 21 - Laying Down Self: Sacrificial Service in God's Name

Imagine, if you will, standing at the edge of a quiet meadow as the early morning sun gently warms your face, and in that stillness you sense a quiet call within your heart, an invitation not to gather honor for yourself, not to chase after personal gain, but to lay down your own desires and needs for the sake of something greater than you have ever known, and though the world around you often shouts that you must fight for your rights, cling to your comforts, and put your interests first, this call beckons you into a different way of living, one that turns upside down the familiar patterns of selfish ambition, urging you to consider what it means to serve God by giving yourself away for others, to find courage not in trumpeting your strengths but in offering your weaknesses and resources to God's hands so that His glory may shine through your humble obedience, and as you think about what it means to lay down self, you realize that this kind of sacrificial service is not a path lined with cheering crowds or easy applause, but one where you must trust that God sees what others do not, that He values acts of kindness done quietly, that He treasures the moments you choose love over comfort, compassion over pride, faithfulness over personal reward, and though it may feel scary to step out and give of yourself without knowing if anyone will appreciate it, you remember that Jesus Himself showed this very example when He knelt before His disciples and washed their feet, doing the work of a servant, lowering Himself to serve those who followed Him, and if the Lord of all creation chose the role of a servant, if He gave His very life to save us, then how can we not follow in His footsteps, trusting that God's strength can fill our emptiness, that His grace can make our offerings worthy, and that His love can sustain us when we pour ourselves out for others, and so you stand there, at the edge of that meadow, realizing that laying down self is an act of courage because it goes against the grain of self-preservation and self-promotion, it requires a faith that dares to believe God's promises over the world's claims, that what is lost for His sake will ultimately be gained, that He who knows every sparrow that falls also knows every tear you shed, every effort you invest, every sacrifice you make in His name, and He does not forget, indeed, this sacrificial service in God's name is like a seed planted in the earth, hidden from sight, its value not always apparent at the start, but given time, watered by grace, warmed by faith, it will sprout and grow into something far more beautiful and fruitful than you ever imagined, and if you wonder how to begin, think of the small steps, the everyday moments when you can set aside your own comfort to listen to a friend who is hurting, to share what you have with someone in need, to speak an encouraging word when you feel tired and uninspired, or to pray for someone else's blessing rather than focusing only on your own requests, and as you practice these small acts of surrender, you strengthen the muscle of sacrificial love, learning that your life is not diminished when you give yourself away, but rather expanded, enriched, and made more meaningful as you join in God's redemptive work, for truly, laying down self is not about denying your worth or suppressing your identity, but about aligning your heart with the heart of God, who is love itself, who teaches that it is in giving that we receive, in losing ourselves that we find who we were truly meant to be, in loosening our grip on our own agendas that we discover the joy of serving a higher purpose, and yes, it takes courage to let go of what you think you deserve, what you have earned, what you fear losing, because the world trains you to hoard, to protect, to grasp at every advantage, yet the path of sacrificial service asks you to release these tight fists and hold your hands open, allowing God to place in them whatever He wills, and take from them whatever He deems best, and though it might seem risky, this openness is where freedom is found, where you no longer have to carry the burden of proving your importance, of building a fortress of pride to guard against rejection, instead, you entrust yourself to a God who knows your name, your story, your struggles, and your strengths, and He leads you toward encounters with people who need what you have to give, whether it's a kind smile, a wise word, a helping hand, or simply your presence, and as you offer these gifts, not seeking applause, not expecting a return on investment, but simply because you love the Lord who first loved you, you find a peace that comes from knowing you are part of something larger, part of God's cosmic tapestry of grace woven through countless acts of humble service, and as you persist in this way of living, your heart shifts, you start to measure success not by how many praise you, but by how faithfully you follow Christ's example, and though your ego might sometimes protest, longing for recognition, you learn to quiet that voice by reminding yourself that real reward lies in pleasing God, in feeling His delight as He watches you serve quietly, courageously, and sacrificially, think of how Jesus offered Himself fully, laying down not only His own comforts and time, but His very life for people who misunderstood Him, who mocked Him, who in many cases did not even welcome His sacrifice, and yet He did it out of love, knowing that through His death and resurrection we would be redeemed, and this ultimate act of surrender stands as the highest model of what it means to give up self for the sake of God's kingdom, if He can do that for us, can we not endure discomfort for our neighbor, can we not spend time and energy helping someone who cannot repay us, can we not choose to let go of personal ambition to lift someone else into the spotlight, can we not forgive even when it costs our pride, can we not pour ourselves out in the name of the One who poured Himself out for us, this is sacrificial service in God's name, this is the heart of laying down self: to love so deeply that no act of kindness feels too small, no inconvenience too great, no sacrifice too costly when weighed against the privilege of bearing Christ's image and extending His mercy into a world hungry for genuine care, and as you walk this path, you realize that the courage you need does not come from a fierce inner strength alone, it is fueled by the Spirit who lives in you, guiding you to see beyond your immediate comfort and recognize the eternal significance of even the simplest loving gesture, He whispers encouragement when you feel weary, reminds you of God's faithfulness when you question whether your efforts matter, and strengthens your resolve when doubts creep in, whispering that maybe it would be easier to just live for yourself, but you know better now, you have tasted the sweetness of following God's call, you have felt the warmth of His presence as you serve others selflessly, and you would not trade that peace for the hollow applause of self-centered pursuits, through the fire of surrender, through the gentle breaking of your pride, you discover a freedom unlike any other—the freedom to love abundantly, to give generously, to trust fully, and to walk forward without the heavy chains of ego dragging you down, and this freedom makes courage sparkle in your soul, enabling you to face challenges that once terrified you, to accept tasks that seem beyond your comfort zone, because you understand that God's grace is sufficient, that when you reach the end of your natural ability,

His power takes over, allowing you to accomplish more than you imagined possible, and all for His glory, not your own, and if ever you stumble, if you find yourself hesitating, clinging to selfish desires or resenting the cost of service, you can remember that this journey is not about achieving perfection overnight, it is about day-by-day surrender, about leaning into the relationship you have with God, who gently corrects and guides you, who helps you loosen your hold on what you idolize, who assures you that your worth does not hinge on the world's measure of greatness, but on His unconditional love, this knowledge allows you to try again after every misstep, to refocus your heart after every slip into self-centeredness, to renew your commitment to serve selflessly, and as time goes on, you notice changes within yourself: your reactions become kinder, your words more encouraging, your willingness to help steadier, and these transformations are not the result of gritting your teeth and forcing yourself, but of the Holy Spirit slowly reshaping you from the inside, gently sanding away the rough edges that keep you from giving your all to God and others, and in this process, your courage is not diminished by admitting your need for divine help, but heightened, because now your boldness rests not on your own fragile ego, but on the rock-solid foundation of God's strength, which never fails, when people see this in you, they may ask what inspires such humble devotion, why you keep serving even when unappreciated, why you lend your resources freely, and you can share the reason: that you follow a Savior who laid down everything for you, who calls you to reflect His character, and who promises that no sacrifice made in His name is ever wasted, that love given in quiet humility ripples out into eternity, touching hearts you may never meet, planting seeds of hope that God can water and grow long after you have moved on, in this grand tapestry God is weaving, your selfless acts become threads of golden grace, shining even when your role is small and unseen, and yes, it takes courage to believe that such small gestures matter, it takes faith to trust that by giving up personal gain, you are gaining something far richer, but this is the mystery of God's kingdom: that in losing your life, you find it, in laying down self, you rise up into your true identity as a beloved child of God, free to love without fear, to serve without calculation, to give without strings attached, and as you embrace this identity, you experience a profound joy that no worldly success can mimic, a joy born of knowing you are living out your divine purpose, channeling God's love into a hurting world, each moment of sacrificial service reinforcing the bond you share with Christ, who understands what it means to give until it hurts, and who celebrates every time you open your heart a little wider, and though the path is not easy, though it involves choosing to do without certain comforts or recognition, though it requires learning to say "yes" to God's nudge and "no" to your ego, you discover that true courage lies in vulnerability, in admitting that by yourself you can do little, but with God's help, you can do wonders, and so you press on, day by day, letting His Spirit guide you toward those who need a helping hand, a kind word, a silent prayer, a shared meal, a listening ear, letting Him set divine appointments you never planned, and through these encounters, your faith grows deeper, your heart more tender, your perspective more aligned with His, and you come to understand that laying down self is not about losing your uniqueness or denying your personal needs, but about allowing God to reorder your priorities so that love leads, humility reigns, and service becomes the natural overflow of a heart set free, and when storms arise, when temptation beckons, or when discouragement tries to settle in, you recall that Jesus promised to be with you always, to empower you, to reward even a cup of water given in His name, no sacrifice slips past His notice, no gift is too small, and this knowledge emboldens you, giving you courage to keep loving, keep serving, keep sacrificing for His sake, knowing that ultimately, everything you do for Him reflects His glory back into the world, lighting up dark corners, lifting burdens, warming cold hearts, and as you reach the twilight of your journey, looking back on a life where you chose again and again to put others first and place your trust in God's plan, you will find peace in the understanding that you have truly lived, that in pouring out your life for the Lord's cause, you have tasted the fullness of life He promised, a life not defined by collecting trophies or climbing ladders of status, but by the quiet heroism of surrender, by the gentle power of compassion, by the unseen battles won through faith and love, and so, here you stand, at the threshold of each new day, reminded that laying down self is an ongoing calling, a repeated decision to serve rather than to be served, a habit of grace formed over time and sealed by God's faithfulness, and as you step forward in courage, fueled by the desire to honor the One who gave everything for you, you embrace the truth that sacrificial service is not a burden, but a privilege, a sacred invitation to join hands with your Creator, to participate in His work of redemption, to become, in some small but meaningful way, a reflection of Christ's own selfless love, and that, at the end of it all, is what ignites your heart with courage: the certainty that by laying down self, you find your place in God's grand story of salvation, written in love, sealed with grace, and carried forward by each humble soul who dares to serve in His name without seeking glory for themselves, but all glory to God alone.

Day 22 - The Power of Yes: Surrendering to God's Will

Imagine a moment when everything around you grows quiet, the noise of daily life fading into the background, leaving you face to face with a decision that seems to hover just beyond your comfort zone—an invitation, not from another person, but from the Lord Himself, a gentle but persistent whisper deep in your spirit asking you to trust Him, to take a step you have resisted, to walk a path you never considered possible, and there, in that secret space of your heart, you encounter the raw essence of surrender, the power of yes, a single, simple word that can change the entire direction of your life; it is not a loud, trumpeting proclamation, but a quiet nod of faith, an opening of your soul's door to let God's will enter, and yet this yes can ignite a courage inside you that you never knew you possessed, fueling your heart to serve the Lord with a fiery passion that outlasts the obstacles, the doubts, the fears that once held you back. Think of all the times you hesitated, weighed the pros and cons, clung to the familiar comforts of what you already knew—saying yes to God often means letting go of what is safe, what is predictable, and stepping into a realm where His guidance is your map, His voice your compass, His promises your only guarantee; yet in that uncertainty lies a peace that surpasses all you understood, for when you say yes to God's will, you align your life with a divine plan that surpasses human logic, a plan woven before time began, a plan that takes into account your fears, your strengths, your weaknesses, and offers a role for you in God's grand story of redemption. The power of yes is not about shouting bravely from a mountaintop, it is about kneeling humbly, bowing your head, and offering your whole self to the Lord's purposes, trusting that He who formed galaxies, who knows the hairs on your head, and who called you by name, will not lead you astray; it is about believing that He can use the most ordinary parts of your life—the routines, the skills you take for granted, even the scars you carry—to accomplish something far greater than you ever imagined, and while you may fear that surrender means losing yourself, the truth is that saying yes to God allows you to become more fully who you were created to be, since His will resonates with the deepest longing of your soul, even if you cannot yet see it. Look at the heroes of faith who have gone before you: Abraham, who left behind everything familiar just because God said "Go," without knowing the destination; Moses, who faced down a powerful king trusting not in his own eloquence, but in the Lord's promise to guide him; Mary, a humble young woman who dared to say yes to bearing the Son of God, even though it meant risking her reputation and enduring confusion; the disciples, who dropped their nets, their secure livelihoods, at a single invitation—"Follow me"—and discovered their ordinary lives transformed into vessels for God's work; each of these stories teaches you that yes is not a burden, but a key that unlocks the door to a life more meaningful, more adventurous, and more aligned with eternal truth than anything you could fashion from your own plans. Yet, let's be honest: surrendering to God's will is not easy, it often means facing the unknown with trembling knees, letting go of carefully built dreams, and trusting that God's dream is infinitely better, even if it does not look like what you expected; it can mean changing your career path, stepping into ministry when you never saw yourself as a leader, offering forgiveness to someone who hurt you deeply, or leaving behind a relationship or environment that hinders your spiritual growth, and while each of these steps may feel like a death to your old ways, it is, in reality, a birth into something new—a life where your values align with God's heart, where your actions flow from obedience rather than fear, and where your devotion is not a hollow ritual but a vibrant relationship with the Creator who calls you His own. The power of yes, at its core, is about trust: trusting that God's perspective outstretches your own, that He knows what you need better than you do, that His definition of success differs from the world's shallow standards, that He measures time differently, seeing not just the immediate moment but the grand tapestry of eternity, and when you say yes, you surrender your limited viewpoint, allowing Him to guide you through twists and turns, uphill climbs and dark valleys, with the assurance that He walks beside you, that His rod and staff comfort you, that He prepares a table before you even when enemies surround, and what does this trust look like in the everyday grind of life? It might mean continuing a difficult ministry even when you feel no visible results, because God whispers that your efforts are planting seeds you cannot yet see; it might mean waking early to pray, though your body craves sleep, trusting that communion with the Lord will nourish your soul beyond physical rest; it might mean speaking truth kindly in a situation where everyone else chooses silence, believing that honesty can bring healing. Saying yes to God's will also involves letting go of control, which can be terrifying for hearts used to holding the reins tightly, you might have envisioned a neat path to your goals—education, career, relationships, and achievements arranged just so—but God's will may invite you to step off that well-trodden road onto a path that is less defined, where He reveals the way step by step, and in this place of trust, you learn that you do not have to see the whole staircase to climb it, that faith grows stronger when you rely on God's wisdom instead of your own limited understanding, and though fear may whisper that surrender is foolish, that you will be taken advantage of, or that your sacrifices will never be acknowledged, remember that fear's voice is not God's voice, He assures you that those who lose their lives for His sake will find them, that He honors those who honor Him, that He notices even the sparrows and adorns the lilies of the field, and how much more does He care for you. The courage ignited by your yes is a quiet flame that sustains you through trials, for when you know you are walking in God's will, you can face adversity with steady resolve, confident that He will provide a way through or a lesson within the struggle, and this is not the bravado of someone seeking danger, but the steady assurance that obedience is never wasted, that the challenges you face while following God are opportunities to refine your faith, to grow in resilience, to learn patience and humility, and to demonstrate to a watching world that your trust is real, not just a pleasant theory. In saying yes, you discover that surrendering to God's will often means serving others in ways that may seem small or unnoticed by human standards, but loom large in the kingdom of heaven—helping a neighbor with their groceries, mentoring a younger believer, volunteering behind the scenes at church, praying faithfully for someone who never knows you prayed, sharing the Gospel with someone who may reject it at first, or simply living with integrity and kindness in a place where dishonesty and cruelty rule, each of these acts, fueled by your yes, becomes a brushstroke in a masterpiece painted by God's own hand, and you may not see the final image now, but in eternity, you will understand that your obedience contributed to something beautiful and eternal. Furthermore, the power of yes is not limited to grand, dramatic decisions; it can be expressed in the simple choices you make daily—choosing gratitude over complaint, forgiveness over bitterness, generosity over hoarding, purity over compromise, truth over convenience, these tiny moments of surrender accumulate, shaping your character into one that reflects Christ, and as your character changes, you become a living invitation for others to discover the freedom and hope you have found, and there is a remarkable humility in this approach: acknowledging that everything you have—time, talents, resources, breath itself—belongs to God, and that your role is to steward these gifts according to His purposes, not your own. Let's also consider that your yes to God's will can spark courage in others, your example of obedience, especially in moments when it costs you something, can inspire fellow believers to step out in faith, to trust that God can use them too, to imagine that their limitations or past failures do not disqualify them from saying yes to the Lord, and even nonbelievers, who do not yet understand your motivation, may be struck by your willingness to take a road that does not promise worldly success, prestige, or comfort, and seeing your peace and conviction, they might begin to wonder about the Source of your hope, and this curiosity can open doors for conversations about faith, about the God who calls us to more than a self-centered existence, about the eternal perspective that shapes your every decision. The power of yes also reminds you that you are not the hero of this story—God is, He is the One who equips you, who opens doors, who transforms hearts, who orchestrates circumstances far beyond what you can comprehend, and your yes is not about proving your worth or earning His love—He already loves you beyond measure—it's about participating in His work, partnering with the Creator of the universe to bring justice, mercy, and truth into places that hunger for them, and this partnership is a privilege, not a burden, because you realize that by surrendering to His will, you align yourself with a mission that transcends your own life's span, it leaves a legacy that endures, weaving your efforts into the grand narrative of redemption that stretches from Genesis to Revelation. Embracing God's will often means letting go of the fear of failure that paralyzes so many dreams, for if your steps are guided by His hand, if your yes is offered in a spirit of obedience, then even what looks like failure to human eyes can hold valuable lessons, spiritual growth, and seeds of change that might bloom in the future, you learn to measure success not by immediate outcomes, but by faithfulness—did you heed God's call, did you give your best with a surrendered heart, did you remain true to His principles even when success eluded you, this perspective liberates you from the relentless pressure to perform and achieve according to worldly standards, freeing you to invest yourself wholeheartedly in tasks great and small, knowing that God's pleasure in you is not based on results, but on your sincere devotion and trust in Him. Surrendering to God's will means acknowledging that He might lead you to places of discomfort—physically, emotionally, or spiritually—places where you must confront your fears head-on, unlearn harmful patterns, break away from unhealthy attachments, and learn to rely on grace rather than your own strength, in these stretches, you may feel stripped bare of your usual supports, forced to rely on prayer like never before, to absorb Scripture's truths as a lifeline in a stormy sea, to cling to the promise that He will never leave nor forsake you, and this forging process hurts at times, but it also polishes your faith until it shines more brilliantly, making you a vessel that can carry His love and truth into the darkest corners of human experience. The power of yes, however, does not mean you should ignore wise counsel or throw caution to the wind, surrendering to God's will involves discernment, prayerful consideration, and sometimes waiting patiently for His timing, it means seeking confirmation through His Word, through the counsel of mature believers, through the peace He grants in your spirit, and when all aligns, when His leading resonates clearly, you say yes, confident that He who called you will equip you, that He will supply what you lack, open doors that seemed bolted shut, and provide strength to meet every challenge; surrender means placing your confidence in His character, knowing that He is good, loving, just, and faithful, so even if you do not understand the immediate purpose of the path before you, you trust the One who designed it. Another beautiful aspect of surrendering to God's will is the healing it can bring to wounded hearts, perhaps you have carried insecurities, regrets, or guilt from past mistakes—surrendering them to God, saying yes to His desire to cleanse and restore you, can break chains that have held you captive, as you say yes to His grace, you learn to see yourself through His eyes, forgiven, precious, and capable of growth, and this inner transformation empowers you to serve Him without shame or fear, stepping forward in ministry, in relationships, in witness, with a new confidence grounded not in your own ability, but in His unwavering love, and just as surrender sets you free from the weight of personal baggage, it also enables you to extend compassion and understanding to others, since you know what it is like to stand in need of mercy. Consider also that saying yes to God's will can lead you to unexpected friendships, alliances, and communities of believers who share your commitment to obey the Lord, as you step into ministries, outreaches, or callings that stretch you, you meet people who are also on a journey of faith, who inspire you with their courage, who support you in prayer and encouragement, and whose fellowship reminds you that you are not alone, this network of fellow servants becomes a source of strength when the road feels long, a reminder that God's family is vast and diverse, each member playing a unique part, and your yes merges with theirs to form a symphony of obedience that testifies to the world about the God who unites hearts across boundaries and backgrounds. The power of yes also touches upon the legacy you leave behind, by surrendering to God's will, you invest in treasures that last beyond your lifetime, maybe you mentor a young believer who will grow into a leader influencing generations to come, maybe your faithful service in a small church or community plants seeds of revival that bloom after you have passed on, maybe your quiet acts of kindness encourage someone to pursue Christ wholeheartedly, leading them in turn to bless countless others, and this legacy is not measured by statues or plaques bearing your name, but by the eternal impact made on souls, and while you may never see the full extent of this influence on earth, surrendering to God's will means trusting that He weaves every yes into a grand tapestry of His redeeming work. In moments of doubt, when you wonder if your yes truly matters, remember that God specializes in turning small acts of obedience into mighty works, consider the boy who gave Jesus his five loaves and two fish, an offering seemingly insignificant compared to the hunger of thousands, yet in Christ's hands, that humble gift multiplied, fed the multitudes, and became a story told through the ages, similarly, your yes, no matter how small it feels, when placed in God's hands, can be multiplied beyond imagining, your single act of generosity can spark a chain of kindness, your willingness to step into a difficult conversation can bring reconciliation that ripples outward, your decision to serve in an unnoticed corner of ministry can uphold a mission that touches hundreds of lives, this multiplication should encourage you to embrace surrender not as a loss, but as a source of abundant fruitfulness. Through this process, as your courage grows, you realize that what you feared losing—control, comfort, image—are nothing compared to the richness of life lived under God's guidance, you discover that when you align your will with His, doors open in unexpected places, fresh inspiration flows, and burdens you carried alone are shared with a God who shoulders the weight far better than you ever could, and as you grow more accustomed to saying yes, you find that it becomes a pattern, a reflex that surfaces whenever a new challenge appears, at each new crossroad, you pause, listen for His voice, and then respond with trust, watching as He turns the unknown into a journey of growth, a path that refines your character and glorifies His name. The power of yes also sets you free from the tyranny of selfish ambition, allowing you to see beyond your personal gain to the needs of others, it transforms relationships, because you approach them not with a "What can I get from you?" mentality, but with "How can I serve you?" you become a peacemaker, a bridge-builder, a source of stability in a world quick to divide, for when your agenda is to fulfill God's will, your ego steps aside, making room for empathy, patience, forgiveness, and kindness to flourish, and the courage that comes from surrender enables you to stand firm in love, even when misunderstanding or hostility arises, because your foundation rests on Christ's example and His unchanging truth. Consider how Jesus Himself said yes to the Father's will, even unto death, and how that single yes changed everything, opening the door for salvation, healing, and reconciliation between God and humankind, His yes serves as the ultimate model and encouragement, showing that surrender is not weakness, but the greatest demonstration of strength and love imaginable, by following in His footsteps, you tap into a legacy of grace that stretches across generations, a legacy of countless believers who dared to say yes, to go where God led them, to care for orphans and widows, to share the Gospel in hostile territories, to live simply so others might simply live, to stand up against injustice, to comfort the grieving, to celebrate with the joyful, and to keep trusting even when the sky looked dark, all these yeses woven together form a mighty chorus of faith, a testament that God works powerfully through surrendered hearts. In this grand narrative, your yes matters, it may seem small, just one voice among millions, but each voice adds richness and depth to the harmony of obedience, and God, who hears every whispered prayer and sees every tear shed in secret, cherishes your willingness to bend your will to His, He pours His Spirit into you, strengthening your resolve, sharpening your discernment, and filling you with compassion that drives you to love even the unlovable, this divine support enables you to persevere, to remain steadfast when challenges intensify, and to keep hoping even when results remain unseen, and as you persevere in this lifestyle of surrender, you find that courage and humility begin to intertwine, producing a spiritual maturity that radiates peace, joy, and a sense of purpose that cannot be extinguished by circumstances. Embracing the power of yes does not mean you will never struggle again, or that you will always know exactly what to do, it means you have chosen to trust a faithful guide rather than stumble alone in the dark, it means that when confusion arises, you pray, you search His Word, you seek wise counsel, and then you move forward in faith, knowing that He can redeem even your missteps, turning them into lessons that deepen your intimacy with Him, surrender is not about being perfect, it is about being willing, about placing your life into the Master's hands and saying, "I am yours, do what you will," and in that moment of offering, you experience a freedom from the crushing burden of self-determination and self-preservation, a freedom that allows you to breathe easier, stand taller, and face each new day with expectant hope. Ultimately, the power of yes invites you into a relationship of trust, where you do not have to force outcomes or manipulate events, but simply walk hand in hand with God, the One who knows your destiny and has prepared good works for you to do, by surrendering to His will, you become a co-creator with Him, planting seeds of grace everywhere you go—at home, at work, in your community, in the hearts of strangers and friends, and these seeds will grow in ways you might never personally witness, but God sees, God nurtures, and God celebrates every time you choose obedience over rebellion, love over indifference, faith over fear. As you near the end of your journey, looking back on a life shaped by yes after yes to the Lord, you will see a tapestry of impact and meaning, a legacy woven with threads of sacrifice, service, and faithfulness, you will know that your life counted for something greater than your own desires, that you participated in God's redemptive story, playing the part He assigned, and though it might not have always been glamorous, and though not all your struggles were resolved as you hoped, you will have the deep satisfaction of knowing you lived by God's wisdom, not your own, that you answered His call when it came, that you learned to love Him more than anything else, and this is the crowning glory of a surrendered life, the ultimate reason to say yes over and over: because in doing so, you discover the full, rich measure of God's goodness, His unshakable faithfulness, His power made perfect in your weakness, and you find that, indeed, giving yourself to His will is not loss, but gain beyond measure

Day 23 - Hope in Hardship: Finding Joy Amid Challenges

Imagine yourself waking up early on a chilly morning, the sky still gray and the world feeling heavy, as if weighted down by unseen burdens, and as you sit quietly, thinking about the day ahead, you can't help but feel a knot of worry sitting low in your stomach, a reminder of the hardships you face—maybe it's the uncertainty of a loved one's health, the strain of finances that never quite add up, the sting of a friendship turned cold, or the looming deadlines and demands that fill your mind with noise—each challenge stacking up like thick clouds threatening rain, and yet, even as you feel these struggles pressing in, something stirs in your heart, a small ember of hope that refuses to be snuffed out, and you realize that finding joy in hardship is not only possible, it's the very thing that can give you the courage to keep going, to serve the Lord even when everything around you cries out to give up, but how do you find joy when so many things weigh you down, when life's trials feel like walls boxing you in, leaving you feeling trapped and alone? Think of joy as a quiet, steady light, not blinding like a sudden flash, but more like a gentle candle that glows in your heart, pushing back the darkness just enough for you to see that there is still beauty, still goodness, still a reason to believe that God's hand rests on your shoulder, guiding you forward, and this joy is not the same as happiness, which can come and go depending on what happens to you—happiness might disappear the instant something goes wrong, but joy, true joy, has deeper roots, because it's tied to hope, to faith, and to the unchanging character of the God you serve.

When you say yes to following the Lord, you are not promised a life free from hardship, rather, Jesus Himself said that in this world, you will have trouble, but He also told you to take heart, for He has overcome the world, and this truth can spark courage in your soul, showing you that hardship does not have the final say, that sorrow is not the end of the story, and that even as you wade through challenges that test your strength and patience, you can hold onto hope, a hope grounded in the knowledge that the God who loves you is bigger than any problem you face, that He works even in the shadows, weaving purpose out of pain, shaping your character through trials, and preparing you to serve Him in ways you cannot yet imagine. Perhaps you have felt this before—when you looked back at a past struggle and realized it taught you compassion, strengthened your resolve, or helped you understand others who suffer, and you saw that what once seemed like a meaningless hardship actually formed a stepping stone on your path of growth, making you more empathetic, more determined, and more open to God's will, and this realization can fill you with hope that whatever hardship you face today is not wasted, that God can use even this storm to deepen your faith, refine your heart, and prepare you for acts of service that require the resilience you are now developing, and though hardship often tries to whisper lies into your ear—telling you that you are weak, alone, and powerless—hope counters these lies with truth: that in your weakness, God's strength shines, that you are never truly alone because He is with you, and that you are never powerless because His Spirit lives in you, helping you do what you cannot do by your own might. Finding joy amid challenges also means learning to see beyond the surface of your circumstances, to recognize that life's difficulties can draw you closer to God; if you let them, think about how, in times of deep sorrow or frustration, you are more likely to fall to your knees, to pray sincerely, to cry out for God's help, and while He does not delight in your suffering, He can use these moments of vulnerability to show you His comfort and presence in ways you might never experience if life were always easy, when you feel the gentle warmth of His nearness despite the pain, you discover a joy that is not based on external blessings, but on the unshakable bond you share with the Lord who knows your every tear, and as your trust in Him grows, so does your capacity to serve Him with courage, because you understand that nothing, not even the hardest season, can separate you from

His love. Another way to find joy in hardship is to shift your perspective from what you lack to what you have, hardship often screams at you to focus on everything going wrong, what you cannot control, what you have lost, but hope invites you to count your blessings, to remember the ways God has provided in the past, to notice the small gifts scattered throughout your day—like a kind word from a friend, a hint of beauty in nature, a memory of a past victory—these reminders show you that even in darkness, there are sparks of light, reasons to be grateful, and gratitude feeds hope, pulling your eyes up from the pit of despair and turning them toward the goodness of God, who has not abandoned you. Consider also that finding joy amid challenges can strengthen not just your own heart, but the hearts of those around you, when you carry yourself with hope and courage during hard times, you become a beacon to others who struggle, they see that hardship does not have to crush the human spirit, that faith can thrive even in deserts, and your life itself becomes a testimony to the Lord's sustaining power, inspiring others to seek Him, to trust Him, to believe that joy is possible for them too, and this ripple effect means your perseverance and hope serve not just your personal growth, but God's broader kingdom purpose, reaching beyond your individual story and influencing people you may never even meet, and in this way, hardship turns into a platform for ministry, where your scars and struggles become tools to empathize, to encourage, and to guide others toward the anchor of true hope. Of course, none of this is to say that hardship is easy, or that you should pretend to be happy when you are hurting inside, acknowledging your pain, grieving your losses, and admitting that you are tired or scared does not mean you lack faith or joy, it means you are human, and God does not ask you to hide your tears or be strong on your own, He invites you to bring your burdens to Him, to rest in His arms, and to trust that even as you weep, He weeps with you, understanding every nuance of your heart, and just as night gives way to dawn, your season of hardship can eventually yield new clarity, fresh strength, and joy that is more profound than any shallow happiness you might have known before. Another dimension to finding joy amid challenges is learning to rely on the power of prayer, prayer can transform hardship into an opportunity for deeper communion with God, when you pour out your heart to Him—your fears, doubts, frustrations—He listens, and though

He may not remove the hardship immediately, He often grants peace that transcends your circumstances, peace that comes from knowing He is in control, that He cares about the smallest details of your life, and that He can work all things together for good in ways you cannot yet see, and when you taste this peace, joy begins to bubble up inside, not a wild, jubilant joy, but a steady, abiding sense that God holds you securely, giving you courage to face another day, to keep serving, keep loving, keep hoping. Reflecting on Scripture can also spark joy amid hardship, stories of biblical characters who endured immense trials—Joseph in prison, David fleeing from Saul, Ruth losing her husband, Elijah running from threats—reveal that hardship is not unusual for those who follow God, but in each of these narratives, we also see God's faithfulness, His provision at the right time, His unseen guidance leading to outcomes that bless not only the individual but many others, immersing yourself in these stories shows you that the God of Abraham, Isaac, and Jacob is the same God who walks with you today, that the hope that sustained them can sustain you, and this knowledge can kindle a quiet joy, because you know that nothing you face is beyond the scope of His care, that you are part of the same redemptive storyline. When hardship hits, it can also tempt you to question your calling, to wonder if you misunderstood God's direction, or if He has left you to fend for yourself, but here is where faith steps in and reminds you that hardship does not mean God has stopped leading you, it could mean He is refining you, teaching you lessons you will need for future service, testing your motives, or strengthening certain aspects of your character, it may mean that you are actually right where you need to be, wrestling through difficulties that will later become testimonies of His faithfulness, and if you hold onto hope, you can press through the confusion, trusting that as you persevere, your calling will not be snuffed out by suffering, but made more genuine and powerful, so that when you do serve, you serve with a humility and love shaped by your own struggle. Another way to nurture joy amid hardship is to surround yourself with supportive community, fellow believers who understand that life can be painful and are willing to stand by you, lifting you in prayer, offering practical help, listening without judgment, these friends can remind you of truth when your thoughts grow cloudy, they can celebrate small victories with you, encourage you to keep trusting when you feel weak, and point you back to the Lord's promises when your heart wavers, and sometimes, witnessing the faith of others who have also walked through hardship, yet hold onto joy, can restore your sense of what is possible, showing you that you are never truly alone in your struggles. Finding joy in hardship also requires forgiveness—both of yourself and of others who may have contributed to your struggles, anger, bitterness, and resentment block the flow of hope, clouding your vision and keeping you stuck in a cycle of pain, but when you seek God's help to release these negative emotions, to let go of grudges, you open the door for His healing light to shine through, and forgiveness does not excuse wrongdoing, it simply places the burden in God's hands, freeing your heart to move forward without the heavy chains of bitterness, and in that freedom, joy finds room to grow again, reminding you that you are not defined by what others have done to you or by your own past mistakes, but by the redemptive love of a God who makes all things new. Sometimes, joy in hardship emerges from discovering a purpose in your pain, asking God how He might use your story to help others, to bring hope to someone facing a similar struggle, or to highlight a need that you can address through ministry, when you realize that your suffering can produce empathy, wisdom, and compassion that serve others, the hardship gains meaning, and with meaning comes hope, because you see that God can transform ashes into beauty, using even the darkest chapters of your life to shine His light into the darkness others face, and there is a special kind of joy that comes from knowing that your tears have watered the ground where someone else's healing may sprout, that your scars can guide others to safety, that your journey through pain qualifies you to minister with authenticity and understanding. In addition, focusing on eternity can help you find joy in the midst of struggles, remembering that this life is not the end of the story, that beyond the hardships, beyond the trials and tears, lies a future where God will wipe away every tear, where suffering and death will be no more, where justice and love reign forever, holding onto this eternal perspective lifts your eyes above the immediate pain, showing you that everything here is temporary, that even the most crushing burden will seem light and momentary compared to the glory that awaits, and though this does not remove your present hurt, it cushions it with the hope that God's plan extends far beyond these fleeting years, that your faithful endurance will be rewarded, that every faithful step you take now echoes into eternity. Joy amid hardship also grows as you learn to celebrate small wins and moments of grace, maybe you didn't solve the entire problem, but you made progress, maybe you didn't find immediate relief, but you discovered a coping strategy that lightened your load, maybe you didn't escape the storm, but you found a sturdy shelter in prayer, each tiny success can remind you that God is at work, that He gives daily bread for each day's challenges, and as you string together these small moments of relief, insight, or encouragement, you weave a tapestry of hope that reinforces the truth: God has not abandoned you, He is teaching you to find joy not because of the hardship, but in spite of it, a testament to the resilience He places in your heart. Reflecting on what you have learned through hardship can also foster joy, look back and see how far you've come, how your faith has matured, how values once taken for granted now mean more, how humility replaced pride, how gratitude replaced entitlement, how dependence on God replaced self-reliance, in seeing these inner transformations, you realize that hardship has acted as a furnace, purifying and clarifying your identity and purpose, and this understanding brings a deep, quiet joy—joy in knowing that no tear was in vain, no struggle went unused, no valley walk was wasted, that in the hands of a loving God, even suffering becomes a tool for growth, and as you stand on this firm ground of purpose, you feel courage rise, enabling you to serve the Lord with greater authenticity and devotion. Another aspect of finding joy in hardship is learning to laugh at times, even when circumstances are grim, humor can be a gift from God, lightening your heart, reminding you that not all is lost, and that His grace can penetrate even bleak situations with rays of goodness, a shared laugh with a friend, a funny memory that surfaces unexpectedly, or the absurdity of a difficult situation seen from a different angle can momentarily lift your spirits, granting a brief respite that restores a bit of energy, and while laughter won't solve your problems, it can restore hope that life still holds brightness, that God's world still brims with unexpected delight, that your soul can breathe even under pressure. Ultimately, finding joy amid hardship involves surrendering your struggles to God, acknowledging that you cannot carry them alone, that you need His strength to endure, and that you trust Him to bring something meaningful out of the mess, and this surrender does not mean giving up or becoming passive—it means actively choosing to place your burdens in His hands, believing that He cares enough to handle them better than you ever could, as you let go of the need to control every detail, every outcome, you free yourself to focus on what matters most: staying close to Him, loving those around you, using your gifts to bless others, and maintaining an open heart that can still receive joy, even when life is far from perfect. This posture of surrender and trust makes joy possible even when you are fatigued, uncertain, or deeply wounded, because you stop relying on your own resources and start drawing from God's infinite well of grace, the courage ignited in these moments is not a human bravery that denies the severity of your trials, it is a divine courage that acknowledges them fully but stands firm in the belief that God's promises hold true, that He will never abandon you, that He can use even this season to refine your character and open doors of service that would remain closed otherwise, when you see your life from this vantage point, joy becomes a quiet companion, walking beside you in the dark, shining just enough light to help you take the next step. Also, remember that hardship can create bonds of solidarity with others who suffer, through empathy and shared experiences, you can join hands with brothers and sisters in Christ who are also struggling, offering mutual encouragement, reminding one another of God's faithfulness, praying together, and carrying one another's burdens, this community support multiplies hope, letting you know that you do not struggle in isolation, that others have walked a similar road and found God's grace sufficient, and that together, you can weather storms that might have overwhelmed you alone, in this unity, joy emerges as you see how God uses each person's story, each person's courage, to lift the entire body of believers, strengthening the collective faith. Finding joy in hardship does not mean you must minimize your pain or deny your feelings, it simply means you refuse to let sorrow define you, you acknowledge the reality of your situation while still holding onto a deeper reality: God is present, God is good, and God's love endures, no matter what, and with this understanding, you can serve the Lord wholeheartedly even when your own heart feels heavy, because serving becomes an expression of trust, a way of saying, "Lord, I still believe in Your goodness, I still want to be part of what You are doing in the world, even as I carry these burdens," and in that faithful service, you discover another source of joy—knowing your life counts, that your pain does not disqualify you from being used by God, rather, it equips you to serve with authenticity, to comfort with genuine understanding, to stand strong as a witness that even broken vessels can shine His light brightly. In the end, hope in hardship and the joy it brings act like a divine alchemy, transforming the base metal of suffering into something golden and precious, not by making suffering good in itself, but by revealing God's ability to bring good from even the hardest seasons, if you remain open to Him, surrendering your fears and disappointments, you will see that every trial can become a stepping stone, guiding you closer to His heart, teaching you lessons that enrich your soul, and strengthening your character so you can serve Him more effectively, with greater compassion and wisdom, and so, as you press on, keep this vision before you: that no matter how dark the storm, there is a sun beyond the clouds, no matter how lonely the road, God's presence is with you, and no matter how fierce the struggle, joy can still blossom in your heart like a desert flower blooming unexpectedly in the wilderness, reminding you that with God, nothing is impossible, that courage can be ignited even in sorrow, and that the hope He offers is an anchor steadying you amid the fiercest winds.

Day 24 - Carriers of Light: Reflecting Christ in a Dark World

Imagine stepping outside late at night, the world around you cloaked in layers of silent darkness, buildings and trees reduced to shadowy shapes, the sky emptied of the day's warmth, and as you stand there, your heart senses that this darkness does not belong solely to the absence of sunlight, but also to something deeper, a spiritual dimness that lies heavy on the human soul, leaving many wandering without clear direction, grasping for meaning in places that yield only emptiness, and as you consider this truth, you realize that we, as followers of Christ, are called to be carriers of light, to bear within our hearts a divine flame that can pierce through the shadows and show the world a better way, a hope-filled path that leads not to despair but to lasting peace and purpose, and yet this calling is not always easy, for darkness can feel overwhelming, making it seem almost impossible for your small light to matter in a universe so large, and you might wonder if you have what it takes, if your faith is bright enough, your courage strong enough, your love genuine enough to reflect Christ in a world where chaos and confusion often reign, but do not let these doubts deter you, because the power does not come from you alone, it comes from the Lord who kindled that light in your soul, who placed a spark of His own goodness, mercy, and grace deep inside you, and who has entrusted you with a mission: to share that light, to let it shine through your words, your actions, your choices, your kindness, your patience, your willingness to stand for truth when lies surround, to choose compassion over indifference, to hold fast to hope when so many are giving in to despair. Picture a single candle flame in a dark room, how even a small candle can shift the atmosphere, allowing you to see shapes and forms you could not see before, how it can guide your steps so you don't stumble, how it can bring comfort just by its gentle glow, and then think about how much brighter an entire community of believers, each carrying a flame of Christ's love, can illuminate neighborhoods, schools, workplaces, cities, nations, even the world, when these individual lights unite, the darkness cannot remain as strong, it must recede, making room for truth, for hope, for healing, and this is not about being perfect or having all the answers, it's about yielding to the Holy Spirit, allowing Him to strengthen your faith and grant you the courage needed to take your light into places that frighten you, into conversations that feel uncomfortable, into interactions where misunderstanding might arise, but where love can break down barriers if given the chance. To be a carrier of light means you reflect not yourself, but Christ who dwells within, so the pressure is not on you to create brilliance out of nothing, rather, you simply allow His presence to shine through you, like a window allowing sunlight to enter a dark room, and to do this, you must remain close to Him, drawing near in prayer, in studying Scripture, in worship, and in fellowship with other believers, because the more time you spend in His presence, the more His light saturates your being, replacing fears with confidence, doubts with assurance, anger with understanding, and selfishness with generosity, so that over time, even your countenance changes, your eyes soften with empathy, your words carry a gentle authority, and your actions become channels of blessing. It might seem counterintuitive that in a world where harshness and cruelty often steal the headlines, something as simple and pure as love can have real power, but remember that darkness thrives on fear, hatred, and lies, and the light you carry—rooted in God's truth and love—exposes these shadows for what they are, empty threats and illusions that cannot withstand the steady glow of divine goodness, and when someone encounters this light in you, they might not immediately recognize it for what it is, they might be drawn to your unusual kindness and wonder where it comes from, or be intrigued by your calmness under pressure, your refusal to return insult for insult, your patience in dealing with difficult people, your willingness to listen deeply and treat each person with dignity, these quiet acts, small as they may seem, stand out in a world accustomed to everyone serving their own interests first, and in noticing this difference, people may be prompted to ask questions, to seek the source of this light, giving you the opportunity to share about the One who lit your flame in the first place. Carrying this light does not mean you never feel afraid or discouraged, there will be days when the darkness feels thick and suffocating, when the brokenness you witness seems insurmountable, when the evil in the world shakes your faith, yet remember that your strength comes not from your ability to remain cheerful in hard times, but from the unchanging character of God, whose love remains steady no matter how tumultuous the world becomes, and by clinging to His promises, you find the courage to keep shining your light even when it flickers low, to guard the flame with prayer and trust, to feed it by returning to the well of His Word, drinking in encouragement and wisdom that remind you God has overcome the world, that He who began a good work in you will carry it through, that nothing can separate you from His love. Reflecting Christ in a dark world also means making conscious choices in the face of moral ambiguity, when others may choose shortcuts, deceit, or cruelty to get ahead, your light compels you to choose integrity, honesty, kindness, even when it costs you something, and though at times this feels like swimming against a powerful current, it's precisely in these moments that your witness shines brightest, for when people see you choosing to remain faithful to God's standards rather than bending to convenience, they glimpse a better way, a way that testifies that truth matters, that goodness can prevail, that righteousness is not an outdated concept but a living force that dignifies human life and fosters trust and peace, and they may not immediately thank you for it or recognize its source, but seeds are planted in their hearts, seeds that might later grow into a yearning to know this God who inspires such courage and consistency. Being a carrier of light also means extending grace to yourself, remembering that you are human, prone to errors and lapses in judgment, sometimes your flame will dim because of weariness, confusion, or even sin, and you'll need to repent, to rest in God's forgiveness, to find restoration in His presence, it is through these humbling experiences that you realize your light is not self-generated, it's a gift, a treasure placed in an earthen vessel, and when cracks appear in the vessel, the light can shine through even more vividly, showing that the glory belongs to God, not to you, this humility keeps you grounded, prevents pride from taking root, and ensures that your service remains authentic, powered by sincerity rather than a desire to appear holy or impressive. The world's darkness can feel overwhelming when you consider the enormity of suffering, injustice, poverty, violence, and despair, how can your single, modest light make any difference at all? But do not underestimate the cumulative effect of countless believers, each carrying their portion of Christ's light, scattered across the globe, in countless neighborhoods, schools, offices, hospitals, kitchens, and marketplaces, together, these lights form constellations of hope in the night sky of human experience, guiding people home to the Father's heart, and though you may not see the full picture now, each small act of faithfulness contributes to a grand tapestry of redemption woven by God's sovereign hand, and knowing this gives you the courage to keep shining, to not give up just because the darkness seems persistent, for the darkness cannot extinguish the light that God Himself kindled. Reflecting Christ in a dark world also involves learning to listen to the Spirit's guidance moment by moment, for not every act of kindness is the same, sometimes you need to speak a bold truth to challenge wrongdoing, other times you need to remain silent and simply be present with someone who suffers, sometimes you must give generously of your resources, and other times you must refrain from offering material help and instead provide prayer and moral support, following the Spirit's lead ensures that your service is not just a reflection of your own assumptions, but a true channel for God's wisdom and love, and as you grow accustomed to listening and obeying His gentle promptings, you become more effective as a carrier of light, because your actions align with the deeper, divine purposes at work. Another aspect of shining Christ's light is embracing diversity and loving people who differ from you, the darkness of the world often tries to separate us into camps, to heighten mistrust and hostility, to make enemies of those who hold different beliefs or come from different backgrounds, but when you carry Christ's light, you recognize that each person is made in God's image, each soul worthy of respect and compassion, and rather than building walls, you seek to build bridges, to understand rather than condemn, to offer empathy rather than judgment, this does not mean you abandon your convictions, but that you present them with grace, willing to hear others' stories, willing to find common ground, and willing to let the Holy Spirit work through relationships that might seem unlikely at first, in doing so, you help break down the darkness of prejudice, letting rays of understanding and reconciliation shine through. To reflect Christ in a dark world is also to know the power of hope, even when circumstances look bleak, you must remember that God's story is one of ultimate victory, that no matter how dark the chapter you find yourself in, the last word belongs to God, who will restore all things, wipe away every tear, and usher in a kingdom of eternal peace, this hope does not deny the pain of the present, but it places that pain in perspective, reminding you that you are part of a narrative that ends in glorious light, when you carry this hope, you diffuse despair, showing others that hope is not naive, but a confident expectation based on God's promises, and when people sense your hope, they become curious about its source, opening doors for you to share about the One who conquered death and darkness. At times, reflecting Christ's light may mean stepping into uncomfortable places where few others dare to go: the bedside of the dying, the cell of the prisoner, the street corner where the homeless gather, the heart of a conflict zone, or even the hush of a family argument that's been left unaddressed for too long, these are the places where darkness sometimes feels thickest, where suffering and despair can make hope seem like a distant dream, but when you enter these spaces, carrying the flame of Christ's love, you bring with you the assurance that God has not forgotten those who dwell in shadows, that they are seen, known, and loved by a Lord who once walked the earth, healing the sick, touching the untouchables, speaking comfort to the brokenhearted, by daring to go where the need is greatest, you become a tangible reminder that light is stronger than darkness, that love outruns fear, and that God's mercy knows no boundaries. This mission is not reserved for a select few—every believer is called to shine, to let their unique gifts and personality reflect Christ's goodness, maybe your light manifests through music, inspiring hope with notes and lyrics that point to eternal truths, maybe it emerges in your ability to comfort the grieving, to counsel the confused, to teach the young, or to lead with integrity in a position of influence, maybe it reveals itself in your art, your hospitality, your quiet acts of service that no one notices but God, whatever shape your light takes, remember that it does not have to be dramatic to be real, even the smallest flicker of compassion can guide a weary traveler closer to God's embrace. Reflecting Christ in a dark world also means learning from your mistakes, because none of us shine perfectly at all times, there will be moments when you fail to represent God's love, when your words are harsh, your patience runs dry, or your judgmental attitude eclipses the light you carry, but grace allows you to repent, to apologize, to learn humility and try again, it is in admitting your faults and leaning on God's forgiveness that you show others the ongoing nature of growth in grace, proving that this light is not about personal perfection, but about a deep-rooted relationship with a merciful Savior who continually transforms you from within, and these moments of honesty and vulnerability can actually intensify the brightness of your witness, because they demonstrate that your source of hope is not your own goodness, but God's unfailing mercy. Over time, as you consistently choose to shine in small but meaningful ways, you may notice that you approach challenges with greater resilience, respond to hostility with surprising gentleness, recover from setbacks with renewed determination, and navigate complexities with a peace that confounds your understanding, these changes are the fruit of living close to Christ, of letting His light shape your perspectives, your priorities, and your responses, and your courage to reflect Him grows stronger with each test, each victory over fear, each instance where you trusted Him more than your doubts, eventually, this becomes more than just something you do—it becomes who you are, a person so rooted in Christ's light that no darkness can persuade you to abandon hope, to compromise on love, or to hide the truth. Your influence may spread quietly, sometimes imperceptibly, but God's ways often work beneath the surface, like seeds germinating underground, one day you might hear a story from someone who found solace in a kind word you spoke long ago, or an act of generosity that planted a thought in their mind about God's goodness, or a moment when your refusal to join in destructive gossip made them rethink their own behavior, these testimonies remind you that every spark of light matters, that God uses your life, with all its imperfections, to illuminate the path for others, and these confirmations encourage you to continue, to not give in to the discouragement that tries to tell you your efforts are in vain, they are not, because God multiplies what you offer, turning your modest flame into a guidepost for those stumbling in darkness. In this journey, remember also to care for your own soul, to ensure the flame of faith within you remains bright, spend time in God's presence, feed on Scripture, lift your worries and dreams to Him in prayer, protect your heart from cynicism and despair by recalling His faithfulness throughout history and in your own story, and share your burdens with trusted fellow believers who can encourage you when your light seems dim, the stronger your connection to the source of all light—Jesus Himself—the more naturally you will reflect His character, even when trials come. Ultimately, being a carrier of light and reflecting Christ in a dark world is about fulfilling the great commandment: to love the Lord your God with all your heart, soul, mind, and strength, and to love your neighbor as yourself, everything else you do flows from this foundation, as you love God wholeheartedly, your life becomes a mirror of His love, and as you love your neighbor sincerely, you transform abstract faith into tangible compassion, bridging the gap between heaven's ideals and earth's realities, showing that the Gospel is not just words on a page, but a living force shaping how you treat people, how you respond to injustice, how you invest your time and resources, how you choose mercy over judgment and hope over despair. And so, as you stand in a world often overshadowed by confusion, pain, and moral ambiguity, know that your calling is to be a carrier of light, to let the reflection of Christ's love guide your steps and influence those around you, to remain faithful when tempted to withdraw or hide, to believe that God can use even your smallest acts of kindness to crack open the darkness and let truth and love stream in, as you keep this perspective, your heart grows more courageous, fueled by the certainty that light is stronger than darkness, that God's grace runs deeper than any struggle we face, and that in Him, we have all we need to shine brightly, illuminating the path for ourselves and for others, and revealing that the darkness of this world is no match for the enduring, radiant glow of Christ's presence reflected through a faithful life.

Day 25 - Ready for the Harvest: Preparing to Serve Others

Imagine standing in a wide, golden field at the edge of the season's change, the sun just beginning its slow arc across a sky brushed with gentle blues and whispers of white cloud, and as you stand there, you can almost feel the earth breathing beneath your feet, waiting for the next step, for someone brave enough to reach in and gather the fruit of months of growth and care, and that someone, in this grand picture, could be you, standing ready for the harvest, which in spiritual terms means preparing your heart, mind, and hands to serve others in the name of the Lord, for the harvest is not just about gathering grain or fruit from fields of wheat or orchards of apples, it is about seeing the world around you as a vineyard ripe with souls who need encouragement, guidance, healing, and a gentle reminder that God is near and cares for them deeply, and as you look across this wide landscape—some places sunlit with hope, others shadowed by sorrow—you know that God has a role for you, a part in this timeless story where love overcomes hate, kindness pushes back darkness, and courage grows from small seeds into tall stalks of faith ready to nourish those who hunger for truth, so how do you prepare for such a calling, how do you fuel your heart with the courage to serve the Lord in a world that often seems cold and hard, how do you ready your spirit to gather what has been growing unseen beneath life's surface, to share grace with people who may not even know they need it, who might be too wounded or frightened to ask? It begins in the quiet spaces of your own heart, before the first step into the fields, before the first conversation with someone who hurts, before you attempt any grand act of service, you must kneel inwardly, offering your fears, hesitations, and selfish ambitions to God, let Him work on you like a gardener prepares the soil, turning it over, pulling weeds of doubt and bitterness, adding nutrients of faith and Scripture truth, so that what grows in you is sturdy and life-giving, you must draw close to Him in prayer, not just rattling off requests, but sitting still long enough to sense His presence, to let His peace settle in your bones, to feel His love surround you like warm sunlight breaking through early morning mist, for the courage to serve others does not come from self-help books or sheer willpower, it comes from the Holy Spirit igniting a flame in your soul, a flame that softens your pride and awakens compassion for those who suffer quietly or openly, who carry burdens seen and unseen, and in receiving this divine spark, you find your perspective shift: the world is no longer a place to simply survive or compete, it becomes a field ready for harvest, filled with opportunities to invest in others' well-being, to speak words of comfort, to perform acts of mercy, to offer guidance and prayer when hope runs thin, but this readiness does not stop at heart preparation, it calls you also to sharpen your mind and train your hands, so that you may serve effectively, with skill and thoughtfulness, consider spending time learning about the struggles people face, understanding different backgrounds and cultures, so that when you encounter someone whose story is unlike your own, you meet them with empathy rather than judgment, seek wisdom in God's Word to ground your service in truth, so you don't rely on empty clichés or hollow advice, but on principles that reflect God's character—justice, mercy, humility, forgiveness—shaping the way you respond to both small and large needs, and remember that sometimes service requires patience and endurance, like working a plow through stubborn ground or gently coaxing a seedling to take root, not every person you try to help will welcome your efforts, not every prayer will see immediate fruit, not every wound will heal quickly, but perseverance is part of preparing for the harvest, believing that God's timing and methods often differ from your own, that a kind word shared today may bear fruit in someone's life months or years down the road, that a single moment of listening and understanding might be the drop of water that allows a seed of faith to sprout in a hardened heart, so do not grow weary when results fail to appear on your schedule, trust the divine Farmer who understands every soil type, every weather pattern, every season of growth, your role is to be faithful, to show up with open hands and a willing spirit, to sow seeds of love and truth wherever you go, leaving the outcome to God's tender care. Another aspect of preparing yourself is learning to let go of the fear of rejection or failure, we often hold back from serving others because we worry about how we'll look if we stumble or say the wrong thing, but in God's economy, even our imperfect attempts can be used for good, He can redeem our clumsy words, our awkward silences, and our trembling voices, molding them into vessels for His grace, do not let the fear of not being "good enough" freeze you into inaction, remember that God frequently used imperfect people throughout history to accomplish His work—Moses had a stutter, David had moral failings, Esther felt unprepared, Peter denied Christ—and yet He worked wonders through them once they surrendered and allowed His strength to shine through their weakness, your weakness does not disqualify you from the harvest; it qualifies you, because it proves that any good thing you do in serving others is rooted in God's power, not your own charm or skill, and that is a beautiful truth that sets you free from the pressure to impress. As you prepare to serve, think also of community, for harvesting is rarely a solo endeavor, gather with other believers who share your passion to shine God's love into the world, learn from their experiences, pray together, encourage one another, because when we serve in unity, our combined efforts brighten the world more than any single light could alone, and in this fellowship, you will find mentors who help you grow, peers who challenge you to keep aiming higher, and younger believers who look up to you and find courage in your example, this network of support can steady you when you face resistance, uplift you when discouragement hovers, and celebrate with you when you witness breakthroughs and transformed lives. And make no mistake, hardship and resistance will come, for the enemy of your soul does not want you to step boldly into your calling, he would prefer you remain timid, silent, and self-absorbed, afraid that you lack what it takes, or too busy chasing trivial pursuits to notice the spiritual poverty around you, part of preparing for the harvest is putting on the full armor of God—truth, righteousness, readiness from the gospel of peace, faith, salvation, and the Word of God—these are not just fancy terms, but essential tools that guard your heart and mind against discouragement, temptation, and deception, with this armor you can face challenges not with dread, but with a quiet confidence that God will guide and protect you, and that even if the path grows steep, He will provide strength for each step. Cultivate a humble spirit as you prepare, remembering that the harvest is not about winning glory for yourself, it's about directing souls toward the Lord, showing them the love you have received so abundantly, humility allows you to serve without expectation of praise, to love the unlovely, to approach brokenness without judgment, and to shine your light without needing center stage, it helps you accept correction when you err, and to be patient with slow progress, humility also reminds you that you are a servant, not a savior, Christ alone can truly heal and redeem, your role is to point to Him, to reflect His light, to be His hands and feet in a world that often struggles to recognize the divine footprints left by His presence, by staying humble, you keep your heart free from pride, which can distort your motives and weaken your testimony. As you prepare for the harvest, remember that joy can coexist with the seriousness of your task, serving others in God's name is not a grim duty, but a privilege, when you see a spark of hope ignite in someone's eyes because of a kind word you said, when a simple prayer you offer brings someone to tears of relief, when your steady presence in a crisis calms fear, you experience the joy of participating in God's redemptive work, and that joy fuels you, gives you courage to keep going, and encourages you to look beyond setbacks, because every soul touched by God's love through your obedience is a reminder that your labor is not in vain, you reap a harvest not of material gain, but of changed hearts, restored faith, and renewed spirits, treasures that moth and rust cannot destroy. Part of your preparation might involve surrendering certain comforts or rearranging your schedule so you can invest time and energy in serving others, perhaps it means learning new skills—listening more attentively, speaking encouragement more clearly, honing your ability to share Scripture in a way that resonates with different audiences—or maybe it means stepping out of your cultural bubble, engaging with people who differ from you in age, background, language, or worldview, this stretching can be uncomfortable, but it's necessary for broadening your capacity to love and understand, to adapt your approach so that the message of hope can pierce through preconceived notions and cultural barriers. Remember that everyone you meet has a story, a hidden complexity, a past that shaped their present fears and dreams, preparing for the harvest means learning to see beyond the surface: the rude customer at the store might be grieving a loss you know nothing about, the teenager acting tough might be terrified of failing, the quiet neighbor might be longing for someone to notice them, when you train your spiritual eyes to look with empathy, the harvest field takes on vibrant detail, you realize that these are not just random encounters, but divine appointments arranged by God to allow His love to flow through you into their hurting hearts, and this realization helps you push past discomfort and awkwardness, encouraging you to risk vulnerability, to ask meaningful questions, to offer help, to show patience, to share a piece of your own story if it will help them see they are not alone. Preparing your heart also involves prayer, continuous, heartfelt prayer, asking God for discernment to recognize the ripest moments to speak or act, praying for the wisdom to know when to be silent, and when to boldly proclaim truth, praying for the humility to see your own blind spots, the courage to address them, and the faith to believe that God can accomplish great things through your surrendered life, prayer knits your heart more tightly to God's purposes, so that your actions flow naturally from His leading rather than your personal agenda, it keeps you rooted in His presence, so you don't run ahead of Him or lag behind, and over time, prayer shapes you into a more sensitive instrument of His will, able to tune into the subtle signals that someone needs a gentle word or a helping hand at just the right moment. Think too about the strength that comes from recalling the promises of Scripture, verses that reassure you that God's Word does not return void, that He will never leave or forsake you, that He is with you always, even to the end of the age, these promises are not empty words, but anchors that hold you steady when fear tries to chase you off the field, when discouragement attempts to whisper that your service is pointless, the promises remind you that it is God who brings the harvest in His time, your role is to labor faithfully, trust Him wholeheartedly, and embrace whatever opportunities come your way. Consider also that preparing for the harvest means embracing a long-term perspective, you might not see immediate transformations, but let eternity shape your outlook, the seeds you plant through simple acts of kindness, truthful conversations, and heartfelt prayers may lay dormant until the right season, and when the rains of God's grace fall upon them, they may germinate and bear fruit that outlives your own time here, this eternal perspective frees you from despair when progress seems slow, because you know the final results belong to God, who orchestrates all things according to His wise plan, and one day, in the fullness of His kingdom, you will see how your small contributions joined with countless others to form a bountiful harvest that glorifies Him and enriches countless souls. Remember too that as you serve, you will learn from those you help, it's not a one-way street, God often uses these encounters to teach you lessons you didn't know you needed, to refine your character as you witness courage, resilience, or generosity in unexpected places, to broaden your understanding of His grace as you see it at work in lives very different from your own, these learnings deepen your humility and gratitude, making you more effective as a laborer in God's field, because your heart grows more open, your understanding more compassionate, and your sense of responsibility more profound, so serving others also serves you, nourishing your own faith journey and stretching your soul's capacity to love and trust. As you prepare for the harvest, embrace the fact that you are part of a divine team that spans centuries and continents, you follow in the footsteps of apostles, missionaries, and ordinary believers who dared to love in Jesus' name, who carried the Gospel to corners of the earth, who quietly served in soup kitchens, classrooms, hospital wards, prisons, homes, and neighborhoods, every act of service you offer links you to this great cloud of witnesses, reminding you that you are never alone, and that the God who empowered them empowers you today, He can turn your trembling into boldness, your hesitation into readiness, your ordinary words into instruments of healing. Finally, as you stand on the brink of this spiritual harvest, let your heart find comfort in the knowledge that God values your willing spirit more than polished perfection, He knows you better than you know yourself, He created you with a unique blend of talents, weaknesses, experiences, and passions, and He places you in situations where your particular light can shine most effectively, trust that He will guide you, step by step, revealing His will as you move forward in faith, and if you stumble, He will catch you, if you falter, He will strengthen you, if you grow weary, He will renew your energy, and as you continue to say yes to serving others in His name, your courage will ignite, your heart will glow brighter, and you will discover the deep, lasting joy that comes from partnering with God to make this world a bit kinder, a bit brighter, a bit closer to the vision He has for all humanity, that vision where every tear is dried, every wound healed, every captive set free, and every soul drawn into the warmth of His everlasting love, and in being ready for the harvest, you commit yourself to joining in that holy work, confident that the Lord who began a good work in you will carry it on, providing all you need to serve faithfully and fruitfully until the final day, when all harvests are gathered into His eternal barns of grace.

Day 26 - Lifted by Grace: Standing on Unshakable Ground

Imagine standing on the edge of a vast, open plain just before dawn, the sky painted with quiet blues and the faint promise of sunrise resting on the horizon, and as you take a breath, you feel a slight tremor beneath your feet, as though the ground itself remembers ages past and the countless lives that have walked upon it, and in that gentle movement, you realize you are not standing on empty air or shifting sand, but on unshakable ground—a foundation more reliable than any human promise, any worldly security, and the name of this foundation is grace, God's grace, a gift that lifts you above your fears and frailties, setting you firmly where you cannot be toppled by the storms that roar through life's unpredictable landscape, and in this moment, as soft light begins to break over distant hills, you feel your heart start to settle, your racing mind slow down, because standing upon grace means you are not balancing on your own limited strength, not trying to hold yourself steady with sheer willpower, but anchored in something far greater, something that roots you in love, purpose, and a truth that runs deeper than all your worries, failures, and regrets. Think about grace for a moment—this quiet, profound force that does not depend on you having everything figured out, or being perfect, or never making mistakes, rather, grace arises from the heart of God Himself, who knows every crease in your soul, every wound you carry, every doubt you whisper in the dark, and who chooses to love you fiercely, unconditionally, and endlessly anyway, it's a love that does not waver when you stumble, that does not shrink away when you sin, that does not vanish when you feel worthless, because it's not based on who you are, but on who God is: faithful, merciful, patient, and kind beyond measure, and this grace, poured out through the sacrifice of Christ, gives you the right to stand, not cowering in shame, but lifted high in the confidence that God is for you, not against you, and as you lean into this truth, you can feel courage begin to stir within you, a quiet flame that says you are not defined by your weaknesses, not imprisoned by your past, not doomed by your failings, because grace has set you free. To be lifted by grace means to understand that your worth is not measured by the standards this world so often uses—appearance, wealth, success, popularity—but by the price God paid to call you His own, He sent His Son to walk among broken humanity, to experience hunger and weariness, to weep at gravesides and feel the sting of betrayal, all to bridge the gulf between our flawed hearts and His holy presence, and on the cross, that act of perfect love, He overcame the chasm that separated you from true life, turning condemnation into forgiveness, despair into hope, emptiness into fullness, so now, standing on the foundation of grace, you see that you do not have to earn God's love by accomplishing great feats or impressing anyone, you begin to realize that He loved you before you even knew His name, that His affection for you runs deeper than the oceans, that He rejoices over you like a parent rejoices over a beloved child, and in that knowledge, you find a security that no human approval can match. Yet grace does not stop at assuring you of love and forgiveness—it also fuels your courage to serve the Lord wholeheartedly, think about it: if you know that nothing can separate you from God's love, that He will never abandon you, that your failures are met with compassion rather than scorn, would you not be bolder, more willing to step out in faith, more ready to attempt the works He sets before you without trembling at the thought of messing up? Grace frees you from the chains of fear, shame, and self-doubt, giving you wings to fly where before you only dared to crawl, now, when God nudges your heart to speak truth in a room that thrives on lies, to show kindness where bitterness reigns, to stand up for the weak when the strong crush them underfoot, you can say yes, confident that even if you stumble over your words or find resistance, God's grace holds you steady, like a hand under your elbow, helping you keep your balance, and by resting in grace, you draw a strength that surpasses your own, enabling you to serve in ways you never thought possible, to face challenges you once believed would break you, and to shine a light that darkness cannot dim. Consider how grace works in everyday struggles, when you wake up feeling overwhelmed by your responsibilities, by the problems you face, by the uncertainty of what tomorrow brings, grace whispers that God's mercies are new every morning, that each sunrise carries fresh possibilities for growth, healing, and understanding, when the pressure of performance and expectations weighs heavily on your heart, grace reminds you that God's approval is not a prize you must earn through frantic striving, but a gift He has already placed in your hands, when you look around and see a world fractured by division, suffering, and injustice, grace encourages you not to sink into despair, but to believe that your faithful obedience, your acts of compassion, your words of comfort can contribute to God's ongoing work of restoration, and when you are haunted by memories of past mistakes, times you hurt others or failed to do what was right, grace declares that those mistakes do not define your future, that repentance leads to forgiveness, that wounds can heal, that broken chapters in your story can be redeemed by the Author who never stops writing new pages of hope and purpose. Standing on unshakable ground does not mean you will never feel the earthquake of troubles beneath your feet, it means that no matter how fiercely the wind howls, how violently the storms rage, you remain anchored because God's grace cements your foundation to the Rock of ages, Jesus Christ, who overcame the worst darkness the world could wield, who emerged from the grave victorious over sin and death, ensuring that the final word in your life is not defeat, not emptiness, but life everlasting, so when trials arise, you can meet them with steady eyes and a calm heart, knowing that while pain and loss are real, they are not ultimate, while suffering may visit your doorstep, it cannot conquer you, for the grace you stand upon is forged in the eternal love and strength of the Almighty God, and He does not yield to any force that tries to tear you down. In practical terms, standing on grace empowers you to love others without the constant fear of rejection or the desperate need for their validation, because your sense of worth no longer hinges on human opinions, you are free to listen to their pain without making it about yourself, to celebrate their victories without envy, to forgive their offenses without carrying resentment, you are free to share what you have, your time, talents, resources, with open hands, confident that God will provide for you as you pour out for others, and when you see the difference your loving service makes—even a small difference like a single tear dried, a single hungry person fed, a single lonely soul feeling understood—you realize that grace has multiplied your efforts beyond what your limited abilities could accomplish alone, this realization deepens your humility, reminding you that this is all by God's doing, not your own cleverness or might. Reflect, too, on how grace transforms your inner dialogue, before standing on this unshakable ground, you may have lived tormented by self-criticism, plagued by endless what-ifs and if-onlys, but now, grace invites you to converse with yourself differently, instead of scolding yourself for every shortcoming, you learn to bring your failures to God, to let Him teach you from them, to accept His forgiveness and move forward rather than wallow in guilt, instead of dwelling on your inability to control the future, you learn to pray with trust, "Lord, You know what lies ahead, lead me according to Your perfect wisdom," and this shift in how you speak to your own soul releases anxiety, replacing it with peace, it allows you to become more patient with yourself and, consequently, more patient with others, extending the same grace you receive to them. Now, consider the times you felt paralyzed by fear—fear of change, fear of loss, fear of failure, fear of not measuring up—and see how grace offers a perfect antidote, if God loves you so deeply that He would redeem your life at the cost of His Son's blood, what can stand against you, what can truly harm your soul if you remain in Him, why should you tremble before human opinions, uncertain futures, or daunting tasks, God's grace assures you that even if you fall, He will catch you, even if you falter, He can correct your course, even if you face hard consequences, He will walk with you through them, strengthening your character and shaping you into the servant He designed you to be, with this assurance, you dare to try what seems impossible, to dream beyond your limited imagination, to say yes to assignments that feel too big for your shoulders, trusting that grace is the sling supporting your arm, the bridge over your fears, the promise that you do not labor in vain. Another treasure hidden in the grace you stand upon is the unity it fosters among believers, when each of us acknowledges that we stand only by grace, not by personal merit, then we cannot boast over one another or look down on someone else's struggles, grace levels the playing field, reminding us that we all need forgiveness, we all rely on God's generosity, we all find strength in His love, this understanding makes us more compassionate, more ready to help rather than judge, more eager to work together instead of competing, and as we unite under this shared grace, our combined efforts shine brighter, making it easier to serve the Lord as a body, supporting each other's weaknesses, celebrating each other's gifts, and moving forward as one force bringing hope to a hurting world. Consider that standing on grace means you can approach God's throne with confidence, not cowering as if He were a distant, harsh judge, but drawing near as a beloved child invited into the safety of the Father's arms, this nearness gives you access to heavenly resources—comfort for grief, wisdom for confusion, strength for weariness, courage for facing giants—and knowing that your relationship with God is secure, not based on changing moods or fragile worthiness, gives you the boldness to ask big questions in prayer, to believe for miracles of healing and reconciliation, to hold onto hope even in the bleakest conditions, because grace is the unshakable ground on which miracles become possible, where faith is not a desperate gamble, but a confident trust in God's character and promises. In a world that often seems to celebrate self-reliance, perfection, and endless achievement, standing on grace offers a refreshing alternative, it says you do not have to perform, you do not have to fight tooth and nail for approval, you do not have to keep score of rights and wrongs, of successes and failures, rather, you can rest in the reality that God has already given you a place in His family, a purpose in His kingdom, and a love that does not shift with your performance, this rest is not laziness, but a secure platform that allows you to serve with sincerity, pouring out your best efforts without burning out from striving to prove something, grace encourages diligence without desperation, excellence without vanity, generosity without fear of running dry, for if God did not spare His own Son, how will He not also graciously give you all you need to fulfill His call on your life. Consider the long road you may still have to travel, the dreams yet to be realized, the growth yet to occur, and know that standing on grace means God's patience accompanies you every step, you do not have to rush to become a finished product overnight, growth takes time, and grace covers the gaps while you learn, while you practice, while you stumble and get back up, this patience with yourself mirrors God's patience with you, inspiring patience toward others who lag behind your expectations, understanding that we are all on a journey, shaped by grace and led by the Holy Spirit at the pace our souls can bear, and this patience becomes another layer of courage, because you understand that you are not running a sprint, but a marathon, and God is not a stern referee waiting to disqualify you at the first misstep, but a loving coach cheering you on, knowing that the grace beneath your feet ensures you will not collapse, but finish the race set before you. As you allow these truths to sink into your heart, you begin to see evidence of God's grace all around you, in the sunrise that quietly proclaims new beginnings, in the kindness of a friend who encourages you when you feel low, in the memory of a past crisis that God carried you through, in the unexpected blessing that arrives just when you need it most, each of these moments is a reminder that grace is not just an abstract theological concept, it is the very air you breathe as a child of God, it is woven into your daily life, showing up in countless forms, fueling your courage not just to survive another day, but to serve boldly, to love fearlessly, to speak truth gently, and to embrace your calling with confidence. Over time, as you consistently choose to anchor your identity in grace rather than your achievements, you will find your heart expanding, your vision broadening, you will no longer be hemmed in by your past or intimidated by the future, because grace teaches you that you are safe in God's hands, that He holds all timelines and outcomes, that His love does not expire, and that He can use you—yes, you, with all your imperfections and uncertainties—to advance His kingdom of light in a world hungry for meaning, justice, and compassion. And as you serve, as you pour out the grace you have received, you create ripples of goodness that touch others, who may then find their own hearts turning toward God, reaching for the same grace that steadies your soul, and in this chain reaction, God's glory shines brighter, drawing more and more people into the transformative power of His love. So stand strong on this unshakable ground, let your feet be sure, your heart serene, your mind clear, and your spirit ready, let grace lift you above the clamor of fear and doubt, and give you the courage to say yes when God calls you to a task you feel is too big, to speak hope into a friend's despair, to stand up for the oppressed, to forgive when it hurts, to keep loving even when love is not returned, remember that His grace is enough for you, that in your weakness His strength is made perfect, and that by relying on grace, not only do you remain standing, but you learn to dance through life's storms, to sing in its deserts, and to serve the Lord with a boldness born from knowing you cannot fall off the firm foundation He has given you, and as you carry this message into the world, your life becomes a living testimony that even in uncertain times, there is a safe place to stand, a ground that does not quake, a love that does not fail, a grace that always lifts you up, giving you courage to fulfill your calling and bring God's light into every place you tread.

Day 27 - A Flame That Spreads: Inspiring Courage in Others

Imagine yourself as a single, small candle flame shining in a darkened room, flickering softly yet steadily, casting a circle of gentle light on faces that once seemed hidden in shadow, and as you stand there, heart pounding with the quiet courage God has placed within you, you begin to notice something remarkable: others are leaning in, drawn to the warmth and glow you offer, curious, hopeful, and longing to understand how your light endures against the darkness pressing close at hand, they see in you a spark of faith that does not falter, a quiet determination that dares to trust in the Lord's promises even when uncertainty howls like a distant wind, and the more they watch, the more they start to believe that perhaps they, too, can carry such a flame within their hearts, that courage is not reserved for extraordinary heroes or distant saints, but can find a home in their own trembling souls; this is how a single flame spreads: by inspiring others to stand firm, to lift their eyes beyond fear's grasp, and to discover that beneath all the noise and doubt lies a steady source of strength and love that never runs dry, for courage, when fueled by faith in God, is contagious, radiating outward in gentle waves until even those who once felt too timid or broken to hope find themselves warming their hands at the fire of your witness, and before long, one candle becomes two, then three, then a dozen, then a hundred, each new flame ignited by another soul who dared to believe that they, too, could reflect God's goodness, and as the brightness grows, you see how once-dim corners of the world begin to glow with new possibilities: families learning to speak kindness instead of anger, schools brimming with respect and empathy, workplaces shaped by integrity rather than greed, communities determined to care for the needy rather than ignore them, and all because your initial flame, though small, was enough to awaken courage in another heart, to show that the Lord's strength can flow through any willing vessel, no matter how fragile or uncertain it feels; the beauty of this spreading flame is that it does not diminish when shared, on the contrary, the more people catch this spark of courage, the brighter the light becomes, and the more hope and love fill the spaces once haunted by despair, like a chain reaction, each believer touched by your example turns around and encourages someone else—maybe a friend weighed down by grief, a neighbor battling loneliness, a young person confused about their purpose, or an elder losing sight of their worth—and as they pass along the flame, a tapestry of faith, hope, and love begins to blanket the landscape, reminding everyone that the darkness was never as strong as it pretended to be, that God's light cannot be caged by fear or crushed by doubt, but shines even brighter when we stand together; yet this spreading of courage is not accomplished by loud speeches or flashy gestures alone, often it is the quiet acts of daily faithfulness that kindle someone else's fire: the gentle smile you offer a stranger, the meal you bring to a family in need, the patient ear you lend to someone who feels unheard, the prayer you whisper at dawn for those you may never meet, each small deed, done in obedience to God's call to love and serve, adds a spark that might just be what another soul needs to find their own courage, and the remarkable truth is that you rarely see the full impact of these moments, how that stranger's day was changed for the better, how that family felt seen and valued, how the person who unburdened their heart to you discovered fresh hope because you listened without judgment, yet God sees it all, weaving these acts into His grand design, turning tiny sparks into a widening blaze of faith that envelops more hearts than you can count; as you embrace your role as a carrier of courage, remember that the strength you share is not your own, it comes from the Lord who pours His love into you day by day, enabling you to face your own trials while still having room to uplift others, think of a tree with deep roots drawing water from an unseen stream—no matter the drought above ground, the tree remains green, producing fruit that nourishes those around it, so too, by staying close to God—studying His Word, praying for guidance, worshiping Him with a thankful heart—you keep your roots sunk deep into His grace, ensuring that even in tough seasons, even when your personal battles rage, you can still provide comfort, truth, and courage to others, because your ability to inspire does not depend on your perfection, but on your willingness to let God's grace shine through your cracks, and in fact, your vulnerabilities and past hardships can become bridges of empathy, showing others that you understand their pain, that you've walked through valleys of doubt and despair and emerged stronger not by your own power, but by God's mercy and faithfulness.

As more souls catch the flame of courage, this collective light can transform entire communities, forging bonds of trust and cooperation where there was once suspicion and selfishness, and when a critical mass of hearts begins to live out their faith boldly—treating enemies with compassion, forgiving old wounds, standing up for what is just, speaking encouragement in spaces drowned by negativity—the culture shifts, and suddenly what seemed impossible before now appears doable, for courage thrives on connection, and as each individual brings their light to the circle, the darkness finds fewer places to hide, ironically, sometimes it takes only one person to break the ice, to be the first to say "I'm sorry," or "I believe in you," or "Let's try," to release a cascade of me-too moments, as others realize they are not alone in wanting something better, a more loving, Christ-centered environment; in this way, your courage becomes a torch passed hand to hand, heart to heart, crossing boundaries of age, race, background, and status, reminding everyone that beneath our differences we share a common longing for purpose, community, and a glimpse of eternity's light, and as you see this chain reaction unfold, you discover that your initial step of faith, your initial refusal to surrender to despair, was never just about you, it was about the countless souls God intended to reach through your example, your story, your willingness to say yes when He prompted you to act, even in small ways, whether that meant offering a quiet prayer with a colleague trembling before a difficult task, or standing up for a classmate being bullied, or gently telling someone trapped in guilt that Christ's forgiveness is real and within their grasp, each courageous choice shining as a beacon for others to follow.

Over time, as you lean into this calling, you find that the courage you inspire in others also comes back to strengthen you, their stories of faith ignited by your influence become a wellspring of encouragement for you when your flame flickers low, it's as if God designed this exchange of courage to be mutual, so that we uplift each other in cycles of giving and receiving, and this creates a resilient community, a circle of believers whose combined faith stands firm against the pressures of a world that scoffs at grace and denies the power of love, and within this circle, you learn that igniting courage is not about imposing your will on others or forcing them to believe, it's about living authentically, letting the truth of God's goodness shine through your words and deeds so that others can freely choose to embrace that light, to pick up the flame and carry it forward in their own unique way.

Reflect on how Jesus Himself lit this flame in His followers, turning a group of unsure, flawed individuals into apostles who carried the Gospel across nations and generations, Christ's example of humility, compassion, bravery in facing the cross, and unwavering commitment to God's mission set a pattern that continues today, and if the flame of courage that was kindled in the early church could spread across centuries, reaching even our time, igniting hearts around the globe, then surely the sparks you send forth can also travel far beyond what you see, maybe a young person inspired by your gentle mentorship grows up to become a leader who influences thousands, or maybe a desperate soul restored by your simple kindness becomes a mentor to others in pain, the point is that courage moves through people like a current, unpredictable and unstoppable, guided by the Holy Spirit who orchestrates these encounters, ensuring that no genuine act of faith is ever wasted.

This flame that spreads is not a grim, forced effort, but a joyful, natural unfolding of God's grace in human relationships, and the more you trust that God can work through your limitations, the more you see surprising results—hearts softening, barriers falling, tears giving way to laughter, and people discovering that they, too, can serve the Lord with courage, even if they once believed they had nothing to offer, perhaps in your personal struggle you overcame shame to share your testimony, and that testimony gave someone else the courage to face their own demons, perhaps your quiet persistence in doing good works day after day, unnoticed by most, showed someone that faithfulness does matter, that not all beauty in the world goes unseen by God, and that realization lit a spark in their heart, pushing them to start their own ministry of encouragement, compassion, or hospitality.

Inspiring courage in others does not require you to present yourself as a mighty warrior, never admitting fear or doubt, on the contrary, honesty about your struggles can be even more inspiring, let others see that courage does not mean feeling no fear, but acting in faith despite the fear, let them know that you have days of weariness, moments where you wondered if God was listening, seasons where your flame dimmed and you needed others to help it burn bright again, this vulnerability helps people understand that courage is accessible, that it's not reserved for a select few, that it can grow in any heart that surrenders to God's guidance, and in this way, your openness becomes a bridge that invites others to join you in walking the path of faith, hand in hand, light meeting light, until darkness is held back by a collective glow that neither scorn nor hardship can extinguish.

As your influence widens, you may never fully know the extent of what God accomplishes through the flames you spark in others, and that's okay, faith teaches you to be content with playing your part, trusting the One who sees the whole picture, who knows exactly where each spark must land to ignite another fire of courage, and on difficult days, when progress seems slow or invisible, remember that seeds planted under the soil remain unseen for a time, but eventually break the surface, emerging as green shoots that promise future fruit, similarly, a kind word you spoke, a piece of advice rooted in Scripture, a prayer offered in secret, may lie dormant in a person's heart until their circumstances shift, their walls lower, and the water of God's grace finally encourages that seed to sprout, and what a joy it will be, perhaps in eternity, to discover how many flames you helped kindle with your obedience, how many hearts found courage because you dared to reflect Christ in a moment that seemed ordinary to you.

Another essential ingredient in this process is patience, because inspiring courage is rarely an instant event, it's more like a gentle, ongoing process that requires you to stick around, to remain a steady presence in people's lives rather than darting in and out, consistency builds trust, and trust gives you a platform to share the truth that courage does not have to crumble under pressure, that the Lord's promises hold firm through storms, by choosing to be there for others, showing up when they are sick, discouraged, confused, or questioning their purpose, you demonstrate that your light is not a flickering illusion, but something lasting, fueled by the eternal flame of God's love, and as they learn to rely on that light, they realize they can carry it themselves, igniting new sparks of courage in people they know, people who might never cross your own path.

Embracing the call to inspire courage in others also means stepping outside your comfort zone, talking to those who might initially resist or misunderstand your intentions, offering patience and kindness in hostile environments, maintaining integrity when shortcuts could earn quick rewards, all these choices are easier said than done, but remember that you are not alone—God's Spirit empowers you, the prayers of fellow believers uphold you, and the stories of faithful servants throughout history encourage you to keep pressing on, no matter how thick the shadows grow, you become part of a long lineage of Christ-followers who dared to believe that the smallest spark can start a mighty fire of renewal, that a whisper of encouragement can echo through generations to come.

As this vision of spreading courage takes root in your soul, you realize that your life's significance is not determined by how famous you become, or how many personal goals you achieve, but by how faithfully you reflect Christ's light and help others do the same, and at the end of your journey, when you look back on the path you've walked, you will find the greatest satisfaction not in earthly honors or possessions, but in the quiet knowledge that you played a part in igniting courage in someone's heart, in lifting their eyes toward heaven, in helping them discover that God's strength can flow through their veins, enabling them to face challenges with hope rather than despair, through your example, they learned to say "yes" to God's nudges, to trust when fear beckoned them to flee, to love when hate pressed them to harm, to believe when cynicism urged them to doubt.

In these ways, you become a catalyst for courage, a humble carrier of fire that can warm cold hearts, guide lost travelers, and illuminate hidden potential, and as the flame spreads outward, radiating from one life to another, you witness how simple faithfulness multiplies, how one spark becomes two, two become four, and soon countless flames dance in the spiritual night, lighting communities, healing wounds, bridging divides, your role might feel small at times, but never doubt that God magnifies what you offer, turning your modest acts of obedience into a beacon that others can follow, so stand tall, even if your knees tremble a bit, and let your light shine, for in doing so you not only honor the God who saved you, but you embolden many weary souls to find their voice, raise their heads, and join in a chorus of faith too powerful for darkness to silence.

This is the beauty of inspiring courage in others: that you step beyond the confines of your own fears and ambitions, and serve a purpose greater than yourself, you become part of a movement that stretches across continents and centuries, connecting you to believers past and future who share the same mission, each playing a role in reflecting Christ's character to a hurting world, and in this grand tapestry, your courage is a single thread weaving colors of hope, trust, and renewal into the fabric of human experience, leaving behind a legacy that transcends your individual story, a legacy of changed lives, enlivened hearts, and faith that thrives under any sky.

So as you find yourself in a moment of choice—do you stay silent or speak hope, do you ignore a need or step forward to help, do you give up or persevere—remember that your courage has the power to start a chain reaction of light, let the love of Christ fill your heart and overflow in your actions, let His words guide your tongue and His compassion fill your hands, let His strength steady your resolve, and let His joy keep you going even when progress seems slow, for the flame you carry is not yours alone, it's a reflection of His eternal flame, shining through your imperfect life to ignite courage in countless others who yearn for a sign that they, too, can stand firm in faith and hope.

Day 28 - Redeemed for a Purpose: Embracing Your Kingdom Role

Imagine a distant, quiet morning where the first rays of sunlight gently touch the earth, revealing rolling hills, quiet streams, and a silent promise that something beautiful lies ahead, and in that hushed moment, before the busy world stirs awake, consider this truth: you have been redeemed for a purpose, set free from past chains and given a calling that runs deeper than any dream you once held for yourself, and as you stand there at the edge of possibility, you realize that your life is not a random series of events, not a meaningless collection of memories, but a carefully woven story in which God, the Author of all creation, has penned a special role for you, long before you knew Him, He knew you, long before you stumbled in darkness, He had a plan to bring you into His marvelous light, and now, here you are, heart pulsing with renewed hope, soul cleansed by the sacrifice of Christ, mind stirring with questions about what to do next, what it means to embrace your kingdom role, because being redeemed does not simply mean being saved from sin, it also means being saved for something, for a task or mission that only you, with your unique blend of personality, talents, wounds healed by grace, and lessons learned along the path, can fulfill, and though you may feel unsure or unworthy, remember that God is never surprised by your weaknesses, never dismayed by your doubts, never caught off guard by your inexperience, He called you knowing exactly who you are, and it's His strength, not your own, that will empower you to step into this role with courage and conviction. To embrace your kingdom role, first understand that God's purposes are rich and varied, the kingdom of God is not limited to church buildings or formal ministries, but spreads through every avenue of life, shining wherever believers choose to stand as living testimonies of His love, maybe your role involves nurturing children who need stable, loving guidance in a world often lacking it, or supporting a friend battling depression with patience and understanding, or bringing integrity into a workplace fraught with compromise, or speaking truth kindly where lies run rampant, or offering hospitality to those who feel isolated and forgotten, or using your creativity to craft stories, music, or art that point hearts toward hope, or serving the poor and marginalized who live in the shadows of society's attention—whatever your calling, be assured that it is important, that it has eternal weight, that it can influence countless lives as God weaves your efforts into His master plan. Don't waste time comparing yourself to others, thinking that maybe your role is too small, too simple, too hidden, for in the kingdom of God, greatness is measured not by human scales, but by faithfulness, humility, and love, a quiet gesture of kindness performed faithfully over years can be more powerful than a thousand loud speeches spoken without genuine compassion, the kingdom role you embrace might never earn you headlines or awards, but it can still shake spiritual foundations, break cycles of despair, and plant seeds of faith that bloom long after you are gone, and as you slowly accept this truth, something stirs within you—a growing courage, a sense that you were not just redeemed to wait passively for heaven, but to bring a taste of heaven's reality into the here and now, to show others that God's grace is not a distant idea, but a living force that transforms hearts, relationships, communities, and futures. To fully embrace your role, you must let go of the notion that you must be perfect before you begin, remember the countless people God used in Scripture who had flawed histories, who carried doubts, who made mistakes but kept turning back to Him, Moses stumbled over words, yet led a nation to freedom, Ruth was a foreigner and a widow, yet became part of Jesus' lineage, Peter denied Christ and still was chosen to shepherd the early church, these examples tell you that your past does not disqualify you, your scars do not prevent you from serving, in fact, they might even equip you to reach those who share similar wounds, to say "I understand, I've been there, and God brought me through," turning your pain into a source of empathy and strength, each shortcoming you surrender to God, each fear you confess, each failure you learn from can shape you into a more compassionate, wise, and effective servant of His kingdom, and this perspective can fan the spark of courage in your heart into a steady flame, reminding you that perfection is not required—just willingness, obedience, and trust. As you step into your role, cultivate a heart that listens for God's voice, learn to slow down, to pray not only to speak your requests but to hear His gentle guidance in return, the Holy Spirit will nudge you when an opportunity arises to offer help, when a conversation could benefit from a word of truth, when a silent act of generosity is needed, when a stand must be taken against injustice, being sensitive to these promptings ensures that your kingdom service does not become mechanical or forced, but remains fresh, authentic, and Spirit-led, this alignment with God's heart keeps your courage fueled, because you know you're not acting on random impulses, but following divine invitations that bring His grace into specific situations, and even when the path is unclear, you trust that God can open doors no one can shut, provide resources you never knew existed, and connect you with people whose lives you can impact for good. Another aspect of embracing your kingdom role involves patience and perseverance, sometimes God's purposes unfold slowly, you may plant seeds of truth and kindness that seem to vanish into hard soil, but don't lose heart—our God is a master gardener who knows the right season for growth, you might mentor a youth who seems distant and uninterested, only to discover years later that your steady presence helped them trust in God when adulthood tested their faith, you might advocate for a righteous cause that faces resistance, yet over time, as more voices join and values shift, your early efforts prove foundational to lasting change, perseverance means refusing to quit when results are not immediate, trusting that God is at work behind the scenes, watering seeds in ways you cannot see, and as you remain faithful, you find that patience can unlock deeper courage within you, the courage to keep loving when love is not returned, to keep serving when gratitude is scarce, to keep speaking hope when despair feels overwhelming, because you know the outcome rests not in your hands, but in God's all-knowing, all-loving will. Don't forget that embracing your kingdom role also means being part of a larger community of believers, each with their own callings and gifts, you are not asked to change the world alone, but to join others who share the same passion for reflecting Christ's nature, this fellowship can encourage you, teach you, challenge you, and help you grow, so seek out people who pray with you, who remind you of God's promises, who celebrate your successes and support you in trials, and offer the same to them, because serving in isolation can strain your courage, while standing shoulder to shoulder with fellow workers of grace strengthens your resolve, pooling your talents and resources to accomplish more than any single individual could, and together, you form a mosaic of God's love—each piece different, but essential to the beautiful whole.

Remember, too, that courage does not always appear as dramatic heroism, often, it's found in quiet consistency, in small acts repeated over time that add up to monumental impact, a teacher who year after year cares for each student as a cherished soul created by God, shaping minds and hearts in ways that ripple throughout lives, a healthcare worker who chooses compassion over cynicism in a system strained by demands, giving patients not only treatments but dignity, a business owner who prioritizes honesty and fairness over cutting corners, showing employees that ethics matter, a neighbor who befriends the lonely elderly man next door, reminding him that he is seen and valued, these everyday acts, done with an awareness that you are serving a bigger purpose—God's kingdom—ignite courage in subtle yet profound ways, proving that grand gestures aren't the only way to reflect Christ, that His love shines just as brightly through consistent faithfulness in ordinary moments. As you continue learning what it means to be redeemed for a purpose, you may face internal battles—feelings of inadequacy, voices telling you that others are more talented, that your gifts are too small to matter, but remember that God delights in using the ordinary to accomplish the extraordinary, the Bible overflows with stories of people who felt unqualified, yet God's strength made their humble offerings bloom into something remarkable, let the truth of His sovereignty settle into your heart, silencing the lie that you must be flawless or spectacular by human standards to be useful, He chose you knowing your limitations, and He can magnify what you offer, multiplying the impact of even your simplest kindness. Consider how your unique story fits into God's narrative: the family you grew up in, the hardships you overcame, the lessons learned from failures, the interests and talents that set you apart, none of these are random, each can be woven into your kingdom service, enabling you to connect with certain people, solve certain problems, or carry out certain tasks that might remain undone if not for you, and as you embrace this truth, courage grows, because you realize you are not trying to force yourself into a role that doesn't fit, but discovering the role God prepared you for long before you realized it, the more you lean into this identity, the more natural serving becomes, like stepping into shoes custom-made for you, shoes that allow you to walk confidently into your mission field, knowing that you were designed for this, that His grace covers your every step, and that you're living out your redemption as it was always meant to be lived—fruitfully, purposefully, and joyously. Embracing your kingdom role also means understanding that challenges will come—opposition, setbacks, misunderstandings, maybe even persecution in some forms—but do not let these discourage you, Jesus Himself warned that following Him would not be easy, yet He also promised that He overcame the world, and by resting in His victory, you find the courage to face obstacles not with despair, but with resilience, trusting that God can use even difficulties to refine your character, sharpen your message, and deepen your dependence on Him, sometimes hardships serve as catalysts, pushing you to innovate, to pray more fervently, to seek greater unity with fellow believers, or to rely on God's strength in ways you never would have otherwise, and each time you overcome an obstacle through His help, your courage is renewed, your faith solidified, and your story enriched with testimonies of His faithfulness. As you live out your calling, never lose sight of the heart behind it: your role in God's kingdom is not about earning His favor—He already granted that through Christ's sacrifice—it's about expressing gratitude for your redemption, about saying, "You saved me, Lord, you lifted me from darkness into light, and now I want to shine that light for others, to show them the way back to You," this heart posture keeps your motives pure, protecting you from the traps of pride or selfish ambition, when you serve with humility, remembering that everything you have and are comes from Him, your actions ring true with sincerity and love, making them irresistible beacons to those who long for meaning, comfort, and guidance. In a world that often seems adrift, where many voices clamor for attention, offering empty promises or shallow solutions, your kingdom role stands out as something rooted in eternal truth, people hungry for authenticity will be drawn to the genuine hope you carry, to the message of a Savior who redeems lives and gives them lasting purpose, by living fully in your God-given role, you offer a contrast to the fleeting pursuits and hollow achievements that so often leave people feeling empty, you present a vision of life that matters, not because of your personal greatness, but because you serve a great God who works through you, accomplishing things that matter for eternity rather than just for a fleeting moment. Over time, you'll see fruit—perhaps a soul that finds new faith after watching you persist in kindness despite difficulties, a broken relationship mended because you chose forgiveness, a community project that uplifts the poor and lonely because you rallied others around God's vision of compassion, or even subtle shifts in the hearts of those who once laughed at your convictions, now softened by the consistent warmth of your love and example—and while you know ultimate results lie in God's hands, witnessing even a glimpse of these transformations will fuel your courage further, reminding you why your efforts matter. And so, redeemed for a purpose, you stand at the threshold of each new day with a heart fueled by courage, prepared to pour yourself out in service, to walk paths that may lead through difficulty but yield abundant spiritual harvest, knowing that you are not alone—God goes before you, the Spirit guides within you, and fellow believers walk beside you—and your soul sings with the understanding that nothing given in obedience to Christ is ever wasted, each prayer whispered, each kind gesture, each word of encouragement contributes to the grand tapestry of God's kingdom being woven across the world, you are part of something far greater than yourself, invited by the King of kings to play a part in His redemptive story, and this knowledge sets your heart on fire, filling you with the courage to keep pressing forward no matter what challenges arise. As you embrace your kingdom role, let gratitude flood your soul, remembering who you once were and how God redeemed you, let gratitude inspire you to give generously, love boldly, forgive freely, and persevere bravely, for gratitude and courage walk hand in hand—gratefulness for God's grace lifts your eyes beyond your limitations, fueling a confidence that He who began a good work in you will bring it to completion, and as your courage grows, you find yourself more willing to try new forms of service, to reach out to new groups of people, to step into areas of need you once avoided, trusting that the One who called you is faithful and will equip you at each step. Consider also that your kingdom role is not static—it may evolve as seasons change, as you grow and learn, God might lead you to unexpected places, shifting your focus to meet new needs, guide new souls, or address new issues that arise in a changing world, this flexibility requires courage as well, the willingness to let go of old, comfortable patterns and embrace fresh assignments, trusting that if God opens a door, it leads somewhere significant, and if He closes one, it is for your good and His greater purpose, this dynamic relationship with your calling keeps your faith alive and active, forging an adventurous spirit that stands firm through transitions. And after you have walked this journey of embracing your kingdom role, after you have poured out your efforts to serve the Lord, leaving behind a trail of seeds planted, hearts encouraged, and souls touched, you will look back and understand something profound: that your redemption was never just about your own spiritual safety, it was also about your impact on others, about multiplying the grace you received so that countless others could taste it too, you have become a conduit through which God's love flows, a bridge that connects people to the Christ who redeems and restores, and nothing can match the joy of knowing your life contributed to eternal outcomes, to shining light in dark corners, to lifting burdens off weary shoulders, to turning doubts into faith and strangers into brothers and sisters under God's compassionate gaze. This is what it means to be redeemed for a purpose, to embrace the kingdom role God has set before you with courage and conviction, to understand that your life story, with all its ups and downs, has been crafted for a reason, and by stepping boldly into the calling He placed in your heart, you not only honor Him, but unlock within yourself a wellspring of strength, resilience, and passion you never knew you had, ultimately discovering that courage was always there, waiting to be stirred to life by the knowledge that you matter to God's plan, that He trusts you with a mission no one else can fulfill quite like you, and that your redeemed life is not a lonely island, but a vital piece in the grand mosaic of His kingdom, shining forth for all to see.

Day 29 - In the Shadow of His Wings: Security in God's Presence

Imagine standing at the edge of a quiet forest at dusk, the air soft around you, the distant rustle of leaves like a gentle whisper reminding you that you're never truly alone, and as the sky shifts from blue to deep purple, a hush settles over all creation, as though the world itself is preparing to rest safely under the watchful gaze of its Maker, and here, at this threshold between light and darkness, you remember the ancient promise that you can find refuge in the shadow of God's wings, a holy hiding place where no threat can truly reach you, where the fears that loom large in your mind shrink to manageable size, and where you feel your heart steadying, breathing slower, each beat echoing a quiet truth: you are safe, not because circumstances have suddenly improved or because you've found the solution to every problem, but because you have chosen to step closer to the Lord who protects, who cares, who loves you beyond measure, and who never leaves your side; under His wings, a beautiful image taken from Scripture, you can picture a majestic eagle sheltering its young, covering them from the cold rain, from harsh winds, from the piercing eyes of predators, and just as those tiny birds trust without question in the strength and warmth of their mother's wings, so can you trust in God's presence to shield you against the storms life sends, to hide you from dangers seen and unseen, to comfort you when you tremble with uncertainty, and it's not a promise that no difficulties will come—trials still roll through like thunderclouds—but rather that they cannot ultimately destroy you, that their power is limited by the One who holds all power in His hands. In the shadow of His wings, you discover a security that no human plan, no locked door, no carefully built wall can provide, it's a spiritual security rooted in the character of God Himself: faithful, unwavering, always true to His promises, always ready to rescue when you call, and in these moments, as you lean into that reality, you realize that courage grows naturally when you know you are cherished and protected, like a young child venturing out to explore the world because they know their loving parent is close by, able to catch them if they stumble, able to banish whatever monsters lurk in their imagination; this courage is not the absence of fear, but the ability to move forward despite it, to do what's right even when your heart pounds, to speak truth in love even when your voice shakes, to stand up for justice even when it's unpopular, and to choose love over hate even when anger tempts you—because you know God has you covered, that He will not abandon you to face life's battles alone. Consider how often you've tried to handle everything by yourself, convinced that it's all on your shoulders, that you must be strong and self-sufficient, that admitting weakness is a flaw, yet this protective shadow, God's gentle canopy, invites you to exhale, to let go of the crushing weight of self-reliance, and to rest in the knowledge that your worth does not hinge on your performance, that your hope does not rise or fall based on your successes or failures, that your identity is not defined by what others say or what you achieve, but by who God says you are—His beloved child, a precious soul He formed and redeemed, one He has drawn near, whispering, "Do not fear, for I am with you," and in the glow of that assurance, you gain the freedom to attempt great things for the Lord, to dare bold acts of compassion, to love when it's risky, to serve when it's inconvenient, and to persevere when challenges seem endless, all because you're no longer depending solely on your limited strength, but on the limitless might of a God whose wings span the heavens, whose presence cannot be thwarted, and whose love for you runs deeper than the ocean's floor. Under these wings, you also find a place to heal from past hurts, to let God's peace seep into old wounds that still ache, to release bitter memories you've clung to like heavy stones tied to your soul, and as you confess your pain and confusion, God does not recoil, He does not say you're too broken to belong, instead, He gathers you closer, as a hen gathers her chicks, making it clear that in His family, the wounded are tended, the weary find rest, and the fearful are taught to sing again, when you realize you can heal in His presence, you start to see that your past does not have to define your future, that you can emerge from dark seasons with renewed strength and a heart softened toward others who suffer, and by offering up your scars to God, you gain empathy, understanding that many around you are struggling, too, searching for a safe place, for some evidence that hope is not a childish dream but a living reality they can hold onto. The shadow of His wings is not a narrow space reserved for a few elite believers—no, it's an open invitation extended to all who hunger for belonging, all who thirst for meaning, all who know that the world's solutions fail to calm the deepest anxieties, you find yourself in a shelter where humility takes the place of pride, where fear dissipates before love's gentle warmth, where old hostilities melt into forgiveness, and where individuals who once stood apart draw near each other because they share a common refuge, a common Protector, this unity born under God's wings creates a powerful bond, showing that we are not solitary soldiers but a united family, each flame of faith brightening the collective glow, each pair of hands joining in the work of caring for the poor, comforting the mourning, welcoming the stranger, and sharing the good news that God's grace is freely given, not earned. From this perspective, serving the Lord transforms from a grim duty into a joyful privilege, for when you stand under His wings, you see that you cannot outgive God, that every ounce of energy poured into His kingdom returns as inner growth, deeper friendships, and a richer, more purposeful life, you serve not to earn His approval, because you already have it, not to impress others, because human applause fades like the echo of a distant shout, but out of gratitude for the One who shields you from the worst storms, who lifts you when you fall, who comforts you when tears blur your vision, and in that grateful service, courage sparks into a flame that brightens dark corners of the world, that sets off a chain reaction of kindness and truth, reaching people you may never meet, places you may never step foot, because the ripples of godly love spread far beyond what we can measure. It's important to remember that staying under the shelter of God's wings requires a daily choice: to tune your heart to His voice rather than the world's frantic demands, to carve out time in silence to listen, to remember you're held by an unshakable presence, to hold tightly to Scripture as a map guiding your steps, to let prayer be your breath of life, inhaling hope and exhaling worries, these disciplines help you remain close, ensuring that your courage is continuously replenished, that you don't run dry trying to serve in your own strength, that you remain connected to the source of all comfort and power, and when the weight of life presses hard, when doubts try to crowd your mind, returning to that quiet communion under His wings renews your perspective, showing that what felt insurmountable is tiny compared to God's greatness, reminding you that nothing escapes His notice, that He orchestrates the details even when chaos seems to reign. Another wonder of dwelling under God's wings is discovering that what once seemed like formidable obstacles to faith—your flaws, insecurities, and fears—can be transformed into conduits of grace, for when you present these vulnerabilities honestly to God, He can use them to connect you with others who struggle in similar ways, enabling you to say, "I understand, I've been there, and God's kindness carried me through," you become a living testimony that weakness, when surrendered to divine love, can become a door through which encouragement flows, this realization humbles you, removing the pressure to appear strong all the time, and instead allowing authenticity, which in turn strengthens the courage of those who see your example and realize they can also trust God with their hidden wounds. Standing under God's wings also brings clarity about your identity—no longer defined by what you accomplish, what people say, or the ups and downs of fate, but by the One who covers you with His feathers and calls you beloved, this stable identity gives you the resilience to handle criticism, failure, or disappointment without losing your sense of worth, you know that nothing can snatch you from God's protective embrace, that no amount of misunderstanding or rejection can separate you from His affection, and this knowledge liberates you to take bold steps of obedience, to attempt what seems risky for the sake of love and truth, because your anchor runs deeper than public opinion or personal comfort, your anchor rests in the eternal commitment of a God who will not let you go. When you realize how secure you are in God's presence, courage becomes not an elusive quality you must conjure up, but a natural outflow of living in the light of His promises, you find courage to stand up for the vulnerable, to speak kindly when others mock, to serve sacrificially without keeping score, and to stand firm in your convictions even when it costs you something, because you know you stand on a foundation that cannot crack, under wings that do not tire, protected by a love that conquers all. This newfound security also reframes how you view life's uncertainties, instead of dreading the unknown or wrestling with anxiety about what tomorrow may bring, you can rest in the assurance that your heavenly Father sees the future as clearly as you see the present, that He has a plan and will guide your steps if you follow His lead, in that trust, you can approach change not as a threat, but as an adventure in God's unfolding story, you can walk into new seasons—be it a career shift, a relocation, or a new phase of parenthood or ministry—with the calm certainty that God's wings still cast their protective shadow over you, that no shift in circumstances can snatch you from His hand. As your heart settles into this reality, you find that you have more emotional space to care for others, you're not so consumed with your own survival, because you know God handles that, so you can turn outward, noticing who is hurting or lost, who needs a listening ear or a shoulder to lean on, who might be longing for the slightest sign that hope still exists, and because you stand on unshakable ground, you can remain steady even as you reach out to help someone else stand, trusting that God, who stabilizes you, will also give you what you need to support them, and seeing others find peace, understanding, or strength through the comfort you share deepens your appreciation for God's design, how He uses each of us as instruments of His mercy in a vast, interwoven pattern of love. Over time, as you continue dwelling in God's presence, you'll look back and realize how far you've come, perhaps you once trembled at the thought of public speaking, but now you find yourself reassuring a group of anxious teens that they are not alone, or maybe you once avoided conflict at all costs, but now you can gently confront wrongdoing with grace and confidence, maybe you once felt helpless amid widespread injustice, but now you invest in causes that bring relief and reform, all because you know your security does not lie in earthly outcomes, but in God's unwavering faithfulness, and in this journey, you see that courage fueled by God's presence does more than strengthen you for a moment, it reshapes who you are, making you braver, kinder, more resilient, and more Christ-like day by day. Throughout this process, you become aware that what started as a personal comfort—hiding beneath the wings of the Almighty—has grown into a source of strength you can share with others, by radiating the peace you've found, you invite others to discover the same refuge, by testifying that you've found unshakable ground in a shaky world, you encourage them to seek God's protective embrace, your story, once marred by anxiety or insecurity, now becomes a beacon of hope that faith is possible, that trust is reasonable, and that living with courage does not mean the absence of trials, but their transformation into stepping stones toward greater intimacy with God and a more profound impact on the world around you. The image of standing under God's wings also reminds you that He remains bigger than any threat you face, more majestic than any power that tries to intimidate you, and when intimidation looms—be it from cultural pressures, from voices mocking your faith, from fears within your own mind—you can lift your eyes above these petty tyrants and see the infinite span of God's presence, dwarfing every fear, overshadowing every enemy, and as you sense His greatness, your heart swells with awe, an awe that makes it impossible to shrink before mere human challenges, for what can the world throw at you that surpasses God's ability to shield and guide? This perspective sets you free from living timidly, from always hedging bets or holding back, enabling you to serve with abandon, to love extravagantly, to hope fiercely, and to march forward under the banner of His promises, knowing that failure cannot define you, that even death itself cannot rob you of the eternal life God secured for you. In the shadow of His wings, your heart learns a new language—the language of faith, where uncertainties no longer translate to panic, but to trust in God's unfolding purposes, where pain does not mean punishment, but an opportunity for deeper reliance on the One who heals, where setbacks do not equal defeat, but invitations to lean on grace more fully, and as you become fluent in this language of faith, you find words of encouragement flowing from your lips more naturally, words that once would have stuck in your throat, you speak these words into weary souls, showing them that they too can find shelter under God's mighty wings, that they too can let go of false securities and find the one true rock that will not crumble beneath their feet. Eventually, you realize something deeply empowering: this whole time, while you were seeking security in God's presence, He was also preparing you to become a source of security for others—a mentor, a friend, a role model of steadfast faith, and though you remain human and imperfect, people can look at your life and see a living demonstration that courage anchored in God's love and promises stands firm against life's tempests, and from witnessing this, they gather the courage to approach God for themselves, to discover that He welcomes them as well, that no one is too broken or lost to find refuge under His wings, and in this way, the cycle continues—those you once comfort now comfort others, spreading the peace, hope, and courage that only God can give, until countless souls find their place in His shelter, forging a community of believers standing strong together in a world that often shakes beneath them. In the end, resting under God's wings is not about escaping responsibility or becoming passive, it's about tapping into the true source of strength so you can engage the world with a bold heart and serve the Lord with renewed energy, it's about accepting that you do not have to be your own savior, that He who cares for you is not an indifferent observer, but an active, involved rescuer, guiding you through valleys and over mountaintops, ensuring that nothing can separate you from His love, with this bedrock assurance, you go forth to share hope with the hopeless, to stand by the suffering, to speak light into darkness, to break bread with the hungry, to clothe the naked, to weep with those who mourn and rejoice with those who celebrate, all because you know you are safe, carried by a grace deeper than any ocean, held by arms wider than any horizon, warmed by a presence that turns fear into courage and doubt into trust. In the shadow of His wings, you have found your true home, a fortress no enemy can breach, and from within this secure dwelling, you can face whatever tomorrow brings, not trembling or retreating, but advancing confidently in service to the Lord who made you, redeemed you, and called you to shine His light in every corner of a weary world.

Day 30 - Pressing Onward: Fueling Endurance for the Journey

IMAGINE STANDING AT the foot of a long, winding road that stretches out farther than your eyes can see, its path disappearing into the haze of distant hills and valleys, and you know that at the other end of this road lies a deeper sense of purpose and closeness to God, a calling that pulls at your heart like the gentle tug of a mother's hand leading her child forward, yet as you gaze upon this journey ahead, you cannot ignore the weight pressing down on your shoulders: the fears that whisper you cannot make it, the doubts that question whether you truly have what it takes, the memories of past stumbles and failures that try to convince you it's safer to stay where you are, rooted in comfort rather than risk the pain of pushing onward, but something inside you refuses to give in to despair, something like an ember glowing quietly in the ashes of past setbacks, and as you lean closer, you realize this is the spark of endurance, God's gift of strength that urges you to take the next step, and then another, and another, even when the way seems long, even when your feet ache, even when the horizon offers no clear promises; this spark is courage, ignited not by your own willpower but by the Lord's gentle voice whispering in your soul, reminding you that He walks beside you, that He is your steady guide, that you need not carry your burdens alone, pressing onward is not a glamorous sprint in the bright sunshine, it is more like a slow, steady climb through changing weather, at times you feel a warm breeze of hope, at times a chill of uncertainty, but through it all, God's hand remains on your shoulder, giving you the confidence to keep moving forward, and as you journey, you realize that endurance is not simply gritting your teeth and marching ahead, it's about tuning your heart to God's promises, letting His truth anchor your steps so that each footfall is grounded in something real and unshakable, when you face obstacles—steep hills of temptation, muddy patches of discouragement, sudden storms of confusion—remember that God's Word is like a lamp shining at your feet, guiding you carefully around pitfalls and through hidden snares, and when fear tries to say you are too weak or too wounded to go on, God's Spirit answers softly that His grace is enough, that His power finds its perfect expression in your moments of frailty, that He is the steady vine and you are a branch flourishing only through His life-giving strength. As you press onward, think of how a farmer patiently tends a field, believing that if he continues to plow, to plant, to water, to weed, the harvest will come, not instantly, not with a single stroke of effort, but through faithfulness over time, and your spiritual journey is much the same: you may not see immediate fruits of your courage or obedience, you might go through seasons where the ground looks barren, where prayers seem unanswered, where you wonder if your efforts matter at all, yet endurance whispers that God is not finished, that beneath the soil of your struggles, seeds of faith are growing, roots of character are spreading deeper, and in due season, the fields of your life will burst into bloom, revealing that none of your tears, none of your prayers, none of your steady steps went to waste, pressing onward means believing that even on days when the road feels lonely, you are not truly alone, for the One who never sleeps keeps watch over your soul, His angels guard your path, and He delights in your willingness to continue despite uncertainties, to trust Him despite the silence that sometimes surrounds you like thick fog. In this process, you must learn to let go of the idea that everything depends on your strength, endurance is not about being a superhero, it's about leaning on God when your knees shake, about confessing your weakness and letting His power work through you, it's about understanding that your part is simply to keep showing up, keep listening to His voice, keep doing the next right thing, and leaving the grand outcomes to Him, in a world that prizes instant results and quick fixes, this steady faithfulness can feel countercultural, even foolish, but remember that God's kingdom often operates by different rules: the small seed grows into a mighty tree, the quiet servant is honored in heaven, the gentle word can break through hard hearts, your perseverance, fueled by God's grace, can shape not only your own character but also reach others who watch your life, even without your knowing, your steady walk can inspire someone else to find their own courage, because they see that you face hardship yet refuse to quit, that you cling to hope when it would be easier to surrender to despair. As you press onward, acknowledge that weariness is real, you will have days when your spirit feels worn thin like fabric that has seen too many winters, days when you question why the journey must be so long and the tests so frequent, in those moments, dare to be honest with God, pour out your frustrations, your aches, your fears, and allow Him to respond with tender mercy, remember that Jesus Himself grew tired, that He slept in a boat rocked by storms, that He wept at gravesides and sweated drops of anguish in Gethsemane, He knows human exhaustion from the inside, so He will not scold you for feeling drained, rather, He invites you to find rest in Him, to lay your burdens at His feet, to drink from the well of His love until your parched soul finds new vitality, and in that rest, you rediscover the fuel for endurance—the quiet assurance that you are precious in His sight, that your hardships do not define you, that His love transcends your understanding but is always present to lift you up. Consider also that pressing onward is not a solo venture, while your personal relationship with God is foundational, He also places you in a community of believers for mutual encouragement, sometimes when your own flame burns low, another's bright faith can lend warmth to your heart, when you can barely shuffle forward, a friend's prayer, a kind word, a shared scripture can give you the extra push to keep going, and there will be times when you are the one offering comfort, reminding someone else that the finish line, though invisible now, truly exists, that God never wastes pain, that perseverance is not pointless but prepares us for greater works of love and testimony, as you stand shoulder to shoulder with brothers and sisters in faith, you find that endurance grows stronger in fellowship, that the journey, while still challenging, becomes more bearable when hearts unite. Another crucial element of fueling your endurance is remembering the times God has already shown His faithfulness, think back to past crises you survived, past problems resolved, past prayers answered in ways you could not have predicted, each memory is a stone of remembrance, building an altar of gratitude in your mind, when the road ahead looks uncertain, these recollections whisper, "He helped you then, He will help you now," and each time you acknowledge His past goodness, your trust deepens, making it easier to press onward with steady determination, even if the present seems bleak, the God who parted seas, who fed multitudes with loaves and fish, who restored sight to the blind and raised the dead to life, is the same God who walks with you, and no obstacle you face today can outmatch His power and creativity. As you advance, let humility guide you, for humility says that you do not have all the answers, that you cannot predict every turn or dodge every hardship, but that's okay, because God does not ask you to know the future, He only asks that you trust His guidance, humility also prevents you from despising small steps of progress or small acts of faith, you begin to see that each inch forward matters, that each day you endure faithfully, each time you choose kindness over bitterness, perseverance over quitting, truth over silence, you are building spiritual muscle that will serve you well when greater challenges appear, humility recognizes that no battle is won in one move, but through a steady series of obedient steps, and this acceptance releases the pressure to be extraordinary overnight, freeing you to celebrate the simple act of rising each morning and saying, "Lord, I'm here, I trust You, show me what to do today." In pressing onward, your perspective on struggle changes, you stop viewing difficulties as meaningless interruptions and start seeing them as opportunities to deepen your reliance on God, to discover new facets of His character, to refine your motives, sometimes it is in wrestling with questions that you find a clearer understanding of truth, it is in facing personal weaknesses that you learn to lean on God's strength, and it is in walking through valleys that you appreciate the mountaintops all the more, endurance teaches you that pain, while never pleasant, can be a tool in the hands of a loving Potter shaping your clay into a vessel that can hold more compassion, more empathy, more resilience, and ultimately more joy. Over time, as you continue pressing onward, you realize that endurance itself becomes part of your testimony, your life's message to others searching for hope, when people see that you did not give up in the face of hardship, that you maintained integrity under pressure, that you clung to God's promises when everything else screamed at you to quit, they glimpse the power of faith in action, your courage becomes a beacon they can follow, showing them that if God carried you through, He can carry them too, and in this way, your perseverance not only sustains your journey but also ignites courage in countless observers, spreading inspiration like ripples on the surface of a still lake, one life touching another. Another gift of endurance is the spiritual maturity it fosters, pressing onward through trials weans you from empty comforts and forces you to anchor in something unshakable—God's word and character, you learn patience as you wait for resolutions you cannot rush, you learn surrender as you yield your desired outcomes to God's better plan, you learn wisdom as you navigate complex moral choices, and you learn love as you serve others even when you're tired or discouraged, bit by bit, hardship carves away superficial faith and reveals a heart deeply shaped by divine hands, and in those moments of clarity, you understand that this journey, while long and sometimes painful, is preparing you for greater usefulness in God's kingdom, making you a vessel of grace who can stand firm in storms and guide others through them as well. Consider too that pressing onward allows you to witness miracles, not always spectacular flashes of power, but often subtle shifts that confirm God's involvement—an unexpected solution to a problem, a timely encouragement from a stranger, a burst of strength at your weakest hour, these miracles remind you that you do not walk alone, that the path, though challenging, is lit by the Savior who promised to be with you always, even to the end of the age, and in experiencing these divine aids, your confidence in God's providence grows, fueling endurance with a surety that what He started in you, He will finish. Another point to remember is that endurance does not mean never resting, it means knowing where to find true rest—at the feet of

Jesus, when you feel overwhelmed, stepping back into His presence, shutting out the noise of demands, letting your soul breathe, recharges your spirit, just as a weary traveler must occasionally pause to drink water and catch their breath, you must also pause in God's embrace, soaking in His comfort, reading Scripture not as a chore but as a refreshing stream, praying not as a duty but as a heartfelt conversation with the One who cares infinitely for you, in doing so, you maintain the strength needed to keep going rather than burning out from constant exertion. Pressing onward also changes how you interpret setbacks, instead of labeling them as failures that disprove your worth or God's goodness, you learn to see them as detours or lessons along the way, perhaps a door closed not to punish you, but to redirect you to a better opportunity, perhaps a delay not meant to frustrate you, but to align you with God's timing, each setback, properly viewed, can add depth to your perseverance, teaching you flexibility, sensitivity to God's nudges, and a more nuanced understanding of what serving Him requires, and over time, this reframing of disappointments into stepping stones fortifies your resolve, making you less fearful of trying new things, less defeated by rejection, more open to God's surprising methods of guiding your path. Another dimension of endurance is that it gives you eyes to appreciate quiet victories that might go unnoticed by a world addicted to spectacle, maybe you managed to be patient with a difficult coworker for one more day, maybe you resisted a temptation that had ensnared you for years, maybe you dared to share a piece of your faith story with someone who was hurting, even if they didn't immediately respond with gratitude or conversion, these small triumphs, taken individually, seem minor, but together they form a mosaic of faithfulness that pleases God, and as you recognize them, you feel your courage swell, because you see evidence of growth, you see that God is indeed working in you, that you are not stagnant, that the journey is moving forward, and that victory does not always wear a crown of fame, sometimes it hides in the quiet act of obedience you choose moment by moment. As you continue, remember that pressing onward is not a phase you outgrow once you become "mature enough," it's a lifelong posture, for even the most seasoned believers face new challenges, new seasons that test their faith differently, endurance is the ongoing choice to keep placing one foot in front of the other, to keep trusting God when logic fails, to keep loving people when they disappoint, to keep believing in redemption when injustice screams otherwise, it's a dynamic process that grows richer over time as you see more of God's faithfulness, gaining perspective that lets you handle today's struggles with more grace than you did yesterday's, and in that sense, endurance is both journey and destination, a constant dance between leaning on God's strength and acting on His guidance, a pattern that shapes your character into a resilient reflection of Christ's own perseverance. One day, when you look back over the path you've walked, you may marvel at how you overcame obstacles you once thought insurmountable, how fears that paralyzed you now seem faint echoes of a distant past, how your understanding of God's goodness deepened as He carried you through storms and deserts, pressing onward allowed you to become someone stronger, wiser, and more compassionate than you would have been had you chosen the easy route, and you will praise God not just for the final achievements, but for every step He enabled you to take, every lesson embedded in hardship, every new facet of courage discovered when you dared not to quit, and by that time, you will have influenced others too, inspiring them to ignite their own courage, helping them find the resolve to serve the Lord no matter what, your endurance leaves footprints others can follow, leading them closer to the heart of a God who never abandons His children. Thus, pressing onward is not just a theme or an ideal, it's a lifestyle rooted in the knowledge that God is with you, that your labors have meaning, that your heart is fueled by grace rather than empty pride, and that no matter how far you still have to go, the One who called you will never fail to supply what you need—hope in the dim hours, courage when shadows lengthen, strength when muscles tire, calm in the face of panic—enabling you to keep advancing in faith and love, stepping toward a future bright with His promises, confident that the journey is worth every struggle, and that the final destination, though still unseen, is glorious beyond your wildest dreams, and this confidence, born of God's unchanging nature, truly fuels your heart to serve the Lord with unwavering courage.

Day 31 - Ignited and Unstoppable: Living Courageously for the Lord

Imagine standing at the edge of a vast horizon, the sun just rising behind you, painting the sky in fierce oranges and glowing gold, its light streaming across the land like a silent promise that this new day holds something extraordinary, and as you inhale the crisp morning air, you feel a stirring deep in your soul, a warmth that does not come merely from the sun's rays, but from a holy flame glowing within your heart, and in that quiet moment, you realize that you have been ignited, that the courage God has placed within you has caught fire, and now you are unstoppable, not because you possess some rare natural bravery, but because you have chosen to live courageously for the Lord who called you by name, redeemed you from darkness, and set you on a path filled with purpose, as you look around, you see that the world needs this fire of courage—there are souls wandering in uncertainty, aching for a sign that truth and goodness still prevail, there are hearts weighed down by sorrow and fear, longing for proof that love and grace can still break through the clouds of despair, and you know that by stepping forward, by letting the light of Christ blaze through your words and actions, you can bring that reassurance, you can change the atmosphere, not by shouting or forcing your will, but by faithfully living out the hope that has captured your own soul, and in this sense, courage is not some distant ideal, it is a living force welling up from within, urging you to be bold in kindness, steady in storms, unwavering in honesty, and fearless in showing compassion, you have tasted what it means to be loved by a God who sees every flaw and still calls you beloved, and that love compels you to stop settling for safe complacency and to start embracing the daring adventure of faith—reaching out to help when it's easier to turn away, telling the truth when silence seems safer, standing by those who are marginalized and oppressed even if it costs you comfort, this courage does not mean you never feel afraid, rather it means fear no longer rules you, no longer dictates your choices or muzzles your voice, because underneath every tremor of anxiety lies the unshakable fact that God is with you, His Spirit strengthening your backbone, steadying your heart, guiding your steps, reminding you that nothing you do in His name is in vain, and as this truth sinks deeper, you find yourself able to attempt what once felt impossible—applying for that mission trip, volunteering for that local ministry, speaking up for the bullied classmate, or gently sharing the Gospel with a skeptical friend, igniting courage means you no longer wait for perfect conditions or total clarity before obeying God's nudges, you trust that as you move forward, He will provide the resources, the words, the timing you need, and that He delights in your willingness to rely on Him rather than on your limited understanding, being unstoppable for the Lord is not about charging ahead recklessly, it's about knowing that obstacles may appear, yet none are insurmountable to Him, it's about understanding that your failures and shortcomings don't disqualify you, but rather keep you humble and teachable, allowing God's power to shine through your weaknesses in ways that leave no doubt that He is the source of your strength, and so you press onward, not because you trust yourself completely, but because you trust Him utterly, each act of courage—each decision to love radically, to give generously, to serve selflessly—is a spark that can ignite others' hearts too, as people watch you face difficulties with grace, handle disappointments with steady faith, and embrace challenges with hopeful resilience, they begin to wonder about the source of your strength, and in their wondering, their hearts open to the possibility that God can ignite their courage too, turning them from bystanders into active participants in the kingdom's work, so you live not only for your own growth, but also for the potential to inspire countless others who yearn to believe that there is more to life than fear and struggle, that there is a purpose worth risking comfort to achieve, that the Lord who overcame death can empower them to stand firm in trials, and as these sparks spread, communities glow brighter, homes become havens of understanding and care, churches become mission hubs radiating compassion to the broken and lonely, and workplaces see integrity and honesty flourish, all because a few souls dared to let courage guide their footsteps, dared to believe that God could use their ordinary lives to weave stories of extraordinary grace, igniting courage does not mean you become immune to pain or immune to doubts, you remain human, still feeling the weight of grief at times, still wrestling with questions that have no easy answers, but now you face these struggles with a different posture: instead of shrinking back, you lean into God's presence, pouring out your fears and disappointments, trusting that He listens, that He weeps with you, that He holds you tightly as you navigate sorrow's valleys, and strangely, this vulnerability—your willingness to admit that you need God—further fuels your courage, because it teaches you that being unstoppable does not require never stumbling, it requires the humility to let God pick you up each time you fall, to let Him mend your broken wings so you can fly again, and each time He does, your faith deepens, your courage becomes more resilient, and your commitment to serving the Lord intensifies. To live courageously for the Lord also involves facing the unknown with a sense of expectancy rather than dread, you know that not all outcomes will match your initial hopes, that some paths may lead to dead ends, that some seeds you plant may lie dormant for years before bearing fruit, yet you keep sowing those seeds—acts of love, words of truth, gestures of mercy—because you trust the Gardener who tends them, you understand that eternity's viewpoint differs from your limited perspective, and that in the grand tapestry of history, every moment of obedience contributes to God's redemptive plan, even if you cannot see how, so you move forward, day by day, step by step, not driven by a desperate need to control results, but sustained by the quiet confidence that God's kingdom grows even where human eyes see no progress, and in that confidence, fear loses its hold, cynicism finds no entry, weariness does not have the final word. Another facet of becoming unstoppable for the Lord is learning to view challenges as invitations to deeper faith, when a door closes, you do not rant against fate; you pray for guidance and look for windows God might open instead, when a relationship sours, you ask the Lord how to show forgiveness and understanding, when resources run low, you rely on His provision, trusting that He can multiply your humble offerings like loaves and fish, turning scarcity into sufficiency, and in each test, your spiritual muscles strengthen, your reliance on God becomes second nature, and before long, you notice that what once terrified you now seems manageable, what once seemed beyond your capability now feels possible by His grace, the courage that once flickered weakly now burns steadily, lighting your path and steadying your steps even when the world around you shakes. Embracing a courageous life for God's purpose also transforms how you see yourself, no longer do you define yourself solely by past mistakes, disappointments, or by what the world values as success, you see yourself through God's eyes: redeemed, chosen, equipped, and loved, this identity, rooted in divine truth, replaces the insecurity that once held you back, enabling you to stand tall not from pride, but from gratitude for what God has done in your life, and this inner confidence radiates outward, people sense that you are not swayed by their approval or discouraged by their rejection, your anchor lies elsewhere, beyond their shifting opinions, and freed from the need to please everyone, you can focus on pleasing God, on following His lead even when it's unpopular, knowing that His smile over you matters far more than human applause. As courage grows, you find yourself stepping into roles or situations you never imagined, maybe you speak out against injustice you once tolerated silently, maybe you mentor a younger believer, investing time and patience into their spiritual growth, maybe you embark on a mission trip that takes you far beyond your comfort zone, or start a Bible study group with neighbors who scarcely understand faith, in each scenario, your willingness to say "yes" stems from the knowledge that the Lord who calls you is faithful, that He does not abandon His servants but supplies everything they need, and even when you encounter difficulties—language barriers, personality clashes, unexpected disappointments—His presence remains your source of strength, turning obstacles into opportunities to learn perseverance, creativity, and deeper reliance on Him. As you move forward, courage merging with love and faith in your heart, you become acutely aware of the spiritual battle underlying life's surface, you see how fear and despair try to corrode hearts, how lies spread doubt, how anger and division threaten to tear communities apart, but with your heart ignited for the Lord, you step into this battleground not as a helpless bystander but as a soldier of light, armed with prayer, truth, empathy, and unwavering hope, you stand in the gap for those who cannot stand for themselves, offer comfort to those who weep, clarity to those confused by lies, hope to those who falter under the weight of their burdens, and in doing so, you discover that courage is not just for your benefit, but a torch you carry to illuminate the darkness for many others, your courage sparks courage in them, inspiring them to break free from apathy, to trust God, to dare something meaningful. Over time, as you remain faithful, you notice that even the smallest acts, when done with courage and for God's glory, weave together to form a pattern of impact that reaches beyond what you can measure, perhaps a child you encouraged grows up to become a leader who transforms many lives, maybe a stranger you helped finds the strength to pass kindness forward, maybe a single prayer you prayed sparks a chain of events that saves a soul from despair, these connections may not be clear to you now, but God sees them all, cherishing each obedient step, each courageous choice as a precious thread in the grand tapestry of His redemptive work. In all these ways, your heart, once uncertain and timid, becomes a harbor of confidence and resilience, not because you no longer feel fear, but because you know fear does not hold the final say, you have learned to bow your knee in prayer rather than in terror, to lift your eyes to the God who defies impossibilities, to trust that when He calls you to walk on stormy seas, He provides the calm in your soul and the power to keep your feet steady on the water's surface, and in this surrendered trust, courage shines like a steady beacon in the night, guiding not only your path but helping others navigate their own. By living courageously for the Lord, you affirm that no circumstance, no failure, no human rejection can strip you of the calling He has placed in your life, that each morning's sunrise brings another chance to rise to the challenge, to reflect Christ's character in a hurting world, and as you embrace this reality, courage stops being an abstract quality and becomes an integral part of who you are, empowering you to serve boldly in quiet corners or public platforms alike, to be a peacemaker in a world at war, a healer where wounds fester, a voice of truth where confusion reigns, a presence of love where loneliness and heartbreak threaten to crush human spirits. Letting courage fuel your heart to serve the Lord makes life an unfolding adventure rather than a static existence, for you never know what door God might open next, what person He might place in your path who needs a listening ear or a gentle push toward hope, what cause He might prompt you to support, what new skill He might ask you to learn for the sake of blessing others, this ongoing sense of purpose keeps your spirit alive and flexible, eager to adapt as God directs, and confident that He will equip you for the tasks He assigns. Even in moments where darkness seems to gain ground, where evil appears to have the upper hand, your courage, rooted in Christ, reminds you that appearances can deceive, that God's plan cannot be thwarted, that Jesus' victory over sin and death was final and ultimate, and that we, as His followers, are privileged to carry forward the mission He began: announcing grace to the guilty, rest to the weary, forgiveness to the repentant, and life to the spiritually dead, this eternal perspective reduces fear and magnifies trust, so that even if circumstances grow dire, you refuse to yield to despair, choosing instead to double down on faith, on love, on pouring out God's goodness into a parched world, convinced that no darkness can snuff out the light He has ignited in your soul. As your journey continues, you become more comfortable with uncertainty, not because it ceases to challenge you, but because you've tasted how God provides when all earthly supports crumble, how He whispers comfort in silent hours, how He orchestrates unexpected encounters that reveal His care, how He grants you wisdom beyond your natural capacity when faced with moral dilemmas, and this ongoing experience of God's faithfulness cements the resolve to press on, to keep shining, keep loving, keep giving, keep hoping, for His sake and for the sake of those who depend on your witness, and as each new chapter unfolds, you realize courage never stops growing; it's a living thing, nourished by God's presence and your consistent choice to trust Him, and thus you never plateau, never settle into complacency, but continually discover new layers of strength, new horizons of service. In the end, to be ignited and unstoppable means you have fully embraced the truth that God's love is stronger than any obstacle, that His promises outlast any trial, that His grace forgives and empowers you beyond human logic, and that your small acts of faith combine with countless others to usher in glimpses of God's kingdom on earth, this reality fills your heart with a quiet, unshakable joy, not the shallow happiness that depends on easy times, but a deep gladness anchored in eternal hope, and this joy, interwoven with courage, drives you forward, day after day, ensuring that you do not just exist, but truly live—live for the One who redeemed you, loved you first, and calls you onward into greatness shaped by service, humility, and endless compassion. So stand tall, child of God, your heart ablaze with courage that no disappointment can extinguish, your mind fixed on the Lord who guides you through unknown territories, your voice ready to speak life where silence once dwelt, your hands eager to lift burdens from weary shoulders, and your spirit poised to radiate the truth: that in Christ, you are ignited and unstoppable, a beacon of hope and faith for a world desperately in need of His light, and as you move forward with this purpose, you discover that serving God with courage does not drain you, it renews you, does not isolate you, but connects you to a great family of believers all shining their part of the light, together forming a tapestry of love that chases away darkness wherever it tries to hide.

Conclusion

Imagine now that you stand at the edge of a quiet field at dusk, the sky painted with gentle shades of pink and gold as the day's last light slowly fades, and in that calm moment, take a breath and remember the journey we have taken together through these pages—an honest, heartfelt walk through fear, faith, love, struggle, and the steady, guiding presence of the Lord who calls you to stand tall and serve with courage. You have learned that true courage does not require you to be fearless, it does not ask that you never tremble or doubt, but that you trust the One who is greater than your fears, the One who breathes life into weary souls and sets hearts aflame with passion and strength. By now, you have seen that your worth does not rest in earthly measures of success or the hollow praise of others, but in the unshakable truth that God knows your name, cherishes your every breath, and has placed you in this world at this time for a purpose that goes beyond what your eyes can see. You have discovered that courage can be found not on distant mountaintops or hidden treasures, but in daily acts of faithfulness—speaking a kind word, standing up for someone who cannot stand alone, choosing honesty when a lie would be easier, holding onto hope when shadows loom large. Each of these moments, though small in the world's eyes, contains a spark of holy fire that can ignite something bigger than you can imagine, for when you serve the Lord with courage, you do more than just face your own fears: you open windows for His grace to flood into dark corners, you offer living proof that love indeed conquers hate, that mercy triumphs over judgment, and that weakness surrendered to God can become a channel of His strength. As you step away from these pages, carry with you the understanding that courage is not a trophy you hold once and forever, but a living flame to be tended, fed by prayer, rooted in Scripture, and shaped by a heart that remains humble before God's majesty. This flame will need nurturing; there will be days when you feel worn thin, when the weight of hardship tries to smother your spirit, when voices of doubt hiss that maybe you should give up. Yet in those hours, remember the truth we have explored: courage does not vanish in hardship, it grows stronger, proving its worth when tested by trials. You have learned that your fears, far from disqualifying you, become opportunities to lean more fully on the Lord's everlasting arms, to see His faithfulness displayed as He guides you through storms and deserts. Embrace this life of courage by choosing to see yourself as God sees you: beloved, forgiven, equipped with gifts to share, and called to walk a path that blesses others. Dare to imagine what might happen if you keep saying yes to God's nudges: you might find yourself connecting with someone who desperately needs to know they are not alone, or shining light into a place of confusion and despair. You might discover talents you never realized you had, stirred into action by a divine whisper in your soul. You might grow in wisdom as you learn to love people who are hard to love, offering grace where others offer judgment. And each time you choose courage over comfort, conviction over complacency, you add another brushstroke to a masterpiece God is painting—a masterpiece that reveals His character through your surrendered life. Never think that your efforts are too small to matter. A single spark can start a wildfire, one candle can break the hold of darkness, one genuine act of compassion can ripple through countless lives. The courage you show today may become the seed that blossoms into hope for someone else tomorrow. Just as you have learned from the examples of faithful believers past and present, your life can be that living example for someone who watches quietly from the sidelines. By being open about your fears yet pressing on anyway, by admitting your need for God's guidance and depending on His Spirit, you show others that courage is accessible, not reserved for the fearless few. When you walk confidently, not in yourself, but in the Lord's promises, people sense something real and lasting. They see authenticity, not a performance. They feel loved and respected, not pressured. They find themselves drawn to the Source of your strength, curious about the faith that fuels your endurance. With time, some may follow your footsteps toward the Lord you serve, discovering their own courage in Him. As you continue forward, remember that courage is not a lonely journey. You are part of a great family of believers spread across lands and ages, each carrying their own torch of faith, each contributing their own light to guide travelers on life's winding roads. Your courage links with theirs, forming a chain of hope that cannot be easily broken. When you stumble, let their prayers and encouragement lift you. When they falter, be ready to lend a hand. Together, united in purpose, the collective flame of God's people can turn even the darkest landscapes into fields of possibility, fields that reflect heaven's gentle glow. Let this vision inspire you, let it remind you that you do not run this race alone, and that your courage strengthens the body of Christ, just as their courage sustains you. In the quiet moments, when uncertainty returns or old fears resurface, do not be discouraged. Turn again to the One who first set your heart on fire, who called you out of darkness and into His marvelous light. In prayer, find comfort; in Scripture, find guidance; in worship, find renewed perspective; in service, find deeper meaning. Each time you reconnect with the Lord, you feed the flame of courage, ensuring it never goes cold. And if at times it flickers, recall the truths learned here: that courage thrives not in an absence of fear, but in trusting God despite it, that your life matters because God says it does, that your efforts, no matter how humble, can play a part in His grand tapestry of redemption. Your journey forward will hold twists and turns, but nothing can sever the bond you share with God. With Him as your strength, even valleys of pain can become places where compassion blossoms, even deserts of doubt can yield rare flowers of wisdom. Every challenge can shape you into a more loving, patient, and courageous servant, refining your faith as gold refined by fire. And each step you take with courage—whether it leads to visible victory or quiet endurance—is a step that honors the God who redeemed you for this very purpose. As we close these pages, may your heart burn brighter than when we began. May the courage ignited in you find expression in how you speak, act, care, and hope. May you never underestimate the ripple effect of a single brave choice, a single moment where you trust God and do what is right, even when it would be easier to do nothing. May you wake each day with a renewed sense that your life is part of something far greater than you can comprehend, and that by serving the Lord with courage, you help bring heaven's light closer to earth. Carry these truths with you: You are valued. You are called. You are empowered by a love that cannot fail. You are not defined by your flaws, but by God's grace. You have nothing to prove to a world that often misunderstands worth. You have everything to offer because the Lord's Spirit dwells in you, guiding each step, blessing each honest effort, turning your kindness, humility, and faith into the building blocks of a better tomorrow. Today, as you stand at your horizon, the ember within has grown into a steady flame. Let it guide you forward. Let courage guide your choices, fuel your prayers, shape your dreams, and anchor your soul in hope. Let your courage, ignited by God's love and truth, become unstoppable—so that you may serve the Lord all the days of your life, spreading grace, stirring faith, and shining a gentle, unwavering light in every place your journey takes you.

Don't miss out!

Visit the website below and you can sign up to receive emails whenever Joshua Rhoades publishes a new book. There's no charge and no obligation.

https://books2read.com/r/B-A-AJLBB-ZJUKF

BOOKS 2 READ

Connecting independent readers to independent writers.

Did you love *Igniting Courage Fueling Your Heart To Serve The Lord*? Then you should read *Enabled- Living God's Purpose With Power*[1] by Joshua Rhoades!

[2]

The 31-day devotional, "Enabled: Living God's Purpose With Power", is a refreshing and empowering guide for believers seeking to deepen their relationship with God and walk confidently in His purpose. Through a month-long journey, this devotional brings readers face-to-face with the profound truth that God equips, sustains, and strengthens us to fulfill His calling. Each daily message is centered on Scripture, rooted in the timeless wisdom of the King James Version, and inspired by I Timothy 1:12, where Paul says, "And I thank Christ Jesus our Lord, who hath enabled me." This verse forms the heart of this devotional, reminding us that just as God enabled Paul to overcome immense trials, He provides us with the strength to navigate our own challenges, live with courage, and stay faithful to His purpose.

---

1. https://books2read.com/u/3Lqy20
2. https://books2read.com/u/3Lqy20

Life often brings uncertainties, doubts, and fears that weigh us down, making us feel inadequate or overwhelmed. Yet, "Enabled" speaks directly to those struggles, encouraging readers to trade their weaknesses for God's boundless strength. Each day's entry includes a Scripture reflection, practical insight, and a heartfelt prayer, making it easy to apply God's truths to everyday life. This book is a powerful reminder that we are never meant to walk the Christian journey alone or rely solely on our own abilities. Rather, God's power is ever-present and available, actively working through us to accomplish His will. Through this devotional, you'll discover the peace that comes from knowing God's strength is made perfect in our weakness, allowing us to live with resilience, hope, and purpose.

As you progress through each day's message, you'll be encouraged by how God empowers us to overcome fear, endure difficult circumstances, serve others with love, and live courageously in every situation. By the end of the 31 days, you'll have a renewed understanding of how to rely on God's strength, not your own, and find that even in the toughest moments, His grace is always sufficient, His love never wavers, and His plans for you are steadfast. Each devotion highlights a unique aspect of God's enabling power, such as courage, peace, endurance, wisdom, and faithfulness, helping you see how His presence enriches every corner of life.

Whether you're facing challenges, feeling uncertain, or simply longing to strengthen your faith, "Enabled: Living God's Purpose With Power" is a perfect companion. This devotional guides you to keep your eyes on Christ, trust His timing, and walk with confidence, knowing you are equipped by His Spirit. It's a beautiful resource for anyone, whether new to the faith or well along in their walk with the Lord. With each day's entry, you'll find yourself empowered, encouraged, and equipped to live out God's calling in your life, discovering that His enabling power isn't just for the heroes of Scripture, but for every believer today—including you. This book becomes a personal guide and source of daily inspiration, helping you build a strong foundation in faith and a life transformed by God's presence.

www.ingramcontent.com/pod-product-compliance
Lightning Source LLC
LaVergne TN
LVHW041020150826
845672LV00001B/160

9798230200413